Max Weber: The Lawyer as Social Thinker aims to relate the categories of Weber's social thinking to the intellectual context of legal thinking and theory in which he was educated. It aims to show how knowledge of these relations illuminates our understanding of Weber's own intentions. The authors submit that Weber radically undermines teleological social theory by providing a thoroughly anti-teleological sociology.

The book identifies some of the key sources of Weber's thought within the legal tradition, notably the jurisprudential theorist Rudolph von Ihering, a typical teleological thinker influenced by Bentham as well as neo-Kantianism. Some of Weber's most famous ideas, for example his claim that explanations of action should be adequate on the level of meaning and the level of cause, the concept of ideal interests, and his stress on "vocations", are shown to be variants of Ihering's concepts. The differences are systematic and profoundly revealing.

Max Weber: The Lawyer as Social Thinker is the only account of the sources of Weber's sociology in the legal tradition, as distinct from an account of Weber's sociology of law. The book leads to a new interpretation of Weber. It should be of interest to scholars in social theory, jurisprudence and the history of ideas.

Stephen P. Turner is Graduate Research Professor of Philosophy, University of South Florida. **Regis A. Factor** is Professor of Government and International Affairs, University of South Florida.

MAX WEBER

The Lawyer as Social Thinker

Stephen P. Turner
and
Regis A. Factor

London and New York

First published 1994
by Routledge
11 New Fetter Lane, London EC4P 4EE

Simultaneously published in the USA and Canada
by Routledge
29 West 35th Street, New York, NY 10001

Typeset in Baskerville by LaserScript, Mitcham, Surrey
Printed and bound in Great Britain by
Mackays of Chatham PLC, Chatham, Kent

British Library Cataloguing in Publication Data
A catalogue record for this book is available from the British Library.

Library of Congress Cataloging in Publication Data
has been applied for.

ISBN 0-415-06751-0
ISBN 0-415-11452-7 (pbk)

In memory of J.P. Mayer

CONTENTS

PREFACE

This book may be read in several ways. It is primarily intended as an introduction to Weber's use of, and response to, the tradition of legal science in which he was trained, which contains a novel systematic account of Weber's core classifications of action and uniformities of action and an account of the underlying anti-theoretical aims of his systematic social thought. The argument is a radical departure from a line of interpretation popularized by sociological theorists, notably Parsons, who have interpreted Weber as a theorist manqué. Our interpretation suggests that he was a self-conscious and systematic underminer of the social theory of his time. Little of the book, however, is devoted to criticism of other interpretations. Indeed, the book is written to stand alone – to be accessible to the reader with a general background in the law or social thought and some passing familiarity with Weber's most famous works. For the specialist, the book may also be usefully read as the third part of a project we began in our examinations of Weber's account of values and its reception in *Max Weber and the Dispute over Reason and Value* (1984) and of his account of explanation in Turner's *The Search for a Methodology of Social Science* (1986). Both of these volumes deal with philosophical issues; this volume is concerned with substantive matters of social theory. The volume also may be read as an intervention into present philosophy of law and social thought – as a reminder of arguments that still have force. The book is based in part on a series of papers we have published over the last fifteen years. In Chapter 4, there is significant overlap between the present text and the previously published text. Material that appeared in "The Disappearance of Tradition in Weber" by Stephen P. Turner and Regis A. Factor is taken from *Midwest*

Studies in Philosophy (vol XV, © 1990, by University of Notre Dame Press). Reprinted by permission. Passages from Stephen P. Turner, "Weber and his Philosophers," *International Journal of Politics, Culture, and Society*, 1990, appear by permission of Human Sciences Press.

Many scholars made useful suggestions or criticisms of the draft of this book and of the previously published work which it incorporates and revises. We are grateful for their help and encouragement. Christopher Adair-Toteff made useful comments on Chapter 2. Guy Oakes made a large number of useful criticisms of an earlier draft – not all of which can be satisfactorily answered. The question of Weber's intellectual sources for his account of the problem of social science abstraction, which is one theme of the book and the focus of Oakes's own work (1988) on Weber and Rickert, cannot be easily resolved. Our intuition is that Weber's conception of the historical individual, though it is framed in the language of Rickert and fits closely with the main themes of Heidelberg neo-Kantianism, is rooted more deeply in the historically prior problem of legal abstraction that is at the core of the Roman Law tradition. Oakes makes a persuasive case for Rickert's influence over Weber. But Weber's resistance to Rickert's major claims, and his selectivity in using Rickert's ideas, suggests that he had a prior set of commitments on these issues. We give an account which shows what these prior commitments might have been, and where in the legal literature Weber might have acquired them.

Stephen P. Turner and Regis A. Factor

1

INTRODUCTION

This book is about three transformations. The first is biographical: Weber's personal transformation from a legal scholar to a social scientist. The second is theoretical: his transformation of the categories of legal science into the basic categories of his sociology. The major thesis this book will document is the claim that Weber's "basic concepts" were taken over and recast from concepts of action and the state, and that the concepts of explanation and abstraction which figure in his methodological writing that had a significant prehistory in the legal writing of his own time had related origins. Among his major sources was the legal philosopher Rudolf von Ihering. There was a paradoxical counterpart to this second transformation, and this counterpart amounts to a third transformation. What Weber found fully developed in Ihering was what we would now call a social theory: in becoming a social scientist he *repudiated* social theory in its conventional form. This radical aim can be revealed from Weber's alterations of Ihering's ideas. He stripped from them all the standard explanatory devices of nineteenth-century social theory – the idea of collectivities, social forces, human nature and a common human *telos*, the idea of developmental principles, the idea of an overarching evolutionary process, and so on. But to effect this change Weber relied on tools from legal science, such as its theories of probabilistic causality and its theories of concept formation, and on meta-legal ideas, such as the idea of the law as a scheme of clarified ideal-typical definitions that self-consciously diverged from reality. Weber's design – the purpose behind his alterations of the legal thinkers of the era – can be seen only through a systematic comparison of the texts. The aim of this book is to provide such a comparison.

THE NEGLECT OF WEBER'S LEGAL BACKGROUND

Although many works have been written on Weber and the law, none of them have grasped either the extent of Weber's reliance on the pre-existing legal science literature or his intentions in using this literature. Among the American studies, Anthony Kronman's *Max Weber* (1983) deals almost entirely with Weber as a sociologist of law, as do such articles as Trubeck's "Max Weber on Law and the Rise of Capitalism" (1972). These studies assume the validity of the sociological enterprise, and do not grasp his challenge to the very idea of social theory or the radical character of his alternative "sociology." The European literature is somewhat more diverse. But it too has concentrated on Weber as a founder of the sociology of law. This literature has rarely attempted to shed light on questions of the philosophy of law or on questions about fundamental "social science" concepts.

One reason for the invisibility of the roots of Weber's thought in legal thinking is historical. The socially oriented philosophy of law that flourished in Weber's youth collapsed into legal positivism – a process that advanced throughout his own lifetime, and with his help. Legal positivism became the defining *topic* of subsequent philosophy of law. The legal writings Weber criticized came to be seen as exemplifications of what G. E. Moore called the "naturalistic fallacy" which, in the case of the law, was the fallacy of accounting for the law by concepts outside the law. Writers such as Ihering became part of the prehistory of legal positivism, and were largely unread. They remained unread even after it became clear that the "naturalistic fallacy" was not so much a fallacy as a debatable form of argument no more troubled than "non-naturalism" in ethics. In overcoming the inadequacies of legal positivism, it might be argued, the Critical Legal Studies movement and feminist jurisprudence might have profitably returned to these writings and to Weber's response to them. But Weber has largely been left out of this literature, and the relevance (and radicalism) of Weber's own approach to issues they share was not made clear.

It is perhaps appropriate to ask why the historical connections to the legal science tradition on which our argument rests have not been explored fully before in the secondary literature on Weber. The absence of discussion is indeed startling in view of the fact, evident to any reader of the notes to *Wirtschaft und Gesellschaft*, that

2

references to the literature of the law and historians of the law far exceed those of other disciplines numerically.[1] A few years ago, a major conference on Weber's "context" was held under the auspices of the German Historical Institute in London. The papers were later published by Mommsen and Osterhammel (1987). In this huge and apparently comprehensive volume there is no discussion of the sources of Weber's thought in jurisprudential theory, the philosophy of law, or (perhaps more astonishing, considering the large portions of *Wirtschaft und Gesellschaft* that are devoted to the subject) the history of law. Aside from a footnote in the chapter by Hennis, in which he concedes that "Among the intellectual connections that are not yet closely investigated are those to the work of Rudolf von Ihering" (1987: 53), there is no discussion of legal writers as a part of Weber's intellectual context.

Yet there are overwhelming reasons for inquiring into Weber's legal sources. Biographical grounds alone are compelling. Weber's academic origins were in the law, and his early writings were for the most part published in law journals. One would expect that Weber's personal transformation from lawyer to social scientist would leave traces. But Weber did not merely acquire a degree in the law. He was steeped in the intellectual culture of the law. Weber's father was a lawyer and politician who served in the German Reichstag from 1872 to 1884 and was a representative of the National Liberal party. The Berlin household in which he was raised was frequented by prominent politicians. At the time, these politicians were concerned with constitutional struggles initiated by Bismarck, particularly the means through which Bismarck had eroded the powers of parliament. Bismarck's claims raised deep legal questions, such as the notion of the supposed "gaps" in the constitution which Bismarck exploited in order to expand his powers. Academics, including Theodor Mommsen, the doyen of Roman Historical studies whose historical contributions included massive studies of Roman public law and later the criminal law of Rome, were frequent house guests and Mommsen later was Weber's academic patron.

Weber's formal academic training exposed him to the best of contemporary legal thinking, at a time when legal science was the discipline at the top of the academic hierarchy. He began his university training in Heidelberg in 1882 and continued it in Berlin, Strassburg, and Göttingen. When he entered university studies in Heidelberg he read Ranke and Savigny, representatives of "conservative" approaches to German legal and constitutional development. In Immanuel Bekker's course on Roman law, a subject in which Weber ultimately was to be habilitated and which was then among the most prestigious of the legal studies disciplines, he was introduced to the work of Ihering (Marianne Weber [1926] 1975: 65; cf. Mommsen [1959] 1984: 4). Later, as a student in Berlin, he attended the lectures of Gneist on German constitutional law and on Prussian administrative law (Mommsen [1959] 1984: 11), Beseler on civil law, Aegidy on international law, and Brunner and Gierke on German legal history (Käsler [1979] 1988: 5). In 1885 he began to study for his first-year law exams in Berlin and Göttingen, where he spent a term in lectures by such teachers as von Bar, an important theorist of legal causality. Weber received a Berlin doctorate in 1889, under Goldschmidt and Gneist, for a study of the law of medieval trading companies. His promotion dissertation of 1891 was for a study of Roman agrarian history in terms of land tenure, a problem demanding great legal skills. The work was done under Theodor Mommsen and August Meitzen, an expert on medieval land tenure.

Weber initially pursued a legal career and held various minor legal posts, passing the exam for junior barrister (*Referendar*) in May of 1886 and serving in this capacity for six years, during which time he continued his legal studies at the University of Berlin (Kronman 1983: 190). After failing in a competition for a position as legal advisor to the city of Bremen, a position previously held by Werner Sombart, he chose the open door of an academic career. He began, characteristically, at the top, in Berlin, where in 1892 he taught Roman and commercial law and in 1893 commercial and German law. In 1893 he was considered for two professorial positions, one in Berlin in commercial law, the other in "national" economics at the University of Freiburg. He was appointed to the latter. This was the beginning of his non-legal academic career, but even in this position he was never far from the law and legal thinking. In Freiburg he encountered the physiologist and probability thinker von Kries, who had applied his theory of "objective possibility" and "adequate cause" to problems of causation in the law of the sort that von Bar had made famous. This, as we shall see, was a crucial "influence."

In 1896, Weber was called to the Chair of *Nationalökonomie* at the University of Heidelberg. The Weber household became a center of Heidelberg intellectual life, with weekly gatherings of leading

4

scholars. The Weber salon continued after he relinquished his teaching duties in 1903, as did Weber's personal relations with other Heidelberg scholars. At the time Weber had close contact with Gustav Radbruch, later attorney-general under the post-war Socialist government of Ebert, who wrote a law dissertation, extensively used by Weber, on the topic of legal causality, and who became an important philosopher of law. The dissertation explicates von Kries, von Bar, and various probabilistic theorists of legal causation. The young philosopher Emil Lask, whose habilitation dissertation was done on the philosophy of law and explicates the problem of the nature of social science categories in terms of Ihering's writings on legal categories, was also a frequent private visitor of Weber's during the period.

Weber's relations with the law were not unmixed. Hennis, in another work, provides a justification for the neglect of Weber's legal background based on other facts of Weber's biography. Weber is depicted by Hennis as having been frustrated with the law and eager to cultivate the new or at least more open field of political economy (Hennis 1988: 111–12). He supports this by some lines in Weber's correspondence and some remarks in Marianne Weber's biography. Economics was, as Marianne Weber said, "still elastic and 'young' in comparison with law" (Hennis 1988: 111). Weber doubtless was bored with the "essentially mechanical" legal work he had performed as a *Referendar* (Kronman 1983: 190) – an experience that is common among beginning attorneys. This evidence speaks, and speaks rather ambiguously at that, to the question of Weber's attitudes toward a career in the law rather than to his intellectual formation and the sources of his modes of analysis. The considerations of career are nevertheless interesting. One is this: in Germany the law lost the centrality to the task of nation-building that it had when Weber was a student. Economics became more central, and it had become more central to the law itself, a fact Weber was acutely aware of. Weber himself pointed out, in his inaugural lecture at Freiburg, that legal issues tended to culminate in questions of economics. He mentions "one of our leading theoreticians, who thinks he can adequately describe jurisprudence as the handmaiden of economics . . . One thing is true," Weber comments,

the economic way of looking at things is inserting itself into the most intimate regions of jurisprudence, in the handbooks of the Pandectists . . . . And in the judgments of the courts we find not infrequently that where juristic concepts reach a limit, so-called economic viewpoints are introduced – and to use the partly reproachful term of a juristic colleague: this is fashionable.

([1895] 1971: 15)

Weber never abandoned his scholarly interest in the law. He wrote extensively, of course, on the historical sociology of law, a much discussed topic that owes much to, yet departed from, the historiographical tradition that informed his dissertations. The framework of the philosophy of law found another crucial application in Weber's continuous reflection on the problems of leadership and the question of constitutional reform. During the Great War Weber wrote a particularly important series of articles on constitutional questions, and later served as a member of an unofficial group of advisors on a new constitution. The Weimar constitution contained some of his ideas on strengthening presidential powers (cf. Mommsen [1959] 1984; Ulmen 1991).

One major biographical fact deserves special consideration – apart from his much discussed "breakdown" and his wartime service, there was no break in Weber's literary productivity. He did not take time out to retrain himself. This is revealing. If he had no need to do so, it is plausible to suppose that he had been provided with sufficient intellectual capital to see him through his scholarly life as an "economist" and "sociologist." Legal science and the history of law did provide, as we shall see, a framework that served his needs. Weber availed himself of it, and adapted it to the new discipline of "sociology" rather than adapting himself to sociology as practiced by others. The continuities between Weber's version of "sociology" and the "sociologies" that preceded him are notoriously difficult to discern. Unlike most of his contemporaries, he is rarely to be found writing commentaries on previous social theory. Weber's comments on the sociologists who were his contemporaries and predecessors are almost exclusively negative, politely distant, or perfunctory. In contrast, the continuities with the legal tradition are obvious, extensive, and, we shall argue, central to his thought.

His methodological writings of the period after 1903, which followed the only break in his productivity as a scholar, illustrate the continuity. Weber's critiques of Roscher and Knies in 1903 and

1905 and of the legal philosopher Stammler in 1907, his "Objectivity in Social Science and Social Policy" ([1904, 1905, 1917] 1949) in 1904, and *The Protestant Ethic and the Spirit of Capitalism* in 1905, all employ the legal science terminology of "objective possibility and adequate cause." Moreover, Weber's conclusions about the methodology of social science, notably his complex conception of value-relatedness, of the necessarily valuative (and consequently arational) character of the primary categories under which social life becomes a subject of scientific interest and description, are connected to concerns that first arose in legal science. When he insisted that there were elements of cause or logic in social scientific explanation which are factual or rational in a general, non-relative sense, but that these considerations did not suffice, on their own, to constitute the explanatory objects of interest to social science, he echoed the writings of his younger scholarly friends, Radbruch and Lask, on the nature of legal abstraction. These uses will be examined in detail in Chapters 6 and 7. Here it will suffice to say that Weber's use of these ideas fits with rather than conflicts with the fact that Weber's personal contact with lawyers and legal thinkers continued throughout his life.

THE PUZZLE OF WEBER'S ORIGINALITY

Friedrich Tenbruck and Wilhelm Hennis have made the point that the sense we have today of Weber's originality, though it is based partly on the novelty of Weber's thinking and is partly the product of Weber's own "addiction to labored originality" (Hennis 1987: 25), is largely the product of scholarly myopia. Tenbruck explains this myopia as a result of two facts: the internationally dominant position of American sociology and its rather limited concerns after 1945 and the lack of "a real understanding of the history of the German social sciences" in German scholarship itself (1987: 263). As a consequence, "the exegesis of Max Weber," as Tenbruck remarks, "is entrusted to disciplines that possess no connection with the historical cultural sciences from which Weber's sociology developed" (1987: 263). Presumably Weber's apparent originality would diminish if we better appreciated his intellectual sources.

Yet Weber's originality is peculiar. Unlike Nietzsche, who inverted and undermined the intellectual forms and prejudices he inherited, Weber was primarily a reconceptualizer of material that had been worked up by others. A typical Weberian text is based on a small number of specialist authorities, whose topics are presented in a new relation to other topics in a structure of headings and categories of Weber's own devising. In the case of many of Weber's most famous writings, such as his work on the non-Western religions, the practice borders on plagiarism, so closely does he rely on particular sources. But the results are novel, often startlingly so.

It is often supposed that this originality is a product of Weber's concealed intellectual vision, of his novel theoretical or philosophical framework. But it must be said that little in the texts points directly to such a framework. Weber makes few concessions to the "philosophical" or systematic expectations of his readers. No neat evolutionary schemes are imposed on the material, and the morals to be drawn, if there are any, do not flow directly. This leaves the interpreter of Weber in an awkward position, compelled to account for him in terms that do not fit him without Herculean effort very well – to find buried in the texts a liberal political theory, or an evolutionary story, or a "sociological theory."

The Weberian texts simply do not include explicit statements of such theories, and textual links between the persons and themes Weber actually discusses and the purposes and themes of nineteenth-century social and political theory generally are difficult to make: Nietzsche, Spencer, Comte, and Marx scarcely appear in Weber's writings, *in propria persona*, and Mill only in a few problematic instances. Weber's commentaries on other thinkers consisted largely in polemics against figures such as Roscher, Knies, Stammler, and many more obscure figures such as the "Energeticist" culture-theorist Wilhelm Ostwald. The texts are entirely within the tradition of internecine German academic quarrelling: the "great tradition" is ignored.

The puzzle we are left with may be stated simply: neither in the case of Weber's "social theory" nor for the bulk of his "methodology" has the direct link to a well-developed intellectual tradition of social thought been established.[2] For example, the basic constitutive categories of his "understanding sociology," as elaborated in the opening pages of *Wirtschaft und Gesellschaft*, have never been linked to sources in nineteenth-century social theory, though it is the categories of social theory that they are designed to replace. Yet the state of development of Weber's ideas, their sophistication and complexity, suggests that Weber *was* relying on a well-developed intellectual tradition: ideas of this sort are not constructed in a vacuum.

In this volume we will describe Weber's transformation of elements of the philosophy of law into central concepts in his own social thinking. We will meet repeatedly with the following situation. Today's readers of Weber will treat a given idea as one of Weber's most distinctive contributions. Robert Nozick, for example, borrows Weber's definition of a state with the remark that "writers in the tradition of Max Weber treat having a monopoly on the use of force in a geographical area, a monopoly incompatible with private enforcement of rights, as crucial to the existence of a state" (1974: 23). But this definition is not "Weber's." It is a close rendering of Weber's *source*, Ihering.[3] Many other concepts deriving from sources in legal science have had a similar fate: they are understood not as a sophisticated product of a developed tradition, but rather as idiosyncratic thoughts of Weber's, expressed in an obscure way and therefore open to free interpretation. The concepts of "adequate cause" and "objective possibility," both of which are technical terms in the legal science of Weber's time, are a case in point. Understanding the technical significance of these terms greatly limits the kinds of interpretation that can be made of such famous texts of Weber's as *The Protestant Ethic and the Spirit of Capitalism* in which they are employed (Turner 1985, 1986). But the technical significance can be understood only within the literature of the law.

These instances suggest a solution to the puzzle of Weber's originality. Weber was no stranger to the major social and political ideas of the nineteenth century, nor was he unaware of the problems of fundamental philosophy that bore on his interests. But he came to these ideas and problems through the well-established and highly elaborated tradition of legal science. The fundamental *historical* thesis this book will substantiate is that Weber's "originality," particularly with respect to the core categories he used to replace the categories of nineteenth-century social theory, was of a kind that historians of twentieth-century science have made familiar: Weber applied the well-developed intellectual skills and technical background of one specialty to the ill-formed problems of another, with revolutionary results. The *genealogical* thesis of the book is that a primary link between Weber and the larger traditions of philosophy and political theory is through "legal science." This argument is not original. Decades ago, J. P. Mayer, in his *Max Weber and German Politics*, suggested that "Weber was a highly trained lawyer. As such Roman Law – and the history of Roman Law – shaped his mind to a considerable extent" (1956: 146). But Mayer did not follow up this thought, saying that "the legal science is – anyway for the time being – beyond my competence."[4] And although a few later commentators have come to similar conclusions, and even, in one case, correctly identified Ihering as a major source of Weber's categories of action (Kelly 1979: 56–7), none have gone from suggestion to analysis.

Weber uses two primary clusters of legal science literature in constructing his basic conception of sociology. One pertains to the problem of legal causality, which arises in the context of assessing liability. The second is the *Interessenjurisprudenz* of Rudolf von Ihering and the general philosophical and historical account of law which underwrites this conception. We shall show how Weber uses these ideas by explicating central concepts in Weber's writings in light of these sources. The aim is to clarify Weber, however, not to provide a complete contextual account of the legal thinking of the period. This would be a worthwhile task in its own right, with implications for many other thinkers and traditions. French social and political thought, American political science and historiography, and German social thinkers other than Weber also relied very heavily on the achievements of German history and philosophy of law.[5] But the present volume has smaller ambitions. Our primary concern will be with Weber's *modifications* of concepts. Weber's real originality, we shall suggest, is that he laboriously emancipated himself from prior social and political theory by proposing concepts of morality, the state, and interest that had no telic implications. Our solution to the problem of Weber's originality is not to make him into a nineteenth-century social theorist who concealed his social theory, but to see him as an enemy of the project of social theory itself.

IHERING AND LEGAL SCIENCE

Ihering is central to this argument – as he was for Weber and to Weber's context.[6] In a textbook on the philosophy of law written by Weber's friend Gustav Radbruch, Radbruch identifies Ihering as the thinker in whose mind "all motifs of thought" of earlier philosophy of law "were gathered and joined" to produce "the renascence of legal philosophy" that had taken place during the time Weber was trained in the law ([1914] 1950: 66). For Weber, Ihering had a different significance. It was Ihering who supplied Weber with a summation of the tradition of social and political theory. Weber's transformation of Ihering fits the thesis suggested above. Weber freely uses Ihering's concepts in the construction of his own "Basic Concepts." The results are radically different, but the full significance of the difference is hidden in Weber's text.

The general analytic thesis of Ihering's major work, *Der Zweck im Recht* (*The Element of Purpose in Law*) ([1877] 1913), was that the purpose of law is to provide a resolution of fundamental conflicts of interest. The compromises between opposed interests which the law embodies are the essence of the law. The premise was that laws were compromises that served practical purposes. The thesis grounded a practical method of analyzing laws in terms of the interests they are designed to accommodate[7]. This was a jurisprudence, a means of aiding judges in the work of finding the law in specific cases requiring judicial decisions: the law to be found is one which preserves the original purpose behind the compromise that the law embodies. Ihering then turned this reasoning into a full-fledged normative philosophy of law in the form of a theory of society. He concluded that legal coercion was *justified* by its indispensability to the preservation of the fundamental agreements of society. But he added that non-legal traditions were also indispensable to society.

Ihering's argument provides us with the solution to part of the mystery of Weber's relation to the tradition of political theory. Ihering's work, unlike Weber's, is directly linked to liberal political philosophy. Ihering was the most prominent German admirer of utilitarianism, and especially of Bentham, whose own discussion of law provided part of the vocabulary for the approach Ihering developed, and whose inadequacies Ihering sought to correct. Ihering's "correction" consisted of identifying a supra-individual or "social" interest in addition to the individual interests of utilitarianism, which he considered insufficient to account, on their own, for legal order. These novel, supra-individual interests arose from associations. This reasoning is familiar to historians of social thought, for it drove such figures as Tönnies and Durkheim to their most controversial formulations. Today, the problem of what holds social institutions or "society" in place where they conflict with the immediate egoistic interests of members of

11

society is a conundrum for "rational-choice" theorists. Weber avoids this problem and, indeed, is virtually alone among the sociologists of his generation in not stating a dubious "solution" to it. So it is worth asking how he avoids doing so and whether his way of doing so is acceptable, or is simply an evasion of a central problem of social and political thought. The same kind of question can be asked about other "central problems" in social thought, such as the problem of ultimate human nature. The thesis of this book is that Weber had no "social theory" and had no "social theoretical" answers to these questions. Indeed, he did not regard them as genuine problems. But he did deal with these questions indirectly, and the way he dealt with them has surprising implications for our understanding of Weber as a thinker.

The purpose of Weber's analysis is to eliminate the concepts that Ihering, Tönnies and others employ to solve such problems as the origins of normative force in favor of categories which do not make such things as traditions or "society" into supra-individual causal forces or objects, and to conceive the state and the law in terms which do not make *them* into supra-individual causal objects. He solves the latter problems by reconsidering an old chestnut in the philosophy of law, the problem of the emergence of law out of a pre-legal situation. The "solution" is to substitute for a "theoretical" account of "the state" an intelligible causal historical narrative involving belief in the legitimacy-claims of rulers, and to redefine "the state" so that this constitutes an explanation.

The strategy of redefinition and substitution, as we shall show, is carried out methodically. The effect of the substitution is to eliminate questions that require "ultimate causes" as answers. But this strategy places a great burden on Weber. He must resolve the problem of explanation and show that these historical narratives are valid. Here again he turns to the legal science literature. He adopts a theory of probabilistic causation directly from jurisprudence. But the importance of the borrowed conception of causality is in the complex account of the epistemic properties of historical explanation in which it is employed. The account as a whole involves a particular notion of abstraction, which has roots in the notion of legal abstraction.

2

COMMON STARTING POINTS
The world created by purpose and the concept of action

Before the nineteenth century, the positive law was seen as a set of conventions or as commands of the sovereign, backed perhaps by the commands of a sovereign God or "Nature." Legal thinking was seen as the use of "natural reason" to deduce applications of the conventions or commands. The idea of law as a world constituting system of concepts is a product of a changed view of the character of "reason" and "fact" that resulted from the appropriation of Kant in the nineteenth century by the neo-Kantians. The period in which this changed view arose has a confusing history, marked by confusing controversies over Kant's meaning. These controversies provided both the means by which the new conception was established and the grounds for believing that a new conception was needed. Today, the conception that resulted is so familiar that it is difficult to "explicate" it. A list of examples might be a better starting point: Kuhn's idea of a scientific "paradigm," the idea that classes have fundamental "ideologies," and the idea of "local rationalities" or culture-specific rationalities are all applications of the key neo-Kantian idea that particular kinds of knowledge require special "presuppositions" that cannot be rationally justified, but which must be accepted as starting points by persons who wish to acquire this knowledge. The thought may be applied, persuasively, to the law: to master the law is not a matter of mastering principles, but a matter of mastering a way of seeing the world; the relation between "fact" and legal conclusions is not properly understood as one in which there are "facts" which are given a legal "interpretation"; legal descriptions are not redescriptions of facts that are properly described in some other way, such as the language of science or ordinary language, but are properly described in the language of the lawyer; moreover, the

13

assessment of legal description is something that can be done only in accordance with tacit criteria of correctness that are part of the legal way of reasoning.

This view of the law as a kind of fundamental, world constituting ideology raises many questions, which we may postpone until the concluding chapter. It is difficult to carry the reasoning through consistently, especially the idea that the law constitutes a separate conceptual domain or sphere. The early appliers of neo-Kantian ideas to the law were sometimes tripped up by these difficulties, and Weber, it is sometimes claimed, was tripped up by the applications of these ideas to "social science." But Weber, as we shall see, avoided some of these problems, and avoiding them was crucial to his strategy as a whole. A brief introduction to the basic ideas of neo-Kantianism is necessary to understand how Weber understood his own project.

NEO-KANTIANISM

The definition of neo-Kantianism is a matter of scholarly dispute. But we may begin with one of Weber's teachers, and later his colleague, Kuno Fischer, who is generally treated as one of the main initiators of the "return to Kant" of the 1860s, a major moment in the development of this body of thought. Fischer eased the path to the return to Kant by his writings on the history of philosophy, which included as its centerpiece his discussion of Kant in his *Geschichte der neuern Philosophie* (1854). It may be noted that Weber was well aware of the book from his student days. In Heidelberg he took Fischer's course in the history of philosophy, and later, as Marianne Weber puts it, Fischer was one of "the stars on the scholarly firmament" ([1926] 1975) at Heidelberg when Weber was first appointed there. It was Fischer, not Wilhelm Windelband, who was the founder of the Heidelberg school. Fischer's was a kind of vulgate Kant: where Kant's sentences were long and his arguments obscure and difficult for readers to locate in a story of the dialectical progression of philosophical opinion, Fischer's sentences were short and his accounts of the great struggles in the history of philosophy were vivid and accessible. With a few phrases of Fischer's on the subject of dogmatism we can get a sense of the not-so-subtly shifted tone that governed the renewal of interest in Kant. Fischer asks whether various questions which arise in "the conflict of opposed systems or dogmas" can be settled by reason ([1866] 1976: 281). The situation with respect to the existence of the soul is this:

> If psychology claims to have demonstrated the existence, immateriality, and immortality of the soul, the exact reverse of this is asserted, and can be supported by just as many pleas. And the same is the case with the existence of God, ... So in Psychology, Spiritualism and Materialism – in Theology, Theism and Atheism – stand opposed in hostile array. . . .
>
> ([1866] 1976: 282)

It should be noted that these are apparent conflicts *within* sciences, within psychology and theology respectively, just as the dispute over vitalism was apparently a conflict within biology. But they are not disputes that can be settled by reason. As Fischer says, "On scientific grounds the existence of God and of the soul can never be demonstrated; just as little can they ever be denied upon the same grounds" ([1866] 1976: 282). The general lesson is this: "None of the opposed systems can refute the other – none can conquer the other – at least, rationally" ([1866] 1976: 284).

One can give, Fischer argues, a *moral* argument for theism and spiritualism. But "if we succeed in such a controversy, our opponent may indeed lose his social *status*, but reason cannot gain anything by it" ([1866] 1976: 283). In the case of conflicts of systems, "victory on the one side, and defeat on the other, is always caused by the influence of a foreign power, which brings other weapons than rational reasons to bear" ([1866] 1976: 285).

The idea that many intellectual disputes were in fact rationally undecidable "conflicts of systems" or conflicts of fundamental presuppositions is the primary legacy of neo-Kantianism. Familiar disputes, such as the disputes between theologians and scientists that were ubiquitous in the nineteenth century, could be seen as disputes between people with different "presuppositions." So could other differences between the points of view of different disciples or professions. Cultural and historical differences could be conceived in the same way. Because the presuppositions differ, there could be no direct conflict between these points of view; fundamental presuppositions were understood to be "dogmatic" (in Fischer's obsolescent language) or simply non-rational.

A second legacy of neo-Kantianism came from a different use of this same reasoning. Kant's famous question "what are the necessary conditions for the possibility of knowledge?" turns the problem of the justification of presuppositions on its head. It takes the fact of knowledge as a starting point, and asks how it is possible. The presuppositions are justified by their necessary role as premises. Kant, however, was concerned with the presuppositions all thinking beings must accept. This left the question of the status of the presuppositions of the special disciplines open. Hermann Cohen came up with a remarkably fecund answer to the question of how to respond to skeptics about the possibility of knowledge in special domains: the fact that there is a science which presupposes given principles shows their legitimacy.[1] "Similar transcendental deductions" reasoning from the *"Faktum der Wissenschaft"* proliferated. Cohen himself wrote a work in 1877 on Kant's ethics which concluded that the *a priori* validity of Kant's categorical imperative was justified by the fact that a science of jurisprudence existed that presupposed it. To claim the validity of some particular principle of justice on the basis of the fact of a supposed science of justice that employs it as a presupposition cannot answer the skeptic's question of whether the science of justice is itself valid. Similar difficulties arise for such special kinds of knowledge as historical knowledge. If one is a skeptic with respect to the possibility of genuine historical knowledge, one's doubts are not likely to be relieved by an account of the practices by which it is constituted, or of what must be presupposed for there to be historical facts. Indeed, the opposite is true: the relation between the presuppositions and the results is revealed to be circular.

Similar puzzles over circularity played a large role in neo-Kantian discussions of the law. The problem of legal validity, for example, was handled according to a standard formula: the concept of validity is not established by legal science, but presupposed by it. The legal theorist Rudolf Stammler, who popularized this argument, became the representative "neo-Kantian" philosopher of law. Stammler used the reasoning to criticize Ihering's attempt to explain legal validity in terms of a social theory of the evolution of the law as an instrument for the realization of interests, on the grounds that the concept of legal validity could not be derived from the concept of interests. Weber used the formula in a similar way to critique "materialist" social science.

Transcendental argument was, then as now, a notoriously trouble-ridden form of reasoning. The arguments were best in their negative use. For example, they could be applied reflexively to show the inconsistent presuppositions of a person who wished to adduce the facts of history in support of the assertion of the historical relativity of all facts. But they were generally troublesome as means of producing univocal positive results. While it was easy to show that claims, like those of the historical defender of historicism, required non-historical premises, for example, about the nature of historical facts, it was not so easy to say what *specific* premises were required by a given *"Faktum der Wissenschaft."* One might, it seemed, constitute the same facts in accordance with presuppositions that were in conflict.

Diversity in conclusions about the conditions necessary for the possibility of knowledge of something undermines the "necessity" part of the "conditions for the possibility of" clause. To say that one can constitute "facts" on the basis of given premises or a given presupposed framework of fundamental categories is not to say that these are the only categories which can be used to do so. And if they are not the only ones, they are not "necessary." Not surprisingly, this was the Achilles heel of neo-Kantianism, which its successor movements, such as phenomenology (with its slogan of "back to the things themselves"), attempted to avoid. The sheer diversity of the transcendental arguments given in this period in relation to particular subjects, such as law and historical knowledge, and the diversity of the presupposed "principles" they purported to establish, ultimately discredited the neo-Kantian project itself. Too many large works of philosophy appeared, each purporting to establish the presuppositions or necessary formal conditions for the possibility of ethics, each arriving at different presuppositions or conditions. So the second aspect of the legacy of neo-Kantianism, the use of the *"Faktum der Wissenschaft"* to establish presuppositions, gradually was attenuated to the claim that science, or various sciences, *had* presuppositions, and that a science without presuppositions was an impossibility. Weber repeated this idea.

The two key ideas, in their attenuated form, could be combined to produce a simple and compelling image of the development of thought: sciences, cultures, and world views were "systems" with presuppositions. These systems are historical, bound to particular groups and epochs. They succeed one another historically, but not rationally, for reasons cannot establish or undermine basic presuppositions directly. This image is the legacy of neo-Kantianism to post-modernism. By the time of what Gadamer called the "dissolution of neo-Kantianism," a process which was well advanced by the 1920s, human reason had come to seem very limited indeed. Historicist relativism prevailed. It was about to be given a further twist, and new life, by Heidegger. In the chapters that follow, it will be useful to keep the broad outlines of this history in mind. The neo-Kantian movement was a complex and fluid affair. Ihering and Weber took from it what they found useful, and tried to come to conclusions that made sense on their own and were not tied to the vicissitudes of philosophical reputation and fashion.

FUNDAMENTAL CONCEPTS IN THE LAW

The law lends itself to characterization as a world constituting conceptual structure. The list of "facts" admissible in a court of law are different from the facts as we ordinarily think of them and from the facts of science. The reasoning about these facts that is admissible or legally valid is distinct from the kind of reasoning that we accept in everyday life as rational. The courtroom is an artificial setting, like the laboratory, and, as with the laboratory, special training is required to understand fully what is going on within it. The fundamental concepts, such as "responsibility," are akin to concepts employed in non-legal settings, but differ from them, as petitioners often find to their dismay. The peculiarity of legal reasoning and the artificiality of the world disclosed by it is part of the experience of every aspiring lawyer. Those who cannot learn to think like a lawyer cannot become lawyers. But the fact of differences between legal reasoning and other forms of reasoning are continually present to the lawyer. Much of the lawyer's time is taken up with explaining to clients the differences between what is, in the idiom of the client, just, fair or true and what is just, fair or true in the eyes of the law.

There are, however, difficulties with any characterization of the law as a separate "world." The sphere of legal reasoning is not entirely separated from the "world" occupied by ordinary people. Much of what the lawyer does in the courtroom is to translate claims of people about their action framed in ordinary language into the language of the law. J.L. Austin made this point in a famous paper, "A Plea for Excuses," by quoting the statement of Finney, an attendant at an insane asylum who had scalded a patient to death and was being tried for manslaughter in an 1874 case. Finney's statement (rendered here as it is presented by Austin, with statements in ordinary idiom of excuse set in italics) described the circumstances thus:

> I had bathed Watkins, and had loosed the bath out. *I intended putting in a clean bath,* and asked Watkins if he would get out. At this time *my attention was drawn* to the next bath by the new attendant, who was asking me a question; and *my attention was taken from the bath* where Watkins was. I put my hand down to turn the water on in the bath where Thomas Watkins was. *I did not intend to turn the hot water,* and *I made a mistake in the tap. I did not know what I had done until* I heard Thomas Watkins shout out; and *I did not find my mistake out till* I saw the steam from the water. You cannot get water in this bath when they are drawing water at the other bath; but at times it shoots out like a water gun when the other baths are not in use. . . .
>
> (It was proved that the lunatic had such possession of his faculties as would enable him to understand what was said to him, and to get out of the bath.)
>
> ([1961] 1970: 196)

Finney's lawyer said the following (with the legal idiom of excuse set in italics):

> The death *resulted from accident.* There was no such *culpable negligence* on the part of the prisoner as will support this indictment. A *culpable mistake,* or some degree of *culpable negligence,* causing death, will not support a charge of manslaughter; unless the *negligence* be so gross as to be *reckless.*
>
> (R. v. Noakes, quoted in Austin [1961] 1970: 196)

The judge ruled as follows (with the distinctions relevant to the legal idiom in italics):

> To render a person liable for *neglect of duty* there must be such a degree of culpability as to amount to *gross negligence* on his part. If you accept the prisoner's own statement, you find no such amount of *negligence* as would come within this definition. It is not every little *trip or mistake* that will make a man so liable. It was the duty of the attendant not to let hot water into the bath while the patient was therein. According to the prisoner's own account, *he did not believe that* he was letting the hot water in while the deceased remained there.

19

The lunatic was, we have heard, a man capable of getting out by himself and of understanding what was said to him. He was told to get out. A new attendant who had come on this day, was at an adjoining bath and he *took off the prisoner's attention.* Now, if the prisoner, knowing that the man was in the bath, had turned on the tap, and turned on the hot instead of the cold water, I should have said there was gross negligence; for he ought to have looked to see. But from his own account he had told the deceased to get out, and *thought he had got out.* If you think that indicates gross *carelessness,* then you should find the prisoner guilty of manslaughter. But if you think it *inadvertence* not amounting to culpability – i.e., what is properly termed an *accident* – then the prisoner is not liable.

(quoted in Austin [1961] 1970: 196–7)

The lawyer and judge rely on the idiom of the defendant: it constitutes in this case the main evidence for the conclusion of no culpability. But the lawyer does something with the descriptions: he restates them into a language of culpability that allows the law of manslaughter to be applied, and cites a case that is similar in the legally relevant respects in which a similar restatement was accepted by a previous court and thus constitutes a precedent.

Austin's purpose was to show that the idiom of the lawyer and judge compared unfavorably with the idiom of the prisoner. He makes two main points:

(i) Both counsel and judge make very free use of a large number of terms of excuse (the terms set in italics), using several as though they were, and even stating them to be, indifferent or equivalent when they are not, and presenting as alternatives those that are not.
(ii) It is constantly difficult to be sure *what* act it is that counsel or judge is suggesting might be qualified by what expression of excuse.

([1961] 1970: 197)

He remarks that "The learned judge's concluding direction is a paradigm of these faults. Finney, by contrast, stands out as an evident master of the Queen's English. He is explicit as to each of the acts and states, mental and physical: he uses different, and the correct, adverbs in connexion with each: and he makes no attempt to boil down" ([1961] 1970: 197). Austin, in short, takes sides: against the redescriptions or translations given by the lawyer and judge, and for those of Finney, given in "ordinary language." A neo-Kantian might reply to this taking of sides by defending the claim that the law and the descriptions of the law are simply different from that of the ordinary person. The world view of the ordinary person in a given society, however, is just one world view among others. Weber himself makes this claim: even the "language of life" abstracts from reality. "Every type of purely direct concrete description bears the mark of *artistic* portrayal ([1904] 1949: 107). To be sure, the language of daily life is governed by different purposes, and abstracts from the full reality of the case in a different way. From this point of view it is entirely appropriate that the lawyer does precisely what Austin complains of: to take as equivalent descriptions that which are *from the point of view of ordinary language* not equivalent, and to define the act itself according not to ordinary usage but in terms of comparisons Austin considers, however correctly from the point of view of ordinary language, to be inexact or excessively abstracted or "boiled down."[2]

Austin himself acknowledges a difference in purposes – the overriding need, in the law, for a decision, the requirement that "the charge or action and the pleadings be brought under one or another of the heads and procedures that have come in the course of history to be accepted by the Courts . . . [and] the general requirement that we argue from and abide by precedents" ([1961] 1970: 188). If Austin had been writing of Continental rather than common law, he might have said rather than "argue and abide by precedents" that categorizations of action must be consistent with the framework of concepts that is part of the Roman legal inheritance. What is common to both forms of law is the need to abstract, and the fact that the "abstraction" is governed by a distinctive "legal" purpose.

Learning the civil law requires learning how to employ a set of concepts with a long history reaching back to the Roman jurists themselves and refined conceptually by the teachers of the Roman legal tradition. But does this make the Roman law tradition a "paradigm" or "fundamental ideology" – a way of making the world? It is easy to see why commentators would have thought it so. Civil law has a well-defined history, and the history is such that the contrast between legal categories and ordinary language categories is one of its central facts. The Roman jurists were rediscovered, an event known as the "reception" by continental professors of the law, and the system of the Roman law was taught to students from the countries of Europe as a closed scientific conceptual system. It was taught for the purpose of application to circumstances alien to those in which it had been originally conceived, namely the society of Ancient Rome. The properly trained student could, it was supposed, return to his own country and apply these categories and forms of reasoning. The conceptual scheme of the law was systematic, expressed in a different tongue than his native language, and precise. Casuistic argument provided the resources to account for difficulties of application, so that the scheme was not fundamentally challenged by novel kinds of facts. But the characterization is difficult to carry through consistently, and the difficulties become evident in Ihering's work, as we shall see.

TWO PARALLEL PROJECTS: IHERING ON LAW; WEBER ON SOCIOLOGY

Ihering's preface to *Der Zweck im Recht* is explicit about its debt to early neo-Kantianism. The author describes himself as a philosophical dilettante, and expresses his regret that when he was a young man "an unfavorable disposition toward philosophy . . . prevailed" as a consequence of the "spell under which philosophy lay at the time of Hegel . . . . The sovereign contempt with which the philosopher of the Hegelian school looked upon the man of positive science" ([1877] 1913: lv) precluded the raising of philosophical questions by practitioners of the special sciences, such as law. Neo-Kantianism broke this spell, and Ihering wrote in this changed atmosphere. He tells us that he searched widely in the contemporary philosophical literature for inspiration. One specific philosophical source, a text by Trendelenburg, was especially useful. From it he took the idea of "purpose as a world-forming principle," which pointed the way to his own central idea "that purpose is the creator of the entire law; that there is no legal rule which does not owe its origin to a purpose, i.e., to a practical motive" ([1877] 1913: liv). But his approach to the law differed from that of his philosophical contemporaries. He characterized himself as a "philosophical naturalist" who brings to light the universal ideas in his domain, and noted that in this

22

domain he has the advantage over the professional philosopher of possessing "the necessary knowledge of his subject" ([1877] 1913: lv). Because the law is a conceptual universe that already exists, yet also changes in time, one may discover, in the manner of a "philosophical naturalist," the underlying purposive order of this universe through a historical reconstruction of its evolution. Ihering had already made a great contribution to this effort in the *Spirit of the Roman Law*, the last volume of which was first published in 1865, which was among other things an historical refutation of Hegel's account of the contribution of Roman law to the world historical spirit.

Weber, writing at a later date and speaking for the *Geisteswissenschaften* in general but with the problem of historical explanation in mind, sought to perform a parallel task – to explicate the explanatory interest of the practitioner of the practical historical sciences (such as historical economics or sociology) – and he employed similar tools: for Weber, the world of interest to the social sciences was a world constituted by the values of the historical scientist's epoch and by the specific cognitive and practical interests of the specific historical science ([1904] 1949: 51, 61). This meant that, for Weber, the various human sciences were each "world-making." But the world they made was already made by the commonsense culture or "values" of their epoch. So it would be better to say that they were "world-remaking." The distinction is important. If the legal way of making the world operates on the unconceptualized stuff of the world, it constitutes an alternative to the way in which, for example, the commonsense outlook of a particular historical epoch makes the world. But the case of Finney suggests otherwise: that the legal way of making the world operates on facts described in the idiom of those whose actions are being examined. The historical sciences, similarly, remake a world already made for them. But it is unclear how the primary world is conceptually constituted: is it made by the subjects of historical inquiry, and controlled by their idiom, or is it made by the commonsense outlook of the epoch in which the historical scientist writes?

These "methodological" questions, as we shall see, are not neatly resolved by Weber. They turn out to bring in their train a series of other questions. But Weber began his efforts to answer these questions in terms of a particular contrast, between the concepts of the lawyer and those of the historical scientist. Weber's sociology and his methodology proceeded from the recognition that legal science had already examined, in light of its own purposes, many of the same concepts, such as action, custom, and the state, that social theory in the nineteenth century examined, and that sociology, of necessity, was engaged in the construction of a parallel conceptual world.

The parallels, indeed, are close in several respects. The opening pages of Ihering's *Der Zweck im Recht* and Weber's *Wirtschaft und Gesellschaft*, his section on basic sociological concepts, have similar content and a similar structure. If Weber had a consciously chosen model for the structure and discursive character of *Wirtschaft und Gesellschaft*, it might well have been this book. Weber cites Ihering in these opening pages on the subject of *Sitte*. The concept is crucial, as we shall see, to Weber's revision of the problems of social theory. In the notes to the opening section, Weber describes *Der Zweck im Recht*, then 35 years old, as "still a significant contribution." He does not often cite Ihering in the *Wirtschaft und Gesellschaft*, even at the points at which the definitions are lifted almost directly from *Der Zweck im Recht*, as in the case of the definition of the state. But if we look for similarities, there are many to be found, as we shall see in subsequent chapters.

The similarities in form flow from the fact that each work generally resembles, in organization, standard civil law texts, such as Sohm's edition of the *Institutes of the Roman Law*. This work, known in the Anglo-American world as "Sohm's Institutes," was the paradigmatic law book in the Roman tradition. It is sometimes said that where the common law is one of writs, a set of commands that the court may enforce, the Roman law is one of categories. The law aspires to conceptual comprehensiveness or "gaplessness." The form of the law books reflects this aspiration. Texts are organized under *Rubrica*, or headings. In a typical text, definitions under each rubric are given and commented on or explicated. Chapters are uneven in length: sometimes the commentary is short, sometimes extensive, as needed. *Der Zweck im Recht* and *Wirtschaft und Gesellschaft* begin with similar headings. Weber has more headings, and the commentary is more fully historical and empirical in character. The strategies of the two texts differ, as their purposes do, and the divergences are evident from the start. But the broad similarities remain, and the texts begin in such similar ways that they may be usefully read as a case of Weber's practice of revising existing material for his own purposes.

Der Zweck im Recht opens, as does *Wirtschaft und Gesellschaft*, with a characterization of human action. Ihering was a child of his times with respect to his way of conceiving the problem of action, and his conception reflected one of the defining issues of nineteenth-century thought: the problem of cause and teleology. The human domain was thought to be the domain of teleology, the physical world that of material causality. Difficulties arose over cases in which the distinctive vocabularies of causality and purpose overlap, such as the case of organic "life." When both causal and teleological language apply to the same cases, there is a metaphysical problem, a problem of which description is fundamental.

The characteristic solution to this problem of overlapping vocabularies was to draw a line between the worlds of cause and teleology, and to assign human action, or life, to one side or another. In France, where the dispute focused on life, with the "vitalists" insisting on the purposive character of life, it was common to believe that the two principles were ultimately incompatible in the sense that the conflict could be resolved only by reducing the universe as a whole to one or the other. Thus, the philosopher Emile Boutroux, a teacher of Durkheim, solved the problem of finding a place for purposes in a world of causes by inverting it and making it into a problem of finding a (subordinate) place for causality in a purposive universe. An alternative, Kantian, approach to the problem was to conceive of causality as a product of human epistemic purposes. Another option was to fuse causal and intentional idioms. The French philosopher of law Alfred Fouillée invented the notion of "*idée-force*" to explain the role of the notion of justice as both a goal and a cause of human conduct ([1878] 1916: 179–83).

Both cause and purpose have important roles in the law apart from the metaphysical issue of which is more fundamental. In the Roman tradition, like the common law tradition, legal responsibility or liability cannot be assigned unless some criteria of intentionality and causality are met. Unintentional consequences and intentions without consequences do not incur the same kind of legal liability. Because Ihering wishes to explicate legal thought as a pre-existing "fact," he is forced to find a place for both. But he is nevertheless aware of assertions about the nature of causality in the human realm by psychologists which purport to give "scientific" answers to the question of the causes of human action which do not accord with the legal tradition. If one claims, for example, as a psychotherapist, that the criminal conduct of an adult is the inevitable causal consequence of events in early childhood, these events are taken as the cause of the crime.

The idea of "purpose as a world-forming principle" provides Ihering with an answer to these psychologists: their purposes form a different world than the world formed by the purposes of the law. But this answer is ambiguous. Ihering might argue that, whatever the metaphysically true relation between causes and purposes, within the domain of the purpose which creates the law, the relation is the one he explicates. But this is not an entirely satisfactory reply. It leaves open the possibility that the world of the law rests on a scientific falsehood or an error about the ultimate character of the subject matter of the law, namely human action. If purpose is merely a concept imposed by lawyers on a reality that is ultimately causal, it would be an imposition of falsity.

Ihering avoids this difficulty by giving what appears to be a general, non-purpose-relative account of the nature of action, and, conveniently, Ihering's non-purpose-relative account of action as it really is, what we might call his metaphysical account of the fundamental character of action, has a place for purpose. Indeed, it would be a source of trouble if it did not: the phrase "purpose as a world-forming principle" contains the term purpose, and if purposes were not part of the fundamental stuff of the human world, they would not form worlds. But it is not clear that Ihering is entitled, on his own account, to *make* metaphysical, as distinct from purpose-relative, claims about action. If his "general," non-purpose-relative claims, such as his conceptual claims about action, require presuppositions of the special sciences, such as legal concepts, they cannot be used, without circularity, to *justify* the presuppositions of the special sciences themselves. This problem bears directly on the issues we noticed in connection with Austin's critique of the lawyer and judge in the case of Finney. What is the status of "special-purpose" conceptual universes? Are they, so to speak, co-equal with those of science and everyday life (and are the various conceptual universes within science and in everyday life in different cultures co-equal)?

Ihering's solution to the problem of cause and teleology itself proceeds on the general, or "non-purpose-relative," level. He proceeds, in short, as though it is possible to speak of human action as such. Because he will define action in terms of purpose and cause, it is necessary for him to begin by defining the terms. He does so by distinguishing the "law of causality" from what he calls the "law of purpose." His "law of causality" is akin to the Kantian category of cause. It is a constitutive rule, rather than a law of nature: it holds that every change in the world is a consequence of an antecedent change. This "law," Ihering reasons, applies to "movements of the will," because "Without sufficient reason a movement of the will is as unthinkable as a movement of matter" ([1877] 1913: 1–2). The psychological antecedents to willing, the sufficient reasons for movements or acts of the will, are *purposes*: "purpose is as indispensable for the will as cause is for the stone. As there can be no motion of the stone without a cause, so can there be no movement of the will without a purpose" ([1877] 1913: 2). The categorical dependence of physical movement on causes and the categorical dependence of will on purpose are thus equivalent. The "law of purpose" is that there is "no *volition*, or, which is the same thing, no *action, without purpose*" ([1877] 1913: 2). The conceptual indispensability of purpose to willing or volition enables him to define action in terms of purpose. To have a purpose, Ihering reasons, one must have an idea of the future, an idea which provides the object of willing. Purpose thus requires understanding and also the possession by the willing being of the "category of possibility" ([1877] 1913: 3, 6). With this we arrive at a definition of action in terms of the indispensable conceptual components of action.

Ihering sought to resolve the apparent conflict between purpose and cause by dividing action into two parts, parts he thought of temporally as stages of action. The "internal stage" begins with an act of ideation consisting of a representation of a possible future state which promises the subject greater satisfaction than his present state. These thoughts of the future are causally conditioned, both by internal influences, such as the residual effects of training, and external influences. But external influences, such as thirst, do not have "direct power" over the will – they acquire power only by being converted into motives. The process of conversion depends on the measure of resistance an influence finds in the subject. Even if thirsty, "a well-trained dog," for example, "will not drink when his master forbids him" ([1877] 1913: 4). The "internal stage" of action proceeds as follows: possible courses of action (or inaction) are presented to the will by the faculties of ideation and desire. The will balances the reasons

and chooses a course of action ([1877] 1913: 8). The stage ends
with the "resolution, the act by which the will relieves itself of
further balancing" ([1877] 1913: 15). The "external stage" begins
here, with overt action. The two stages thus operate under two
different "principles." The external stage is governed by the law of
causality. The internal stage is governed by the "law of purpose."

The "law of purpose" that governs the internal stage is a bit
mysterious. It has the same form as the Kantian category of
causality, and is justified on the ground of conceptual necessity:
"an act without a purpose is just as much an impossibility as is an
effect without a cause" ([1877] 1913: 9). To "prove" this as a "law"
Ihering proceeds in a way that parallels Kant's own procedure in
the discussion of space in *The Critique of Pure Reason*. Ihering
responds to the two objections to this conceptual claim that he can
conceive, and shows that they are not tenable. The first objection
is that we may be *compelled* to act, for example, by duty or by the law.
The second is that some actions, such as the actions of the insane
and actions that are habitual and therefore "we no longer think
anything in the doing of it" ([1877] 1913: 10), are purposeless but
are nevertheless actions. His response to both objections is to
point out that the terms "because" and "in order to" may be used
interchangeably in the case of action, but *only* where the reason it
connects to the action is *intelligible as a reason*. He gives the example
of a person who said he drank "because it rained yesterday" rather
than "because I am thirsty." In this case, he says, there is no visible
connection between the reason assigned and the drinking ([1877]
1913: 10). Ihering's discussion of this important point is slight.
Weber, in contrast, gives the criterion of intelligibility a large role.

Ihering's response to the first objection is to say that acting out
of duty or legal compulsion *is* acting with a reason. Acting under
physical compulsion or threat is also action, because such cases
require "an actual act of the will and not merely the outward
appearance of such" ([1877] 1913: 11). Ihering points out that the
Roman jurists established this distinction. This raises the question
of whether his reasoning at this definitional stage reflects the
special *legal* interest in the subject of action, or pertains to action
as such and in general. Here, it seems, he falls into circularity: his
justification for a special purpose language is given in the special
purpose language itself (or by appealing to the special purpose
language itself). His response to the second objection is that
habitual action is action with a purpose, but the purpose is hidden,

even from the agent, as a result of repetition. The purpose has been, as he puts it, bound to the act itself to such an extent that "the purpose has ceased to be a consciously perceptible element of the voluntary process" ([1877] 1913: 15).

Ihering's reasoning here extends the notion of acting for reasons beyond the paradigm case of action, which is action for conscious reasons. The extension is crucial to the contrast we will discover between Weber and Ihering, and it marks a major line of division in social explanation generally. For Ihering, actions do *not* have to have conscious reasons, at least where there is an appropriate causal explanation of the reason having fallen out of consciousness, in the case of habit. His discussion of the problematic case of animal "purposes," which provides Ihering with the philosophical germ of the concepts of "interest" and interest-relativity, also extends the application of the concept of action. He rejects such formulations as "animals drink because of the instinct of self-preservation" by denying that animals have a sufficient concept of the self to make its preservation a conscious purpose. The motive, he says, is actually the discomfort the animal feels and the pleasure of relieving this discomfort. But when "the animal turns to the water," Ihering says, "it establishes a practical relation between itself and the water." This "purpose-relation" or "self-relation" is part of the internal stage of action. It comes after the condition that occasions volition, in this case the animal's discomfort, which is part of the domain of cause, and the desire to remove the discomfort, which Ihering says is the "first beginning of purpose" ([1877] 1913: 22), but before the "external deed" ([1877] 1913: 23). The "purpose-relation," Ihering says, which is expressed in the animal as a feeling of dependence on the water, "is the same element which we will find later in man as Interest" ([1877] 1913: 22).

The section on basic concepts of sociology in *Wirtschaft und Gesellschaft* opens with a definition of *sociology*, rather than action. By beginning with a definition Weber avoids the problems of circularity Ihering gets entangled in. He does not make claims about action as such. Weber simply stipulates a purpose for sociology, and defines sociology accordingly. The emphasis in Weber's text is on the epistemic problems of understanding and explaining action that his definition creates, rather than on the fundamental or metaphysical character of the phenomenon of action. Nevertheless, the definitions of sociology and action in the sociological sense closely parallels Ihering's discussion of action. Sociology is defined as "a science concerning itself with the interpretive understanding of social action and thereby with the causal explanation of its course and consequences" ([1922] 1978: 4). Action is defined, for the purposes of "sociology," as behavior to which the agent attaches subjective meaning. The model of action Weber explicates is almost identical to Ihering's, and consistent with their common source in legal science. For Ihering, actions need have no visible manifestations. For Weber, purely inward passivity, acquiescence, and omission are all actions ([1922] 1978: 4). For Weber, action is "social" if it takes account of the behavior of others. But even inward acts may have this quality.

There is, however, a crucial difference in terminology. Where Ihering speaks of purposes, Weber speaks of meaning (*gemeinter Sinn*). But Weber uses this term interchangeably with "purpose" ([1922] 1978: 7–8). When he discusses explanatory understanding, by which he means understanding of motives, he uses "meaning." If we recognize the close connection between "meaning" and "purpose" in Weber's own account, the parallels between Weber and Ihering become clear. In speaking of the meaning of an intentional action, Weber is speaking of what Ihering thought of as the teleological aspect of action. Weber, thinking epistemically rather than metaphysically, stresses that this aspect of action is open to being known only by comparing the course of events in a given case with typical patterns of visible manifestations of courses of action. We shall return to the question of how ideal-types aid in understanding in the next section. One reason for the difference in terms is that Weber wishes to make an epistemic point about understanding which holds both for actions and for the understanding of propositions, such as "2 x 2 = 4," which do not have purposes. *Sinn* covers both cases.[3]

Ihering considered the teleological part of action to be a *stage* of action, the stage governed by the law of purpose. Purposes are not directly accessible, but the "law of purpose" does something to constrain the attribution of intentions to agents. It implies that no aims can be attributed to an agent that are not intelligible as reasons for the actions that the agent takes. Weber restates this constraint as a condition for an adequate *account* of action. An explanation of an action, he says, must be adequate both on the level of cause and on the level of meaning. Where Ihering has "stages," Weber has aspects of a whole: the whole, the "causal interpretation," "is arrived at when the overt action and the motives have both been correctly apprehended and at the same time their relation has become meaningfully comprehensible" ([1922] 1978: 12). The "relation" which must be made comprehensible, however, is simply the relation specified by Ihering's "law of purpose": the relation of being an intelligible reason for an action. Weber adds that the overt manifestations of action that are relevant to the attribution of intentions are not limited to the manifestations of action the individual decides on, that is to say the intended consequences. Visible expressions of emotion, such as "anger as manifested by facial expression, exclamations, or irrational movements," may also bear on interpretation ([1922] 1978: 8).

Weber makes a broad distinction between natural processes and processes with meanings, or intended purposes, which parallels Ihering's distinction between mechanical "causes" and psychological "purposes." In Weber the distinction is between processes which are meaningless, such as natural processes, and those that are meaningful; in Ihering, it is between influences on conduct that have or have not been converted into psychological motives, to which the will has or has not capitulated ([1877] 1913: 12). Both accept, of course, that natural processes are involved in various ways in action. For Weber, the category of natural processes includes memory, habituation, and such phenomena as can be attributed to racial or biological sources. Moreover, as we shall see, he grants that these processes govern an extremely large portion of human conduct. Both agree that conscious ends may be either ultimate or intermediate (that is to say ends that are, or provide, means to other ends). They also agree that actions with clear, single, conscious intentions are rarities and that most conduct is habitual or causally determined by bodily needs and the like. Yet in spite of their general agreement on these points, they come to strikingly different conclusions about how to handle conduct that does not fit the paradigm of conscious intentional action.

Our first hint of this major difference comes with the category of action proper, action with an intended purpose, Weber defines it differently and more narrowly than Ihering. Weber phrases the problem of "what is action" in terms of the "subjective meaning" an individual attaches to his action, and collapses the concept of subjective meaning into the concept of "intended purpose." Subjective meaning must, implicitly, be conscious. Yet it was evident to

Weber, as it was to Ihering, that many of the cases in which the concept of purpose is employed in ordinary usage do not fully share the properties of those cases where the agent is fully conscious of the purposes toward which the action is directed and where these purposes are articulable and comprehensible to others as purposes. They approached this fact in different ways.

LOOSENING GROUNDS FOR ATTRIBUTING INTENTION

The traditional "social theoretical" approach to the understanding of the stable features of social life, such as the law, was to employ the full range of historical knowledge and knowledge about the stable features of human motivation and attempt to fit these facts together with what is known partially and imperfectly about the particular actions of individuals. If one is permitted to discern hidden purposes in actions and quasi-actions, one can construct chains of purposes of a utilitarian type, based on general ideas about human motivation, and see various actions and quasi-actions as contributing to some larger or collective purpose, such as social order. One may be able to arrange actions in relation to one another in a way which exhibits them as satisfying purposes of a larger, collective kind. One may then even identify mechanisms by which these arrangements change and adapt to circumstances through feedback mechanisms. Ihering did all of this in his account of law in *Zweck im Recht*, which is a model "social theory."

Social teleological analysis of this sort inevitably requires one or another kind of loosening of the standards by which intentions or purposes are attributed. Ihering loosened the standards in two directions simultaneously: first, by assuming that one can attribute purposes in the absence of conscious articulation, at least under appropriate circumstances, and, second, by assuming that there were more or less fixed human interests which could be widely attributed. These are such commonplace variations on the idea of intentional action that one might reasonably ask whether one can have a social theory or theory of the law without *some* such loosening. Functionalism and Marxism, with its idea of objective interests, could not proceed without attributing motives in the absence of conscious articulation. Functionalist sociology and anthropology typically proceeded by taking the patterns of action it explained as "functional" regardless of the professed purposes of those who performed the acts: thus the purpose of primitive rituals which were performed for the conscious purpose of providing magical protection could be said to serve such purposes as reducing anxiety or increasing social solidarity. This can be done, of course, only if one has in advance some notion of the "real" purposes that are there to be served.

As we have seen, this kind of reasoning is accepted by Ihering. He followed the rule that an attribution of purposes had to be made to fit with the observable features of conduct. But while this rule eliminates many possible attributions of intention, at least for actions with a familiar course, for many actions it leaves open a wide range of possibilities, some of which cannot be eliminated by identifying features of the situation with which they are in conflict. Given Ihering's theoretical purposes this was a convenient sort of underdetermination. It left him free to select from the possible imputable purposes. He could then reason circularly, on the basis of the larger social ends he thought he could discern in legal evolution, and attribute to agents, as their "real" interests and motives, the intentions that served the larger social ends he could observe being fulfilled.

The divergence in Weber's and Ihering's views of animal behavior is revealing in this respect. In the first edition of his book, Ihering had insisted that two fundamental differences between animals and humans were that animals used other animals only as means and that animals do not learn and transmit their learnings. In later editions he recanted both claims. In particular, he recognized many cases of mutual aid and he accepted that "even the idea of society, i.e. of regulated living together for the purpose of pursuing common ends, already appears in the animal world" ([1877] 1913: 59). In this case, as elsewhere, Ihering is satisfied to *infer* purpose, on the basis of apparently purposive behavior. He refuses to deny the animals' "purposing power the name of will because of a defective self-consciousness which is less complete than man's own" ([1877] 1913: 6). Even "the idea of a future event," which is readily attributed to animals, he argues, "means an idea subsumed under the category of possibility," and this implies the "use of the categories of purpose and of means" and therefore the control of these by "understanding."

Weber considered such imputations of purpose to be epistemically unwarranted anthropomorphization. Like Ihering, he accepts that "many animals 'understand' commands, anger, love, hostility, and react to them in ways which are evidently often by no means purely instinctive and mechanical and in some sense both consciously meaningful and affected by experience" ([1922] 1978: 15–16). But where Ihering used this fact to collapse animal behavior into the category of purposive action, Weber's strategy was more complex. He suggests that "biological analogies" may prove suggestive in connection with "the question of the relative role in the early stages of human social differentiation of mechanical and instinctive factors, as compared with that of the factors which are accessible to subjective interpretation generally." He argues that these factors are "completely predominant" in the earlier stages of human development. But he also claims that they are "often of decisive importance" in *later* stages, particularly in connection with "traditional action" and charisma. He observes, for example, that "the seeds of certain types of psychic 'contagion'" are at the root of "many aspects of charisma," and claims that they "are very closely related to phenomena which are understandable either only in biological terms or can be interpreted in terms of subjective motives only in fragments" ([1922] 1978: 17). Compared with Ihering, this is quite a drastic extension of the domain of the biological. Moreover, this reasoning went hand in hand with the expression of strong doubts about the relevance of "interpretation in terms of subjective motives" to understanding phenomena that are primarily determined by biological causes. At one point he remarks that "In a way our ability to share the feelings of primitive men is not very much greater" than our ability to share those of animals ([1922] 1978: 16).

Loosening the grounds for attributing purposes or intentions is at the core of many approaches to the problems of social science. Modern economic theory and rational choice theory, which have made their way into writing on the law (cf. Posner 1991), depend on loosening as well, and in practice the loosening is even more radical than Ihering's. Purposes are attributed to the actions that make up aggregated patterns of action, such as those of buyers in a market, without regard to evidence of actual individual intentions. The much weaker requirement of "plausibility" with respect to rational-choice attributions is the economist's substitute for this constraint. The economist, however, employs a test of attributions of preferences and choices to economic agents. The "test" for these attributions is that they "explain" *as rational choices of individual agents* the aggregate pattern they are constructed to explain. Yet, this test, in contrast to the "test" of fitting with supposed "social ends" is a quite stringent one – sufficiently stringent that many social patterns, such as the act of voting, appear to be beyond explanation, at least if one applies to the situation such basic assumptions, widely employed in rational-choice accounts, as regarding voting as instrumental and supposing that individuals have some sort of relatively coherent set of at least partially transitive preferences which allow for the substitution of ends. The difficulty in explaining voting is quite simple: a decision to forego almost any good, such as ten minutes of sleep, in favor of voting makes no sense in instrumental terms, because the probability of an individual vote affecting an electoral outcome is so low.

Economic analysis has, since the nineteenth century, been reluctant to associate itself with the concept of *homo economicus* as anything other than a kind of abstraction. The criticisms of economic man leveled by the "Historical School" of economics in Germany, which stressed the historical variability of economic motivation, was part of the background to Weber's own economic and methodological writing. Though Weber defended classical economic theory as a useful abstraction, he rejected it as a philosophical anthropology. Such a defense of the explanatory utility of economics may be made on various grounds, but it must overcome a central problem. If economics is an abstraction, it must be an abstraction from something with explanatory force if it is to have any explanatory force.[4] Economists of the Chicago school sometimes have been relatively open about this, as Ronald Coase is when he suggests that

> human preferences came to be what they are in those millions of years in which our ancestors (whether or not they can be classified as human) lived in hunting bands and were those preferences which, in such conditions, were conducive to survival.
>
> (1988: 4)

Coase then comments that

> It may be, therefore, that ultimately the work of sociologists (and their critics) will enable us to construct a picture of human nature in such detail that we can derive the set of preferences with which economists start.
>
> (1988: 4)

35

This serves to root the abstractions of economic analysis in facts of the science of evolutionary biology – albeit a not yet consummated science. "Preferences" have explanatory force because of these roots in human nature. Weber defended the model of rational action quite differently. He associated classical economics with a particular type of action, the kind of action that fits the model of decision-making rationality, and he considered this to be the most fully understandable type of action. But where rational-choice theory attempts to assimilate other forms of action to this model, Weber argued that rational decision making was unusual. This argument, like the difference of opinion with Ihering with respect to animal intention, is a sign of Weber's divergence from competing approaches. Characteristically, however, the point of the argument is concealed.

Weber makes claims about the rarity of particular kinds of action and, more generally, about the distribution of actions between various categories of action in a large number of places in *Wirtschaft und Gesellschaft*, the text in which he introduces his classification of action. These assertions, which are usually ignored or "corrected" by interpreters, have a peculiar character. There could be no serious "empirical" basis for such assertions, if only because there is no way to count "actions" and sort them into categories. Weber himself recognizes this. Indeed, he acknowledges that there are no boundaries between his fundamental types of action, and therefore there is nothing in the way of categories of the kind one could sort things into. But by dividing action into ideal-typical categories, Weber is able to undermine any sort of general reduction of action to human nature and provide an alternative picture of the causal basis of the domain of human conduct that undermines the rational-choice project.

Weber divides actions into a set of four ideal-typical categories: *zweckrational, wertrational,* affectual, and traditional (see the Appendix). Each of these categories is somewhat strange, as is the means of classification. Weber seems to be distinguishing not different types of *intention* so much as different fundamental *causes* of action. So the classification is one of predominant *causes.* Traditional action, for example, is described as "determined by ingrained habituation" ([1922] 1978: 25). Affectual action is "determined by the actor's specific affects and feeling states" ([1922] 1978: 25). *Zweckrational* action is "determined by expectations as to the behavior of objects in the environment and of other human beings." But in this case the character of the beliefs of the agent has something to do with the classification. "These expectations are used as 'conditions' or 'means' for the attainment of the actor's own rationally pursued and calculated ends" ([1922] 1978: 24). Similarly for "value-rational action": it is "determined by a conscious belief in the value for its own sake of some ethical, aesthetic, religious, or other form of behavior, independently of its prospects of success" ([1922] 1978: 24–5). The causal strength of the determinants is the distinguishing element in the classification.

Traditional action is the largest category. Most human behavior is repetitious and routine. But the category is something of an oddity in the classification itself. It is properly not a subcategory of "intentional action" but an extension of the non-intentional notion of habit. Weber argues that only a vague borderline separates such "actions" from pure reactions, like "the reactive type of imitation," which are non-intentional and therefore not actions proper. The "great bulk of all everyday action to which people have become habitually accustomed approaches" the category of non-action, for it is "very often a matter of almost automatic reaction to habitual stimuli which guide behavior in a course which has been repeatedly followed" ([1922] 1978: 24–5). In short, then, even the conduct that falls into the category of traditional action is at the limits of the category of action, and close to thoughtless "reaction." The only reason "its place in a systematic classification is not merely that of a limiting case [is] because . . . attachment to habitual forms can be upheld with varying degrees of self-consciousness" ([1922] 1978: 25). Thus *because* one can act in a "traditional" way with full self-consciousness and intentionality, habitual conduct resembling intentional traditional conduct can be regarded as quasi-action. "Affectual" behavior, in its pure form, "also stands on the borderline of what can be considered 'meaningfully' oriented, and often it too goes over the line" as, for example, when it is an "uncontrolled reaction to some exceptional stimulus" ([1922] 1978: 25). Thus both in this case and in the case of traditional action there is a continuum. Each of these kinds of action is the intentional case of a type of conduct, either "reaction" or "habit," that is usually not performed with conscious intentions and is therefore beyond the borderline of "action" proper.

The only categories that are action properly and unequivocally are *zweckrational* (instrumentally rational) action and *wertrational* (value-rational) action. The paradigm cases of *wertrational* action involve "clearly self-conscious formulation of the ultimate values governing the action."

> Examples of pure value-rational orientation would be the actions of persons who, regardless of possible cost to themselves, act to put into practice their convictions of what seems to them to be required by duty, honor, the pursuit of beauty, a religious call, personal loyalty, or the importance of some "cause" no matter in what it consists. In our terminology, value-rational action always involves "commands" or "demands" which, in the actors opinion, are binding on him. It is only in cases where human action is motivated by the fulfillment of such unconditional demands that it will be called value-rational.
>
> ([1922] 1978: 25)

How often does this happen? How often is conduct determined by these motives? Weber is unambiguous about this: "for the most part only to a relatively slight extent" ([1922] 1978: 25), though in a few cases people are motivated to a high degree by these "commands."

Zweckrational action is also a "limiting case" – not because, as in the other cases, it stands at the border with non-action, but because the orientation of action wholly to the rational achievement of ends requires ends, or, as Weber puts it, a "relation to fundamental values," which cannot themselves be chosen rationally.[5] Thus, by definition, no action can be wholly *zweckrational.* This argument is Weber's response to rational choice analysis. *Zweckrational* action is defined in terms of decisions, in terms of the weighing of consequences of different courses of action. But the ideal-typical case of *zweckrational* action is fully conscious. There is no place – in the ideal-type – for tacit "decisions" hidden behind actions in the form of decisions to follow "preferences" that can only be "revealed" through their manifestations in action. Moreover, a transitively coherent set of ends – the essential premise of economic or rational-choice analyses – has no role in Weber's account, *save where* coherent ends are part of a conscious ideal or conscious situation of choice. Most actions, indeed, may be satisfactorily characterized by comparing them with a standard pattern of simple intentional action. These actions do not need to be interpreted as a decision, nor do they need to be connected to higher or more ultimate purposes unless these connections are part of the consciousness of the individuals in question. Ideals of rational decision making can usefully serve in the rational reconstructions of particular complex actions, such as military decision making in battle. But in this case the goal is to make sense of the meanings attached to particular courses of action by the agents – to approximate their understanding of their situation and to identify the causes of the errors of the decision-makers.

"UNDERSTANDING" ON THE MARGINS OF ACTION

The effect of Weber's alternative picture of human conduct is to place conscious intentions and biological causes on par with one another. Each can serve as a cause of human conduct, but in most cases the determinants are largely or wholly biological. Action, as Weber depicts it, is a small island of self-conscious intentionality in a sea of conduct which is determined largely biologically – "reaction," "habit," and the like. Most of the island is itself a swamp, made up of a kind of quasi-action, largely determined – causally – by the biological forces of habit and reaction but distinguished from purely habitual and reactive conduct by the fact that there is some "meaning," often only dimly apprehended by the agent, to the action. Our intellectual access to these quasi-actions – the possibility of our "understanding" it – is limited. Understanding is understanding "meaning," and these quasi-actions are on the borderline of the meaningless. In some cases – charisma, the doings of primitive man, and group feeling or contagion – we are simply unable to "understand." The causes are not "meaningful" but are rather biological, and "meaning" is not a clear guide to causation in these cases. In a crowd situation, for example, "the most diverse kinds of feeling – gaiety, anger, enthusiasm, despair, and passions of all sorts" – may arise much more readily than "if the individual were alone." And "for this to happen there need not, at least in many cases, be any meaningful relationship between the behavior of the individual and the fact that he is a member of the crowd" ([1922] 1978: 23). In these cases there is a discrepancy between the feelings that the persons would have if they conformed to the ideal-type of persons acting in accordance with meanings alone and the feelings they have in the crowd. Feelings are heightened by the crowd situation, and this heightening suggests that other causes, rooted in the biological character of humans, contribute to the feelings.

When Weber speaks of biological causes he does not seem to think that he is describing action from a special "biological" point of view that is simply different from the sociological point of view. As we have seen, he characterizes the subject matter of the sociological point of view, namely action, in terms of facts about causality and claims about which actions are and are not predominantly determined by biological causes. In this respect he is in the same dilemma as Ihering. He cannot characterize action from the point of view of sociology without characterizing it as such, just as Ihering could not avoid giving a general character-ization of action. But if Weber believed that all characterizations of causes were "from a point of view" it would be contradictory for him to make claims about the "predominant causes" of actions as though he had access to the causes in an absolute, "no point of view" sense.

Is Weber entitled to these assertions about causes? Do they contradict his own account of "points of view?" Whether Weber's argument here is adequate is a matter to which we shall return in the last two chapters. It raises all the troubling problems we noted in relation to Austin – questions about whether certain forms of description from certain points of view, such as the point of view of natural science, are privileged. More generally, it raises the question of whether the notion of "points of view" is adequate as a picture of these differences. But Weber may be interpreted in ways that do not lead quite so directly to these difficulties. His basic argument is negative. It is based on the recognition that meaning attributions are limited in their power. They apply well in only a narrow range of cases. But they are nevertheless indispensable to us, for the ideal cases, the cases in which intentions are conscious, are the only ones that we can "understand" with full clarity. So if we pursue understanding, we are condemned to this strategy and to the few cases to which it applies.

The question Weber is compelled by the limitations to ask is this: what does the universe of human conduct look like as seen through this admittedly limited instrument? What is the whole of human conduct as seen from the point of view of the problem of understanding? Weber's answer is that it is a mixture of the under-standable, the non-understandable, and the semi-understandable.

The understandable is that which matches the ideal types that we already understand. The semi-understandable is that which partly matches them. And the non-understandable is that which does not match them. We know, simply as a result of our general familiarity with human beings, that some of what does not match may be attributed to biological causes, though we may be vague about what the precise scientific character of these causes might be.

As we have seen, when we account for "actions" that do not fully fit the model of conscious intentionality, which is to say the quasi-actions that constitute the overwhelming proportion of human conduct, we are forced to match ideal-types, for example the ideal-type of a person shooting someone out of revenge ([1922] 1978: 9), with a pattern of conduct which fits it only imperfectly. The reason for this is to be found in the causal character of the actions themselves.

> In the great majority of cases actual action goes on in a state of inarticulate half-consciousness or actual unconsciousness of its subjective meaning. The actor is more likely to be "aware" of it in a vague sense than he is to "know" what he is doing or to be explicitly self-conscious about it. In most cases his action is governed by impulse or habit. Only occasionally and, in the uniform action of a large number of individuals, often only in the case of a few individuals, is the subjective meaning of the action, whether rational or irrational, brought clearly into consciousness. The ideal type of meaningful action where the meaning is fully conscious and explicit is a marginal case.
>
> ([1922] 1978: 21–2)

Explaining this conduct requires some sort of loosening of the application of the notion of intention or the standards of evidence of intention, and Weber accepts this. But Weber assimilates his loosening to the general epistemic problem of the gap between reality and purified abstractions. He argues that the sociologist must often work with ideal-types because of their clarity, but should keep in mind that he is in fact imputing motives and meanings on the basis of an ideal-type ([1922] 1978: 22). In cases of conduct in which intentions are not fully conscious, the sociologist must match up the external features of the conduct with the ideal-type. The problem of what something meant for a person can be solved by this kind of matching – by identifying an

41

insult which made them angry, for example, by determining what, in some course of events, preceded the visible manifestations of anger and insult. Doing so supplies us with a motive for their subsequent action ([1922] 1978: 19). Needless to say, however, this is an uncertain process, in which we begin from a base which is secure, namely the ideal-type of insult in which the meaning is clear to us, and extend its application to material which is not clear to us and will always be partially obscure.

Weber opens a very large loophole by this argument. It allows him to say that even in the face of lack of self-consciousness about meaning the sociologist "may reason as if action actually proceeded on the basis of clearly self-conscious meaning" ([1922] 1978: 22). In the case of uniformities of action, for example the conscious intentions of persons, the few cases of the conduct in question in which conscious intentions figure can be taken to be indicative of the unconscious intentions behind the conduct of the rest ([1922] 1978: 21). In Weber's *The Protestant Ethic and the Spirit of Capitalism*, for example, the habitualized patterns of Protestant behavior are explained by reference to the explicit statements of such persons as Benjamin Franklin. Weber treats Franklin's formulations – maxims of the "early to bed, early to rise, makes a man healthy, wealthy and wise" variety – as the conscious idealizations to which the behavior of Protestants is an approximation. One important implication of this reasoning should be noted. "Meanings" must, implicitly, be conscious, but they may be peripheral to our consciousness. So one may, and indeed in the great majority of cases *must*, treat these peripheral semi-conscious meanings as the explanatory equivalents of fully conscious "meanings."

For Weber, there is no point to the quest for underlying hidden purposes that are *not* part of at least the semi-conscious awareness of the agent or, in the case of "uniformities of action," his or her peers. Social theorists, as we have seen in the case of Ihering, have typically reasoned differently. The key argument of Weber's contemporaries was that the individual's purposes and especially moral feelings were a product of social purposes that could be discerned by observers to be operating in a person's actions, much as they could be discerned in animals. Both Ihering and Weber's closer contemporary Ferdinand Tönnies supposed that the underlying purposes were to be discerned in something lying beneath the surface; both of them regarded the reasons people gave for their conduct to be rationalizations of habit.[6] So did Durkheim, who had an even stronger interest in studies of animal social life. These thinkers supposed that the habitual responses in which "morality" and moral feeling consisted could not be accounted for without appeal to social purpose or will, or deeper social "causes." Weber looks at the same actions and concludes that they are actions rather than mere behavior because and only because we can attribute meaning – that is, we can believe that the agent consciously, though perhaps dimly, attributes the same meaning to the act that we as observers attribute to it. Our only grounds for such an attribution, however, is on the basis of similarity to ideal-types of meaningful action. So sociology, as Weber defined it for himself, could not be about underlying purposes – not because there were no underlying purposes but because they were outside the domain of meaningful social action and therefore inaccessible to the sociologists' methods of attributing meaning. This leaves open, as we shall see, the question of the true nature of society, the fundamental causes of human action and indeed virtually all of the moral questions that social theories like those of Ihering were constructed to solve. This "leaving out" was obviously by design.

Weber's larger design is still unclear. This much, however, is evident. Weber faced a fundamental problem as a result of the definition of sociology he gave. It is so restrictive that it is difficult to see what sorts of things a sociology limited to this approach *can* explain. Yet the structure of basic sociological concepts in *Wirtschaft und Gesellschaft* is comprehensive: few if any of the topics of importance to nineteenth-century social or for that matter legal theory are omitted from the text. So Weber's aim, we may hypothesize, was to show *what* such a limited sociology could explain, and thus to show why it was preferable to alternative social theories. But if this was his aim, he did not pursue it in the usual way: he did not provide a foundationalist philosophical justification for his preferred terms, claim them to be uniquely "scientific," or embed them in a reflexive, self-justifying doctrine of historical development in which his terms represented the pinnacle of intellectual development – the model of Marxian "Critical Theory." In the following chapters, we shall see how he created and filled out the comprehensive structure of basic sociological concepts in *Wirtschaft und Gesellschaft* within these self-imposed limits, and how this achievement bears on the claims of his competition. In fact, as we shall see, Weber was careful to account for all of the kinds of puzzles and anomalies on which "social theory" traded, and to answer, in his own fashion, the main questions it raised – or to give grounds for dismissing the questions.

One of the "main questions" was the problem of human nature. Ihering believed that there was a common core of human wants. History, for him, was the quest for the fulfillment of these wants through the creation of social institutions, such as the law and the recognition of rights in the law. Weber was concerned to account for the same set of institutions and their history. But his methodological views, and especially his denial of hidden purposes, made it impossible for him to account for social institutions in terms of a hidden social teleology. In the next chapter we shall see how Weber varied Ihering's account of fundamental human motivation. Both dealt with the problem in terms of the concept of "interests." But each conceived of interests in different ways.

3

INTERESTS AND IDEALS

Weber and Ihering both employed the term "interests" lavishly. Ihering had a proprietary sense about the term. He originally used it in *The Spirit of the Roman Law*, completed in 1865, in which he claimed that interests, rather than will, constituted the basis of the law. As he saw it, this was a startling departure, and indeed it was – from the Kantian tradition, in which disinterestedness was the mark of the moral. Ihering's early uses of the term, however, are not easily distinguishable from the notion of utility. Only later, with *Der Zweck im Recht*, was the concept integrated into a broader historical theory. The broader theory accounted for the properties of legal relations (such as contracts, associations, and the state) in terms of the individual interests which they realize. Accounting *historically* for these legal forms and their changes required an expanded notion of individual interests and human purposes – expanded, at least, from the Benthamite principle of pleasure and pain.

Weber adopted Ihering's distinctive contribution – the categories of "material" and "ideal" interests. One of Weber's most famous statements could, indeed, have been written by Ihering:

> Not ideas, but material and ideal interests, directly govern men's conduct. Yet very frequently the "world images" that have been created by "ideas" have, like switchmen, determined the tracks along which action has been pushed by the dynamic of interest. "From what" and "for what" one wished to be redeemed and, let us not forget, "could be" redeemed, depended on one's image of the world.
>
> (Weber [1915] 1946b: 280)

"Interests" constituted, for both Ihering and Weber, a level of

45

explanation that was prior to and distinct from the level of intention. But they disagreed about the contents of the category and in particular about the way in which interests arise. The key to the difference is in their divergent conceptions of ideal interests.

IHERING ON ASSOCIATIONS AND SOCIAL INTERESTS

Ihering's "theoretical" premise is that the source of all interests is to be found in "egoism." But he acknowledges that "He who knows no other motive of action than egoism will find insoluble riddles confronting him in human life" ([1877] 1913: 36). One of these riddles is the fact that self-denying actions occur. So simple egoism is false. But some modifications to the thesis that an individual's own pains and pleasures are at the root of all that individual's actions may suffice to preserve it. As Ihering notes, self-denying actions do not occur indiscriminately:

> I make sacrifices for my children, for my friends, for a common purpose, but not for the Shah of Persia, not for the building of a temple in India. My self-denying motive is not impelled blindly, finding every purpose equally acceptable; for it criticizes and discriminates between purposes. They must all have some definite reference to me if I am to warm up to them.
>
> ([1877] 1913: 39)

This was the core of the idea that made Ihering's reputation in Germany as a critic of utilitarianism. The purposes for which one denies oneself are *social* purposes. Social purposes have a particular genealogy. Egoistic interests or purposes create social interests by virtue of the fact that the realization of most egoistic interests is possible only through other individuals ([1877] 1913: 36–47), and in particular through "associations" which have distinct supra-individual purposes, which is to say social purposes. Ihering's critique of utilitarianism consisted of an argument to the effect that utilitarianism conceded the interest of society and therefore the independent reality of social purposes.

The utilitarians' mistake was in identifying egoism with *individual* purposes. This, Ihering said, led them into a fundamental conceptual difficulty. Even Mill conceded the propriety of the interest of society in various regulations designed to keep an individual from acting against the interest of others. But in doing this, Ihering pointed out, he conceded the validity of the standard of the "interest of society." Mill made this concession in the course of his attempts to draw a line between justified and unjustified intrusions into individual freedom. These attempts were, as Ihering showed, hopelessly *ad hoc*. On the one hand Mill denied the propriety of laws that have the purpose of forcing an individual to act for his own good against his will. On the other hand, he said that the law could forbid a person selling himself into slavery, on the grounds that freedom cannot be used for its own destruction. But *every* contract, as Ihering observed, "contains a partial renunciation of freedom" (translated in Stone 1950: 302). This argument was used to establish the claim that there were "interests," "social" interests, above the interests of individuals. The difficulty for Ihering was to make sense of these interests historically, as something more than the expressions of the will to power the state.[1]

The conceptual consequence of admitting the validity of collective interests (such as the interest of society) is that "individual" interests become only one set of ends among many interests, some of which may have equal or superior force. The interests are also different in kind. "Associational" interests have a degree of autonomy from individual interests. They persist historically over longer periods than the particular individual egoistic interests that give rise to them. But, like individual interests, they are subject to evolution and alteration. Moreover, new circumstances and conflicts create new coincidences of interest between individuals, which in turn make new associations possible and desirable. Associations and their activities, of course, produce new circumstances – under which new purposes may be created. This process made for the evolution of interests.[2] These core facts about associational interests are the basis for Ihering's evolutionistic social theory. The ideas impressed social theorists and jurisprudential thinkers throughout the world, and echoes of them may be found preserved in many settings. In what follows, we shall give a very schematic introduction to the core concepts and ways of arguing that are distinctive to Ihering, with an eye to Weber's ultimate uses and modifications of these ideas, but this discussion should not be taken as a full account of this important thinker.

Ihering's argument begins with a simple theory of human nature, a philosophical anthropology. The "world," Ihering says, has four levers. The first two are given by nature and take the individual form of pleasure and pain; or, from the point of view of the user of the levers to influence action, of reward and coercion ([1877] 1913: 26–7, 73). These primary objective positive and negative levers have "subjective" or psychological forms as well: honor is the carrot and psychological coercion is the stick.³ Ihering said of psychological coercion that it is a kind of "indirect compulsion" ([1877] 1913: 34). In contrast to external compulsion, the "mastery of another's will . . . [in which] the resistance which the foreign will opposes to our purposes is broken by summoning physical power superior to its own," in cases of psychological coercion "the resistance of the foreign will is overcome by itself from within" ([1877] 1913: 176–7). The second set of levers are moral or ethical, involving the feelings of duty and of love.

Cooperation, "*connecting one's own purpose with the other man's interest*" ([1877] 1913: 28, italics in original) and securing "agreement of wills" between parties, is the basis of all social forms or forms of association, including the state. The model is the valid contract⁴ in which the decisive fact with respect to validity is *not* the objective reality of the interests or the naturalness of the community of interests, but *subjective* interest and assent. Interests may be created "artificially" in the sense that a buyer or seller may offer inducements. Moreover, because the "subjective conviction of interest" is decisive to securing agreement in wills, in such paradigmatic cases as commercial agreements this may depend on salesmanship, which Ihering calls "business eloquence" ([1877] 1913: 29). Ihering's insertion of the notion of "subjective conviction of interest" marks a step away from reductive naturalism, the idea, central to Hobbes, for example, that social institutions may be explained by reference to a simple list of more or less fixed human needs or wants.

The concept of ideal interests is another step in the same direction. The reasoning behind it is characterically legal. Ihering points out that forms of work that are not considered, legally, a proper subject for exchange and therefore of material reward may be rewarded in non-material ways, and that these rewards may have a large significance in society. He notes that in Rome it was considered ignoble to pay for intellectual work ([1877] 1913: 81).⁵ But the gift of non-manual services by free men to the state was not unrewarded: the reward was honor. When money was needed to support an intellectual worker, a novel legal form, the

48

honorarium, was invented for the purpose of distinguishing it from mere money payment for labor. Interest in honor is the paradigmatic "ideal" interest. Such interests may, as in the case of administrative intellectual work in the later Roman Empire, come to be mixed with monetary reward. But honor is conceptually distinct from monetary reward, and cannot be reduced to it. It is a distinct "lever" that can be used in the process of securing agreement in wills or more generally in inducing particular forms of behavior.

Ihering uses the "levers" of reward, coercion, honor (or ideal interest) and psychological coercion as a means of categorizing the social relationships that employ them. Commerce is organized compensation, reward given for reward. Revenge is the return of evil for evil.[6] These are, so to speak, the primitive social uses of the two lower "levers." Commerce has two forms, exchange and association. "Exchange presupposes a *difference* of need on both sides, and accordingly also a difference in the means whereby the need is to be satisfied, viz., in the mutual services" ([1877] 1913: 95). Identity of purpose is the basis of association or, in legal terms, the contract of partnership "when the purpose exceeds the powers of a single person, or when the combined pursuit of it gives a prospect of economy in the means to be expended, or greater security in the attainment of the purpose." The Roman legal term for this sort of association is *Societas.* Commerce is egoistic in essence, and largely self-regulating. Competition and supply and demand set prices and define "equivalence." Each person, acting egoistically, constrains the others by rewarding them with remuneration. Under ordinary circumstances, law is *not* necessary. But there is a role for legal coercion in the regulation of commerce in checking excesses of egoism, such as those that produce the extraordinary circumstances of force, fraud, and the like. Legal coercion, then, has only a supplementary role, albeit a necessary and in some circumstances important one, in relation to commerce. But the idea of *replacing* commerce by state power, replacing reward by coercion, is not practical: "Coercion is effective only so long as the whip is in sight; remuneration works continually" ([1877] 1913: 105).

These ideas appear in Weber. Weber comments that "only a limited measure of success can be attained through the threat of coercion supporting the legal order" and that "This applies especially to the economic sphere" ([1922] 1978: 334). In the opening section of basic sociological concepts in Weber's *Wirtschaft und Gesellschaft*, Weber defines the concept of "social relationship" ([1922] 1978: 26–8) in a way that stresses the "subjective meaning" that is attached to it and distinguishes "communal" and "associative" relationships (the latter corresponding to *Societas*) ([1922] 1978: 40–3). He also discusses the problem of membership ([1922] 1978: 43–6), relationships of representation (or agency) and mutual responsibility ([1922] 1978: 46–8), and "organization" ([1922] 1978: 48–50). In each case his discussion of a "social" relationship is modelled on the discussion of legal relationships. In the sections of *Wirtschaft und Gesellschaft* devoted to the sociology of law, contracts are distinguished and the history of their forms is discussed ([1922] 1978: 641–729), much as they are by Ihering. The details vary between Weber's treatment and Ihering's, but often they do not vary by much. In Weber's definition, "'Exchange' is a compromise of interests on the part of the parties in the course of which goods or other advantages are passed as reciprocal compensation" ([1922] 1978: 72). The definition is Ihering's as well ([1877] 1913: 28). Both of them typically stress that actual cases are often of mixed character. Ihering distinguishes between "organized" purposes and "unorganized" purposes, meaning collective purposes which are achieved without direction. He gives science as an example of unorganized purposes, a concept he explicates in a manner reminiscent of Michael Polanyi's later treatment of science. When Weber makes a parallel distinction between "Consensual and Imposed Order in Organizations" (which he says "coincides in its broad lines ... with the distinction between public and private law") he comments that "it goes without saying that the majority of actual organizations partake of both characteristics" ([1922] 1978: 52).

Weber's treatment varies with respect to the subdivisions or subcategorizations of exchange, among other things. The significance of these variations is obscure. But there is a large systematic difference between Ihering and Weber with respect to interests that has its roots in the problem of the agent's consciousness of his or her purposes, a problem discussed in Chapter 2. Ihering reasoned that while various social ends might easily be recognized *retrospectively* to be concealed in the practices of a society (its manners and its statutory laws) or in the individual purposes subjectively significant for action, it is not characteristically the case that people have a self-conscious understanding of the connection between their practices or subjective interests and the social purposes they serve. In his discussion of "ideal interests," for example, Ihering argued that such acts as dying for one's country or for particular principles in fact served societal purposes. So part of his own analysis is a kind of *Ideologiekritik*, the general aim of which is to show the real societal purposes behind apparently non-egoistic, non-societal, ideal aims.[7] His thesis is that

> Behind the so-called ideal interests, which we pursue, behind the idea, for which we set our strength and life, stand real personalities, whose well being, be it what it will, ought to be fostered, we ourselves, our supporters, our comrades in belief, our fellow citizens, the poor, scientists, etc., at a higher power, a whole *Volk*, at the highest, humanity – every idea of a practical motive of our action ends finally in living essence.
>
> ([1883] 1886: 89)

This consideration informs Ihering's practice as a social theorist: if we wish to explain an apparently anomalous but causally important interest, we are advised to seek the hidden purposes it serves.[8]

Weber handled ideal interests differently, and the difference points to a fundamental difference in design. Weber does not deny the reality of group interests. Nor does he deny that ideological superstructures may be built on these interests. The ideology of the common lawyers, he thought, was an articulation and institution of their status interests, for example. But the term status interests itself suggests that these interests are distinct from and perhaps not reducible to either "material interests" or group interests of the sort Ihering has in mind. Indeed, in some of the crucial cases, the ultimate explanation is to be found elsewhere. The "emotional foundations" of political community, for example, are to be found in the subjective realm, in the fact, as Weber puts it elsewhere, that on the battlefield "the individual can *believe* he is dying 'for' something." The "location of death within a series of meaningful and consecrated events," rather than common interests in well-being, "ultimately lies at the base of all endeavors to support the autonomous dignity of the polity based on force" ([1915] 1946a: 335). The contrast to Ihering is direct: for Ihering, the basis of the state is interests, and the basis of ideal interests are

MAX WEBER: THE LAWYER AS SOCIAL THINKER

social interests. For Weber, the significance of consecrated death on the battlefield stands on its own as an explanation, and does not need to be backed or supplemented by reference to "social" interests.

The same differences in approach are evident in the contrast between Ihering's attempt to follow the strategy of reduction to social interests in discussing the concept of "vocation" and Weber's later treatment of the concept in *The Protestant Ethic and the Spirit of Capitalism*. Ihering examines "vocation" in a chapter on the lever of "reward," and defines it as follows:

> By vocation ("Beruf") in the social or objective sense . . . of the word, *i.e.*, the subjective qualification, the inner voice, which calls ("vocare," "rufen") a man to a task, we understand a definite kind of activity, for which the individual puts himself permanently at the disposition of society: his *social post*. If the vocation is combined with the economic purpose of the subject to make his living thereby, it is called a *trade or business*. A trade or business is therefore a branch of work *for which* or *from which* the individual intends to live. In the phrase *for which* we have the relation of the business to society; in the phrase *from which* we have its relation to the subject.
>
> ([1877] 1913: 106–7)

Ihering's point is that having a vocation means serving a particular social purpose that confers rights of a sort on the clients of the person who is "called," as a result of the obligation to perform the services to which one is called. The "honor" of the businessman is to provide services. "[H]onor in the objective sense (the respect of the world) is the recognition of the social worth of the person; in the subjective sense it is one's own feeling and the actual living up to his worth" ([1877] 1913: 108–9). Work understood as work in a calling is no disgrace, and neither is the acceptance of pay for such work. He notes, anticipating Weber's thesis in *The Protestant Ethic and the Spirit of Capitalism*, that the notion of vocation is alien to the classical world and to the distinctions he describes in relation to *honoraria* ([1877] 1913: 107).

The difference between Weber's and Ihering's treatment is simple: Weber ignores the claim that callings serve or can be explained by higher "social" purposes. Thus in "Politics as a Vocation" he advances a distinction between "living for" and "living off" politics identical to Ihering's. For Ihering, "living for" and "living off" are two aspects of any vocation: the "for," however, is the social purpose "for which" the individual works. Weber's use of the contrast is different. As a practical matter, he observes, everyone in politics lives both "for" and "off" it to some extent, but a few have independent wealth and can live predominantly "for" it, meaning that such a person "makes politics his life, in an internal sense," either because he "enjoys the naked possession of power" or because "he nourishes his inner balance and self-feeling by the consciousness that his life has *meaning* in the service of a 'cause'" ([1919] 1946: 84). No concealed social purposes stand behind these interests or explain them. In *The Protestant Ethic*, work in vocation is something that becomes the subject of a theologically motivated value-choice, an other-worldly ideal interest sanctioned by Calvinist theology. It does not "serve social purposes" in Ihering's sense, but nevertheless has material consequences of the greatest significance: it is an ideal interest that remade the world by bringing about modern capitalism. Here, as in the case of death on the battlefield where consecration is an independent causal fact, the consecration of worldly callings *precedes* its effects on the material interests of the called, and the effects are unintended. With these examples we can begin to see the significance of the difference between Weber and Ihering noted in the previous chapter with respect to their willingness to attribute purposes to actions, as it bears on substantive explanations. Weber is careful to identify unintended consequences. But he is equally careful not to construe these consequences as serving hidden purposes, much less reduce them to social purposes. On the contrary, he *alters* Ihering's examples or redescribes them in a way that eliminates the notion of social purposes. Yet, as we shall see, Ihering's argument itself may be seen to pave the way for Weber's repudiations of social teleology, for Ihering's account of ideal interests provides Weber with one of the means by which he undermines the concept of social purposes.

FROM INTERESTS TO VALUES

Ihering was curiously ambivalent about the naturalness of the interests to which he appealed, and the ambivalence runs through his explanations. As we have seen, when Ihering discusses the contract as a form of association, he notes the role of what he calls "business eloquence" in bringing about a conviction of interest, or subjective interest. There is of course a legal issue here: the distinction between fraud, a bringing about of a conviction of interest on the basis of lies, which annuls a contract, and the kind of persuasion which does not. But Ihering makes little of this distinction or of the role of persuasion, doubtless because he thinks that material interests so widely predominate, are so present, and are so numerous that the possibility of a person making fundamental errors about self-interest is not terribly significant from the point of view of social theory.

Nevertheless, the concept of interest itself undergoes a peculiar change in his hands. One list of ideal interests he gives includes "entertainment, distraction, pleasure, vanity, ambition, social considerations, etc." ([1877] 1913: 30). Later he adds more: satisfying the feeling of duty and security from the dread of *ennui*. These lists serve an important purpose for Ihering: they help him make the point that the role of "interest" in social life is persuasive. But they also represent a dilution of the explanatory power of the concept of interest. Interest becomes not a fixed factor which explains diverse purposes, but a term that is the virtual equivalent of the specific purposes for which one acts – which is to say the thing which the concept was designed to explain in the first place. Expanding the concept of interest to include ideal interests, in short, collapses the concept of interest into the concept of intention.

Ihering's distinction between objective interests and subjective interests creates another loophole. If "interests" can be made subjectively convincing without being in accordance with causally important interests, is it not at least possible that the causally important interests in a given domain are these subjectively convincing but objectively false interests? Could it not be that people very often act in terms of what they have been persuaded, wrongly, to believe are their interests? The explanatory significance of objective interests or purposes would disappear utterly if this were so, unless we could say, with the Marxists, that "in the last instance" objective interests would be determinate or that there was some sort of limit to the possible substitution of subjective interests for objective interests.

Ihering gives no argument for believing that the pursuit of objectively false interests is not the general condition of social life and law, apparently because he did not consider this to be a real issue. Perhaps he would have argued that there are genuine (but not general) *de facto* constraints on the process of creating a "conviction of interest" that would preclude the wholesale rise of novel objectively false interests. He did provide some grounds for responding in this way: he was greatly concerned with the genealogy of such things as moral feelings and judicial sense, which he explained by habituation and the emergence of novel mutual interest in the continuation of practices or customs, such as tipping. In each of these cases, however, objective interests, individual or social, could be found to be served. He might have argued that this is the only way novel ideal interests may arise, and that business eloquence or persuasion alone could not produce an ideal interest, but only something more transitory, such as a "conviction of interest." If Ihering supposed that "business eloquence" and its variants have limits, for example if he thought that human nature and human motivation are fundamentally plastic, he might have thought that the means for transforming them are limited. But he did not say this. In all likelihood he simply believed that the utilitarians were fundamentally correct in their image of human motivation, and that this image simply needed to be softened, reconciled with evolutionism, and extended to account for such interests as honor, rather than discarded.

Ihering presented a famous lecture called "The Struggle for *Recht*," in which the issue of subjective convictions of interest is clarified in part. The lecture begins with a Nietzschean-sounding paradox: "The end of the law is peace. The means to that end is war" ([1872] 1979: 1). He argues that our sense that this claim is paradoxical is produced by the conceptual error of thinking about law statically, as a mere set of principles or ideas. But "The law is not mere theory, but living force" ([1872] 1979: 2). The law is always in a process of change in which the existing law conflicts with rights that are being claimed. If the struggle for the recognition of these rights succeeds, they become law. Where Savigny and the Romantics went wrong, Ihering suggests, is in their image of organic growth – violent struggle is in fact the norm in legal change. But struggles to establish legal rights have a property that distinguishes them from material–interest struggles: they are fought with a tenacity that is out of proportion to the material interests involved. Ihering explains that, like a lawsuit that costs more to pursue than a person will gain from its successful resolution, these are struggles to force the recognition of rights

([1872] 1979: 28). This is, as Ihering says, an "ideal end" ([1872] 1979: 28) and rights have an "ideal value" ([1872] 1979: 59).

The basis of the struggle for rights is not material interests but pain, the psychic pain of transgression of the feeling of legal right ([1872] 1979: 61), which accounts for the disproportionate response. This feeling of pain, however, has roots in social interests:

> In defending his legal rights [the person] asserts and defends the whole body of law, within the narrow space which his own legal rights occupy. Hence his interest, and this, his mode of action, extend far beyond his own person. The general good that results therefrom is not only the ideal interest, that the authority and majesty of the law are protected, but this other very real and eminently practical good which every one feels and understands, even the person who has no conception whatever of the former – that the established order of social relations is defended and assured.
>
> ([1872] 1979: 74)

The inchoate feeling of pain is the experienced form of what is only dimly apprehended: that the practical good of social order itself is at stake.

We may observe here that certain forms of the present-day case for a feminist jurisprudence fit Ihering's model very closely. The quest for legal protection of rights begins in inchoate feelings of pain which are the product of fundamental natural desires (for example for recognition). These desires come to be articulated as a demand for the recognition of new rights, demands that initially are seen to be alien and threatening to the existing legal order. Ihering, of course, had in mind the recognition of workers' rights. The pattern, however, is identical: for Ihering the process in each case was part of a larger evolutionary process of expanding social utility through the extension of legal rights.

Weber wrote at a time in which Ihering's assumptions about the social utilities of ideals – in sociological terms, his normative functionalism – had been challenged by Nietzsche, who was Ihering's contemporary and by some accounts was influenced by Ihering (Gromitsaris 1989). Nietzsche understood Ihering's genealogical reasoning well, and his attack on this style of reasoning is memorable. On the idea of purpose as an explanation of the legal practice of punishment, Nietzsche offers a word on the origin and purpose of punishment – two problems that are separate, or ought to be separate: unfortunately, they are usually confounded. How have previous genealogists of morals set about solving these problems? Naïvely, as has always been their way: they seek out some "purpose" in punishment, for example, revenge or deterrence, then guilelessly place this purpose at the beginning as *causa fiendi* of punishment, and – have done. The "purpose of law," however, is absolutely the last thing to employ in the history of the origin of law: on the contrary, there is for historiography of any kind no more important proposition than the one it took such effort to establish but which really *ought to be* established now: the cause of the origin of a thing and its eventual utility, its actual employ-ment and place in a system of purposes, lie worlds apart; whatever exists, having somehow come into being, is again and again reinterpreted to new ends, taken over, transformed, and redirected by some power superior to it; all events in the organic world are a subduing, a *becoming master*, and all subduing and becoming master involves a fresh interpretation, an adaptation through which any previous "meaning" or "purpose" are necessarily obscured or even obliterated.

([1887] 1969: 76–7)

This is to say that to explain the transformations of a thing is to identify the power that transforms it and reinterprets it to serve new ends:

purposes or utilities are only *signs* that a will to power has become master of something less powerful and imposed upon it the character of a function; and the entire history of a "thing," an organ, a custom can in this way be a continuous sign-chain of ever new interpretations and adaptations whose causes do not even have to be related to one another but, on the contrary, in some cases succeed and alternate with one another in a purely chance fashion. The "evolution" of a thing, a custom, an organ is thus by no means its *progressus* toward a goal, even less a logical *progressus* by the shortest route and with the smallest expenditure of force – but a succession of more or less profound, more or less mutually independent processes of subduing. . . .

([1887] 1969: 77–8)

For Nietzsche, the struggle to subdue underlies "the continuous sign-chain of interpretations." But the relations between the "sign-chain of interpretations" and the struggle to subdue are contingent rather than systematic.

The Nietzschean picture, in which there are more or less independent processes – of interpretation on the one side and subduing and resisting on the other – raises many questions. What precisely is the power of a new interpretation? Is it a matter of the relative strength of the vital forces to which it is allied, however contingent the alliance? Or is it in some sense a matter of the power of the interpretation itself? Here again it is useful to consider the parallels to the claims of feminism. Are they a new interpretation which is to be victorious because of the political force of the movement behind it? And, if so, what are the interests behind the movement? Superior fidelity to the experience of women's reality seems to be a plausible ground for women to accept a given articulation of their interests. But what if these interests are not reconcilable with articulations of interest that are faithful to the experience of men? And what if no change in the character of gendered experience – through social reform or the reinterpretation of experience – can produce a common articulation of interests? Is struggle inevitable, and is all "justice" then merely victor's justice? These are deep questions that any theory of justice that employs the distinction between interpretation and force in its various forms, such as the paired notions of "false consciousness" and "objective interests," must face. For Nietzsche, at least, the "struggle to subdue" is an explanatory end-point – a more or less fixed feature of human existence rooted in natural differences in strength between people. He proposes an alternative form of *Ideologiekritik*: the "values" people adopt are, for Nietzsche, expressions or intellectualized forms of their urge to subdue, or intellectualizations of their resentment at being subdued, as in the case of the "slave-morality" of Christianity.

Weber rejects both the kind of reasoning that reduces values to objective utilitarian interests and the Nietzschean idea of the underlying urge to subdue. His grounds for doing so are given both in his own work and in that of his friend and contemporary Gustav Radbruch, a legal scholar and philosopher of law. The core idea they shared, and which Radbruch applied in his own philosophy of law, was that the value choices that are available to us are rationally irreconcilable. By this they meant specifically that certain kinds of value disputes were not open to rational resolution.

A Tolstoyan Christian, for example, would choose to reject all worldly legal orders. Against the consistent Tolstoyan Christian, the reasoning of an Ihering would have no force. The Tolstoyan choice is "other-worldly", Ihering's values are "this-worldly." There are no common grounds for choosing the one over the other. The Tolstoyan would reject any resolution that rested on worldly goods. The utilitarian would reject any resolution that rested on the "other-worldly" goal of obedience to divine edict. In another passage Weber gives the example of the presumably "factual" question of whether the Mormons or the Indians were better adapted to the Salt Lake area. He observes that

> one person may assert that the greater numbers and the material and other accomplishments and characteristics which the Mormons brought there and developed, are a proof of the superiority of the Mormons over the Indians, while another person who abominates the means and subsidiary effects involved in the Mormon ethics which are responsible at least in part for those achievements, may prefer the desert and the romantic existence of the Indians. No science of any kind can purport to be able to dissuade these persons from their respective views. Here we are already confronted with the problem of the unarbitratable reconciliation of end, means, and subsidiary consequences.
>
> (Weber [1917] 1949: 26)

Weber's and Radbruch's insistence on the ineliminability of these ultimate moral conflicts led them to a view of morals radically at variance with Ihering's. Ihering responded to value conflicts by ordering purposes in an impersonal, "objective" hierarchy in which, for example, the choice of individual values over collective values can be understood as a kind of self-contradiction, and by explaining "ideals" by showing them to be affirmations of concealed social purposes. Weber and Radbruch, in contrast, insisted on the cognitive necessity of choice. It was for them a kind of dishonesty or torpor to refuse to accept the implications of this cognitive necessity. Thus they stressed, in their "normative" writings, the *moral* desirability of self-conscious value choice, that is, of recognizing the potential conflicts between choices and the need to make "responsible decisions", conscious decisions between fully understood alternatives, and of ordering value choices in a *personal* hierarchy (Weber [1917] 1949: 18; Radbruch, [1914] 1950: 112). But they did not think that there were general rational grounds for choosing to live a life of self-conscious decision. Radbruch called this doctrine, whose premises Weber shared,[9] "decisionism" or "relativism."

Their argument is developed on the level of "logic." Its implications for the explanation of social life and historical development are unclear. Weber's famous statement, in the lecture "Science as a Vocation," that "so long as life remains immanent and is interpreted on its own terms, it knows only of an unceasing struggle of these gods with one another" ([1919] 1946: 152) fits the notion that the ultimate moral reality is unceasing struggle. But it is clear, and Weber acknowledges this, that there are long periods in which particular moral schemes, such as Christianity, are dominant, and the "struggle" is irrelevant or inactive. In some contexts Weber and Radbruch went beyond the notion of unceasing struggle to the thought that ideas had their own causal powers. Radbruch is most explicit about this when he writes that

> ideas do not fight the struggle of the interests all over again in the clouds like the Valkyries above the battlefield; rather, like the Homeric gods, they descend to the battlefield and fight, powerful forces themselves, side by side with the other forces. Granted that, on the one hand, legal philosophy is the struggle of political parties transferred into the realm of the spirit; on the other hand, the struggle of political parties in turn represents a grandiose legal philosophical discussion. All great political changes were prepared or accompanied by legal philosophy. In the beginning there was legal philosophy; at the end, there was revolution.
>
> (Radbruch [1914] 1950: 55)

Moreover, when Radbruch used the term "relativism" he was careful to insist that it was not, as he put it in one book,

> cognate to Pilate of the Gospel, in whom practical as well as theoretical reason becomes mute: "What is truth?" It is cognate rather to Lessing's Nathan, to whom the silence of theoretical reason is the strongest appeal to practical reason:

"May each of you vie with the other then in bringing out the power of the gem in his own ring."

([1914] 1950: 58)

With this formulation, Radbruch comes close to affirming a model in which moral ideas themselves have a kind of historical force. Weber may also be found making claims which appear to grant a kind of anthropomorphic causal power to ideas. His conclusion to *The Protestant Ethic*, in which he observes that "Since asceticism undertook to remodel the world and to work out its ideals in the world, material goods have gained an increasing and finally an inexorable power over the lives of men as at no previous period of history" ([1904–5] 1958: 181), seems to grant causal powers to the ideal of asceticism. However, in the specific case of Protestant asceticism there is a mundane causal interpretation of the usage. There is a potential causal effect, a feedback effect, of the ideas or ideals of a person on the success of that person's ventures, and this effect may hold for groups of persons holding the same ideas or ideals. Thus "asceticism undertook to remodel the world" may be construed as a literary conceit, a personification of a large-scale historical process involving many individuals acting on similar "ascetic" ideals.

Yet Weber wants to make a stronger point as well. Ideals, such as anarchism or Tolstoyan Christianity, may be powerful and historically effective whether or not they lead, through such feedback mechanisms, to self-continuation. The fact that odd, other "worldly ideals" are logically possible, and that they are frequently historically important, has an important implication. Not only are *justifications* of ethical systems by appeal to ultimates of human nature not possible, it is not always (and perhaps not often) possible to give historical *explanations* of ethical systems by reference to fundamental common interests. The effect of this reasoning is to reject explanations in terms of "material interests" or "human nature" understood as ultimate causes. They retain their role as proximate causes, and despite these "in principle" disclaimers, in Weber's actual explanations and analyses, material interests play the predominant role. One reason for this central role is relevant to law: material means are essential to the achievement of many "ideal" interests, and intermediate ends may be shared between persons who have radically diverse "ultimate" values. Radbruch quotes a French jurist to this effect:

61

Peace, security – these are the first benefits the law is to afford us. Even if we should be in profound, irreducible disagreement on the higher ends of the law, we could nevertheless arrive at an understanding so as to make it achieve these intermediate ends in which we are all interested.

(quoted in Radbruch [1914] 1950: 108)

There is, in short, a community composed of persons with common intermediate aims, such as "order," which each needs to pursue different ultimate values. But some persons – such as the Tolstoyan or the radical anarchist – because of their ultimate values, stand outside this community of intermediate aims. The unusual case in which the law itself is rejected is a major concern of both Weber and Radbruch. Radbruch recounts the long history of religiously motivated denunciations of the law ([1914] 1950: 107, 129). "This-worldly" value choices may also conflict with the law, of course, as the facts of criminality and revolutionary terror ([1914] 1950: 92) show. As value conflicts, they are not, as both Radbruch and Weber agree, rationally adjudicable. From this it follows that "the law" itself cannot be rationally justified as a value in the manner attempted by traditional normative legal theorists. There is no extra-legal goal of the law, such as peace, that all rational persons share and that overrides all other goals.

Religiously motivated rejections of the law are historically exceptional. For the most part the law secures "intermediate ends in which we are all interested," as Radbruch concedes. So in their accounts of the ordinary case, Radbruch and Ihering are close. Where Ihering says we achieve our egoistic ends through others, and the associations we make with others are means to these ends, Radbruch would say that many people share the intermediate ends secured by law. But Radbruch adds an important disclaimer: the sphere of the law itself requires "decisions" between rationally irreconcilable options, for example between the legal values of certainty, expediency, and justice (Radbruch [1914] 1950: 109). Radbruch argued that in law the choices were structured by the fact of the mutual dependence of the three basic values – individuality, collectivity and community – that constituted the sphere of law.[10] The achievement of each required, he argued, the achievement, to some extent, of the others. Radbruch was a socialist, and held to what he called a "social view" of the law. His analysis of private property illustrates his reasoning about "mutual dependence": "even the individualistic theories of ownership," he observes, "were never purely individualistic. They were based on the assumption of a prestabilized harmony between individualistic selfishness and the common weal" ([1914] 1950: 166). Consequently, "even in the legal view of today, private ownership appears as an area of activity for private initiative, entrusted to the individual by the community, entrusted in the expectation of its social use, always revocable if that expectation is not fulfilled" ([1914] 1950: 167). This formulation, he thought, turned the question of nationalization into a factual question of its effects rather than a matter of ultimate values: the individualist believer in property "rights" who concedes the necessity of the intermediate good of legal order and the state concedes that the domain allotted to private initiative is a matter of policy rather than an absolute. The "mutual dependence of values" argument thus has implications that are similar to Ihering's notion of a "social interest" created by association, but does not depend on general claims about human nature or objective interests.

EXPLAINING INTERESTS

To understand Weber's approach to the explanation of interests, his surrogate for Ihering's genealogical accounts of the basis of ideal interests in social interests, it will be useful to introduce some technical terms. Charles Taylor used the term "explanatory asymmetry" to characterize forms of explanation in which a certain condition did not demand explanation (for example, because it was "natural"), whereas other conditions ("deviations from the natural") require explanation (1964: 21–5). Taylor had in mind the difference between teleological explanations, in which there was a favored end-state which, if reached, did not demand further explanation, and causal explanations, which he took to be symmetrical because there is no favored "unexplained" state. Asymmetries, however, arise in causal explanation as well, in a different way. The causal laws of science, as understood in textbook philosophy of science, are themselves a kind of explanatory dead end: some laws may be explained by higher or more comprehensive laws, from which they can be deduced, but the "highest" laws cannot be explained at all; as John Stuart Mill remarked, explanation is the substitution of one mystery for another. If we substitute a form of explanation for another form of explanation which has different asymmetries – for example a causal explanation that appeals to general scientific laws that are not themselves explained by other laws for a teleological explanation which appeals to purposes that are ultimate in the sense that they are not themselves explained by higher or more encompassing purposes – we have displaced the explanatory problem. Typically, to "displace" an explanatory problem is to accept new asymmetries, to change the dead end which the explanation reaches.

The concept of "objective interests" depends on an asymmetric explanatory structure in which the fixed and unproblematic character of the normal case is assumed and only deviations from it are explained. Failure to act in accordance with one's objective interests may be treated asymmetrically as intellectual "error," as the product of false consciousness, alienation, fetishism, and so forth. This structure is of course open to many variations. The problems vary according to one's conception of objective interests: for a Marxist, the problem to be explained by a sociology of knowledge is the failure of the proletariat to recognize its "objective" historical class mission; for Pareto, it is non-logical conduct of various kinds. We may ask what sorts of novel asymmetries are produced by a conceptual revision of the concept of interest along the lines specified by Weber and Radbruch. Ihering's concept of interest was more or less fixed. It was ultimate in the sense that it was not further explained, for example, by placing human motivation in the perspective of biological evolution.

What is the dead end in Weber's explanations? Weber does not make it easy to answer the question. He uses the notions of "interest," "material interest," and even "objective interests" in his explanations without treating any of them as ultimate. Some ideals, moreover, are not traceable to interests at all. Consider his comment on the "sense of justice":

> Experience shows . . . that the "sense of justice" is very unstable unless it is firmly guided by the *pragma* of objective or subjective interests. It is, as one can still easily see today, capable of sudden fluctuations . . . . Being mainly emotional, that "sense" is hardly adequate for the maintenance of a body of stable norms. . . .
>
> ([1922] 1978: 759–60)

Weber acknowledges that "the sense of justice" has some effects, even if it is "unstable." These seem to be effects that are not causally traceable back to interests, though sometimes the "sense" is "firmly guided" by their "pragma." Doubtless Weber would also argue, as indeed Ihering had before him, that the sense of justice was largely a matter of habituation. But Weber makes no attempt, as Ihering did, to trace such habituations back to "interests" or "purposes." "Subjective interests" raise similar difficulties. What explains them? And how do they relate to objective interests or material interests? Weber must be taken as believing that there are subjective interests that are not reducible or explained by objective interests. But the category of subjective interests undermines the stability of the concept of interests itself. If "subjective interests" are, sometimes at least, simply decisions about what ideational ends to seek, a conclusion that seems to fit Radbruch's discussions of religious rejections of the law, it seems that the notion of subjective interest is not very different from the concept of subjective purpose or value.

If we think of this set of issues in terms of the problem of the explanatory displacement and the substitution of explanatory asymmetries, it is evident that by substituting Weber's and Radbruch's scheme for Ihering's we displace an explanatory scheme with one large explanatory asymmetry, namely Ihering's unexplained concept of interest, and substitute a large group of asymmetrical appeals to the various interests and values that individuals have. Solving explanatory problems by breaking them down into smaller components that are more readily explained is of course a strategy that is often successful. Breaking one problem into many, however, is only a first step: the component problems must still be solved. But Weber made no attempt to solve the problem of the origin of values, at least not by providing a general formula.

Many of Weber's successors considered this inadequate and sought to provide alternative accounts that remedied this deficiency. Talcott Parsons, Weber's expositor to American sociology, sought to correct Weber by employing ideas about the underlying normative patterns that were functionally necessary for society. This was, in effect, a return to Ihering's views. But Weber himself, it appears, did not consider "values" to be deficient as explanatory facts. He argued that explanations that stopped at the point of ideas were no less legitimate than those that stopped at material interests. His position was that all explanations and causal chains come to an end someplace, and there is no general reason for accepting one asymmetric stopping point over another, that is to say for accepting chickens rather than eggs as an answer to the question "what came first?" In practice, action explanations do come to at least a temporary stopping point – the point at which a person makes a decision. And the acceptance of a value, when it is done consciously and intentionally, is a kind of decision. If we grant, as Weber would, that the causes of the decision may include influence through imitation or group emotional contagion, we have an explanation of value choice that is similar in kind to other action explanations. Weber considers this sufficient, and does not consider a general theory of values to be necessary for the task of explaining values. Although Weber did not provide a general theory of values, such as Ihering's, he was nevertheless greatly concerned, as Ihering was, with the historical development of ideals. In particular, he sought to provide accounts of the practical consequences of ideals and the ways in which these practical consequences affected the development of the ideals. This suggests that Weber believed that piecemeal accounts of the development of values and ideal interests could be given. In Chapter 5, we shall see how he employs the concept of charisma to serve this purpose.

Parsons, who speaks for the tradition of teleological social theory represented by Ihering here, had a point. The crucial "values" of a society are not easily assimilated to the model of conscious choice, even a model relaxed to include contagion and imitation. The difficulty is not with the element of consciousness (which Weber, with his notion of semi-conscious quasi-actions, has a response to) but with the element of choice. Tolstoy's followers, it may be said, made a choice. They fit Weber's model of value-rational action, in that the choice "involves 'commands' or 'demands' which, in the actor's opinion, are binding on him" ([1922] 1978: 25). But the edict "Thou shalt not steal" not only has the form of a command and is in the actor's opinion a command, but also is experienced as something external to the self. It is thus very different from a choice. Weber understood this objection. But he did not, as Parsons would have preferred, try to explain the phenomenological sense of the externality of morals by appealing to the social forces that backed the "command." His response, as we shall see in the next two chapters, was to break up the problem of the force of morality into a series of separate topics. For example, the case of stable normative patterns, Parsons' focus, was addressed under the heading "uniformities of action," and not treated as a matter of choice at all.

4

THE COMMANDS OF MORALITY

Though it is presented as part of the section on basic sociological concepts in *Wirtschaft und Gesellschaft*, Weber's classification of uniformities of action appears, on the surface, to be of little importance. It is concerned with distinctions between *Sitte, Brauch, Wert, Mode,* and *Recht.* Although Weber uses some of these concepts in his sociology, his discussion of the distinctions does not prefigure anything of importance in his "sociological" analysis, except in the case of the concept of *Recht.* The section, indeed, appears to be no more than a pedantic diversion.

Why is the discussion presented at all? One answer to this question is that Weber's competitors supplied parallel sets of definitions, and granted the concepts, especially the concept of *Sitten,* a much larger theoretical role. So Weber's contemporaries would have read these passages in the way they will be read in this chapter: by comparing them with the definitions of his competitors, especially Tönnies and Ihering. Thus the section amounts to a critique of these competitors and of their approach to the problem of the nature of morality which is central to their approaches to social theory.

In one sense, the section is redundant. As we shall see, it makes the same point that Weber makes in his methodological writings against collective concepts (such as "society") by pointing out the bad consequences of granting any sort of "reality" to the objects they denote. But it is important to distinguish two kinds of issues about the "reality" of collective entities. One is the ontological issue of their reality, to which Weber's methodological attacks are directed. The point of his demonstration of the possibility of reductively eliminating such concepts as "the state" in favor of descriptions of individual belief, for example, concerns the supposed *existence* of the state as a real supra-individual entity. But Weber's competitors understood these objections, and considered themselves to have substantial grounds for rejecting them. The grounds were highly persuasive. They claimed that one could not account *causally* for some of the main phenomena of social life, including the law, without granting that some "social" or "supra-individual" objects have causal reality.

The idea of the power of customary morality or moral attitudes, of *Sitten* (which we shall, for convenience, translate as "mores"), exemplifies the problem. One might ontologically "reduce" custom to individual descriptions of beliefs and expectations, as Weber did with the social relationship "marriage," but this would remain an empty enterprise if one did not go on to account for the ingrained sense that customary morality does have a kind of power beyond human will and is thus causally real – an effective force – apart from the way in which it is described by philosophers, sociologists, or lawyers.[1] Ihering and Tönnies attempted to give a theoretical account of this pre-theoretical fact, and considered that they were compelled to grant the causal reality of *Sitten* as a force. Weber, in contrast, had to make the pre-theoretical fact disappear, and this required an alternative *causal* argument. The concept of *Sitte*, which was central to German social thinking, was, aside from the state and "society," the major conceptual obstacle to the program of providing an alternative to supra-individual concepts.

THE PROBLEM SITUATION: SITTEN AND MORALITY

One need not speculate on Weber's immediate targets in this discussion: they are identified by Weber himself. Weber not only cites Ihering, describing his major work, *Der Zweck im Recht*, then thirty-five years in print, as "still worth reading" ([1922] 1978: 29), he also cites Tönnies's *Die Sitte* ([1922] 1978: 34), which is itself in significant part a commentary on Ihering.[2] Tönnies's work concludes with a discussion of some passages from Nietzsche's 1881 work, *Morgenröthe*. For Weber and his contemporaries, including Durkheim (who began his own published work with a commentary on "German moralists" which included a discussion of Ihering), these writings were the standard statements on the nature of morality and the moral basis of law. They defined a common problem domain for both ethics and social theory. The core problem which motivated these works was the problem of the relation between morality as such, which is presumably universal, and the particular or local practices to which moral significance is attributed (for example, such things as sexual *mores*, which are highly diverse). Many strategies were employed to resolve this conflict. In social theory, the typical solution was to identify a source of morality specific to particular societies which included elements, such as incest prohibitions, that were common to all societies and in this sense universal. In ethics, one solution was formalism – some version of an argument to the effect that the good in a practice was separable from the specific *content* of the practice, so that superficially conflicting practices could be treated as equally ethical in form.

The point of formalism was to avoid a certain kind of reasoning, exemplified by Nietzsche's early formulations, in which the universal claims of morality were reduced to the status of local custom, and custom to tradition, on genealogical grounds. Nietzsche claimed that

> Morality [*Sittlichkeit*] is nothing other (therefore no more!) than obedience to customs [*Sitten*], of whatever kind they may be; customs, however, are the traditional [herkömmliche] way of behaving [*handeln*] and evaluating. In things in which no tradition commands there is no morality; and the less life is determined by tradition [Herkommen], the smaller the circle of morality.
>
> ([1881] 1982: aph. 9)

This reductive reasoning employs distinctions and a strategy of analysis with a complex prior history, of which the history of law forms a conspicuous part. Nietzsche had the aim of parodying these arguments. But the arguments had a positive, respectable form as well. Savigny, for example, dealt with the diversity of law between societies through an assertion of the basis of law in custom, and he took this historical origin to establish the continuing primacy of custom or customary morals over law, at least with respect to the questions of the moral authority or force of the law, the shared feeling of inner necessity which gave mere statutes their moral force. This doctrine was based on a conception of the *Volksgeist* that was discredited by its subsequent uses by the Nazis. Weber, however, faced *völkisch* thought as a living tradition.

Handling the claims of this tradition was crucial for Ihering as well. His approach was to assimilate the explanation of *mores* to the same general pattern of explanation that he applied to law. Throughout the text of volume I of *Der Zweck im Recht* he refers to the forthcoming discussion of this general topic in the first chapter of volume II, chapter 9. The chapter itself Ihering regarded as a significant achievement ([1883] 1886: xii). The basic argument of the chapter parallels his justification of legal order. The claim that legal coercion was warranted by its indispensability led him to a recognition of the indispensability of the *Sittlich* realm both to the societal purposes served by law and to law itself. As we have already seen, Ihering argues that while coercion is indispensable to the law, it is also insufficient. Here he argues that coercion needs to be supplemented by *Sitten* ([1883] 1886: 179–80).

From the point of view of the teleological side of his analysis, law and *Sitten* are analogous: both serve societal purposes and both are indispensable. But Ihering did not consider this teleological argument, the argument from "necessity," to be sufficient. To understand this, it is necessary to have an overview of the problem Ihering's philosophy of law attempted to solve, and the specific problems he faced. One generic problem with teleological justifications for the law derives from the fact of diversity. We might say "legal order is justified by virtue of the fact that it is necessary to bring about something we all desire, namely peace." But peace might be achieved by quite different legal orders, so this assertion, even if true, is not a reason for accepting the particular legal order that one wishes to justify. Particular legal orders vary considerably. Ihering was impressed by the fact that the various legal systems of the historical world have secured quite different ends. So the problem, as he saw it, was to salvage the possibility of a teleological justification of the law in the face of diversity. A teleological justification that applies to one group in society with one set of interests but not to another group is not adequate. The law is binding on all. So what is needed is a justification that is binding on all.

The concepts of "interest" and "peace" provide Ihering with a neat solution to this problem. "We," that is to say those of us in a given society, do have a common interest in peace, which we can secure through compromise and the acceptance of a binding legal order. The particular compromise that will secure peace varies according to societal circumstance, particularly the circumstances of "interest." Different societies have different conflicts of interest

71

to resolve, and therefore different threats to peace for the law to overcome. Nietzsche, as we have seen, exposed the weak link in this reasoning. Peace is *not* a universal "purpose." It is at most the purpose of the weak. The hero, or the "great birds of prey," do not share this purpose and are therefore not bound by the conventions that secure it.

If Ihering was right he would have a theory of the law which in addition to explaining the diversity of legal systems, would explain why they are binding on us. It would *justify* the binding character of the law by showing us that it is necessary for our goals of peace in our particular society. So if Ihering was right he would have provided an explanatory sociology of law. To this extent, then, he and Weber had the same purposes, and provided conflicting solutions to the same explanatory problem. Establishing an explanation of the law in its various historical forms, an explanation which incidentally established the binding character of particular legal orders for members of the societies in which they are found, is an attractive strategy, if it can be brought off. The temptation to extend the strategy from the explanation of law to the explanation of *Sitten* is overwhelming. By doing so one might hope to resolve the problems with peace as an explanation of legal order, for example. If war-like peoples have a morality, it too can be understood in terms of its goals, and the goals can be theoretically reconciled, or seen as variants of the same goal.

As sociological thinkers later showed, "normative functionalism," that is to say the explanation of "norms" or moral practices by reference to their desirable consequences for a group, is illuminating. Customs and moral ideas whose point is mysterious or hidden to the individual can often be analyzed to exhibit their valuable social or collective consequences. But "normative functionalism" in sociology had difficulty with causal or genetic analysis, and so did Ihering; as we shall see, the bridge-concepts that served Ihering in the case of law did not serve as readily in the case of *Sitten*. Put simply, there is a kind of feedback mechanism in the case of law. Given legal orders create, or allow for the development of, particular interests and conflicts of interest and these motivate new laws, which resolve the conflicts or protect the interests. If they fail to do so the pressure of the new interests or the conflict continues, perhaps even resulting in revolution and the creation of a new legal order. The threat to (or loss of) peace shows the necessity of a new order, which, once imposed, is recognized as necessary and consequently accepted as binding. But laws are consciously articulated things, and legal orders have visible effects. *Sitten* are quite different in character, and the mechanisms by which they change and come to fit new circumstances necessarily differ. There is no moment of "recognition of necessity": something else has to happen to make customs binding.

Ihering deals with this difficulty, but in a roundabout manner. He explains the phenomenological character of moral feeling and how "history" continually evolves different "imperatives." His key point is made through a discussion of Locke's criticisms of the doctrine of innate moral ideas. Locke, he suggests, was close to the truth. His error was one of emphasis. He should have stressed not only the negative side of his argument, that is to say his case *against* the theory of innate moral ideas, but his positive suggestion that moral ideas are learned. "Man," Ihering says, "has to learn that he may not rob, steal, kill; [or else] common living cannot exist. Man must learn much through injury" ([1883] 1886: 112). This learning initially takes the form of an insight: "One rises to the *Sittlich* when one gains the insight that one's individual survival is conditioned via one's societal survival" ([1883] 1886: 198). But *individuals* do not acquire morals by learning in this way. The lessons or insights in question are transmitted in the form of a "description of a *geistige* world" ([1883] 1886: 100), that is to say the conceptual structures that are constitutive of the individual's moral life. Moral imperatives, consequently, are felt as *conceptual* necessities, and experienced phenomenologically as an "emanation of [one's] own *sittliches* essence" ([1883] 1886: 101) in the form of an inner sense of correctness or conscience. Morals, to put it in the language of Weber's statement on interests quoted at the beginning of the last chapter, inhere in the "world-images" or cognitive "railroad tracks" which a person acquires through socialization into a society.

The history of the practice of tipping, which Ihering reconstructs, is illustrative of the process by which *Sitten* emerge ([1883] 1886: 249). The process involves three steps: first the initial act, second the imitation, third the attachment of obligation. "When individual action is imitated it becomes custom, and if the element of social obligation is attached to it, it is now *Sitte*" ([1883] 1886: 242). Customs, in the sense of the non-obligatory "simple facticity of continued universal action," become obligatory if they serve not only the individual's interest but that of others or of the public at large by being linked in a chain of mutual interests ([1883] 1886: 247). Chains of mutual interests are *local* historical phenomena. A practice that is beneficial in one setting may not be in another. So different *Sitten* emerge in different times and places.

This account never overcomes its weak link. The connection between a practice and its benefits still must at some point and in some sense be "recognized" for a practice to become obligatory. In the case of many obligatory moral customs, it is doubtful that there was such a moment of recognition.[3] Moreover, one may ask whether the mere recognition of the mutual benefit of a practice is sufficient to transform it into an *obligation*. Nietzsche seized on this point in his own critiques of utilitarian social theory and ethics. Tradition is, he wrote, "a higher authority which one obeys, not because it commands what is *useful* to us, but because it *commands*" ([1881] 1982: aph. 9). Utility *per se* does not "command." Moreover,

> if an action is performed *not* because tradition commands it but for other motives (because of its usefulness to the individual, for example), even indeed for precisely the motives which once founded the tradition, it is called immoral and is felt to be so by him who performed it: for it was not performed in obedience to tradition.
>
> ([1881] 1982: aph. 9)

The social theorists who followed Ihering took up the problem in this form and sought some way of accounting for *mores* that respected the sense of externality and command that distinguishes them.

TÖNNIES'S ORIGIN STORY

Tönnies's book *Sitten* begins with a definitional problem, the problem of properly relating "three ideas related to custom [*Sitte*] which must be differentiated conceptually. These are the ideas of actual usage, of norm, and of social will" ([1909] 1961: 112). The concept of social will, which had been introduced in his *Gemeinschaft und Gesellschaft*, provided his solution to the problem of the feeling of command. Ihering himself, Tönnies noted, had argued that custom and habit differ with respect to the normative,

74

"command" element. Ihering had based his argument on an analysis of language which indicated that *Sitten* invariably command, but habits do not ([1909] 1961: 36). Tönnies argued that this analysis of language was erroneous. *Contra* Ihering, some *Sitten* command and others do not. Yet language does attribute "commanding" and "permitting" to some *Sitten*, as in the expression "custom permits that the sexes bathe together." Tönnies suggests that this language points to an "authority" or "powerful will." If so, it must be a social will, which must be perceived and analyzed "in analogy to individual will" ([1909] 1961: 37).

That Tönnies would propose such a strange thesis is evidence of the intensity with which the conceptual difficulties over the binding character of morality were felt. Strange as it was, the thesis solved a key problem. He did not need to posit, as Ihering did, a historical moment at which the benefits of a social practice were consciously recognized by individuals and became binding or obligatory. But the price he paid for this, that he was forced to claim that "society" had a "will," was high. As the familiar expression "society demands" suggests, this is not a totally unintelligible step. But it is fraught with difficulties. One effect is that it makes moral consciousness itself largely an illusion. We believe that we are making free moral choices, but we are not – we are controlled in our feelings, to a large extent, by the social will. Tönnies accepts this consequence and denies that the conscious will has the role attributed to it in the Kantian tradition:

> The real and essential will is not what lies on the surface of consciousness. These are only the busy servants and messengers who pave his way while the sovereign sits unseen in his coach. The real and essential will is habit – that is, will which has become lord and master through practice.
>
> ([1909] 1961: 34)

The individual, Tönnies argues, is governed by force of habit, meaning unconsciously ingrained habits. The habits are expressions of will. But the "will" that is consciously accessible to the individual is but a small part of the will governing his or her actions. The hidden will is social.

Tönnies was already committed to this thesis, and his analysis in this book merely extends it. His characterization of the "social will" is reminiscent of Durkheim with respect both to its being hidden in part from consciousness and to its effects. But Durkheim constructed a causal, nomic model of the collective consciousness and its effects on action. Tönnies's reasoning differed. He insisted that the act of command implies the existence of autonomy and freedom whether it is the command of an individual to itself or the command of an association of individuals ([1909] 1961: 38). So the command-like character of *Sitten*, Tönnies held, itself implies the existence of a social will, for only such a will could "command."

Tönnies uses the fact that habit inherently "points toward the past" ([1909] 1961: 42–3) to account for the distinctive reverence and honor which attach to *Sitten*. *Sitten* fall in the category of things learned by the "obedience and imitation through which the young and disciples follow their parents and masters and learn from them" ([1909] 1961: 43).[4] Reverence "results from the actual state of affairs as an inference and a claim" ([1909] 1961: 45). The child makes an inference from the fact of parental power and superiority, and generalizes it to include all "past" things. The reverence accorded past practice is a special case of the reverence of the living for the dead, which is itself a special case of the reverence of children for parents and the young for the old ([1909] 1961: 44). This reverence, in the last analysis, is based "actually on nature, on 'natural law' that is, on a tacit understanding about what has to be" ([1909] 1961: 45) that arises from the natural fact of the child's dependence on parents. This "natural" feeling of reverence, fear, and honor toward the parents attaches to the *Sitten* that are transmitted by the parents. The sense of reverence later produces, or becomes articulated as, a conscious belief in the sacredness of the *Sitten*. Tönnies called this belief in the sacredness of established practice a "custom of customs . . . as a custom which rises above custom, links itself with it, and sanctions it" ([1909] 1961: 48).[5]

This account of the inferences which produce the belief in the sacredness of custom is "naturalistic" – the belief is presented as an intelligible, albeit erroneous, intellectual conclusion of primitive thinkers and children from natural facts of infantile dependence and parental superiority. It solves the problem that Ihering cannot solve – the problem of how a sense of obligation arises from practice. It solves it, at least, if we consider acting out of fear, reverence, and honor to be equivalent to acting out of obligation. For the cases Tönnies has in mind, those of an unchanging "traditional" society, this is perhaps plausible. But it does not enable Tönnies to explain how novel obligatory customs arise, or why different customs arise in different societies. A "social will" governing through habit may be, as Tönnies suggests, conceptually necessary to account for the sense of the externality and commanding character of *Sitten*. But it is a *deus ex machina*: the social will does not itself seem to be governed by, or part of, the causal processes of social life. Tönnies does have a few words to say on this subject:

> Every will is directed toward self-preservation, the will of the people to the life of the people, and hence to the *welfare* of the people. We note that the word "well" recalls "will." But as we said before, the will of the people is a more *general* will in distinction from and in contrast to individual will, insofar as it wants to order, regulate, and establish.
>
> ([1909] 1961: 41–2)

But this explains nothing about such things as how the will is caused to change, or indeed how this will is affected by causal processes. There is thus a logical gap between the naturalism of Tönnies's account of the process of transmission between generations that makes for reverence for past practices and the non-naturalistic concept of the social will.

WEBER'S REMAPPING

The conscious belief in the sacredness of custom, of course, is a familiar "Weberian" idea, which Weber applies to legitimacy. But Weber's appropriation of this argument was highly selective. Weber ignores the notion of a personified "social" will which is the mysterious source of the power of custom. But his scheme for classifying the *Sittlich* realm carefully covers precisely the same ground as Ihering and Tönnies, and he cites them as sources.[6] The differences in their classification schemes are, we may infer, a matter of design. But Weber's intent in formulating the categories is not made explicit. He does not, for example, directly criticize the classification presented by his predecessors. His own explanations of what he is doing, as given in the text itself, are curiously self-deprecatory. At one point, he denies that he has any "intention here of attempting to formulate in any sense an exhaustive classification of types of action" ([1922] 1978: 24–6) and he goes on to suggest that "The usefulness of the classification for the purposes of this [sociological] investigation can be only judged in terms of its results" ([1922] 1978: 26). But he does not say what sorts of results it is supposed to achieve, except perhaps "clarity." Nevertheless, the effect of the presentation is clear: it is a radical remapping of the domain of human conduct, a remapping in which the problem Ihering and Tönnies sought to solve, the problem of the commanding force of *Sitte*, does not arise. Thus the subtext may be read by noticing, at each step of Weber's discussion, how one portion after another of the domain of *Sitte* that was explained, however badly, by the theories of Ihering and Tönnies is explained differently or described in a way that makes further explanation, such as explanation by appeal to a personified social will, unnecessary or irrelevant. One can also see, as Weber's classification unfolds, the extent to which Weber builds on these predecessors by altering their emphasis to avoid the difficulties on which they each become impaled.

Ihering and Tönnies gave "insufficiency" arguments for their constructions. Collective purposes in Ihering and the "social will" in Tönnies were held to be *necessary* to account for the facts of obligation and normative force. To genuinely supplant their analyses, Weber must show that these arguments are wrong, and he must do so by providing an alternative account of the same facts. We distinguished two aspects of the issue of collective concepts, the causal and the ontological. It is useful to see that these aspects have a concealed as well as an overt form. Authors like Tönnies and Ihering, and behind them Marx and Durkheim, may be read as the purveyors of defective theories of collective causation, as anthropomorphizers of "society," "history," or "class." Subsequent writers have been more careful about these usages. But it is unclear whether they actually improved on these arguments, or simply concealed their dependence on them more effectively.

Sociologists such as Parsons and Luhmann replaced the older language of collective causation, will, and purpose with the language of systems theory, and applied these revised explanatory concepts to the question of the place of law in society. These and other concealed forms of anthropomorphic attributions of causal powers to collective entities or historical forces, however, have flourished, both in social thought generally and in connection with the law. Feminist jurisprudence is a problematic case in point. To make assertions about the "sexism" of "society" or its "practices" is to grant causal powers to collective entities. Similarly, jurisprudential thinkers like Stanley Fish, who are ordinarily sensitive to the absolutization of such rhetorics by other authors, fall unconsciously into similar usages, and treat such concepts as "community" as foundational. Weber's classification of *Sitten* raises the more subtle question. He is not merely concerned to stigmatize the overt appeal to collective concepts. He wishes to deal with the question of whether appeals to collective concepts are avoidable. *Sitten* is a test case, the phenomenon most difficult to explain "individualistically." As Tönnies says, even ordinary language, in sentences like "custom permits," seems to side with the appeal to collective facts with powers of command. So it is a test case for Weber's approach as a whole.

Knowing in advance that there is a problem with the notion of "command," and seeing that Weber's approach in this section is to rearrange boundaries, enables us to ask what happens to the notion of "command," and more generally to the sense of the externality of morality, in his classification of action. Weber does not tell his readers what he has done with the topic. But in fact the notion of command does not appear in the section on *Sitte*. It appears only in the treatment of value-rational action, which we discussed in Chapter 2, and in his later discussion of authority. In both cases, the structure of the reasoning is the same. The sense that one is subject to valid external commands is presented as the product of choices – the choice to believe a particular legitimacy claim in the case of authority, the choice of a "value" in the case of morals. This assimilation of "command" to choice is itself an instance of conceptual assimilation of the sort we have become familiar with already, as when Ihering sought to turn "beneficial practices" into "obligatory practices" through recognition, or when Tönnies sought to transform the commands of parents into sacred customs through the child's mistaken generalization of reverence for parents to reverence for past things. Weber's strategy is slightly different. The transformation of choice to command can be performed, with some plausibility, for the specific cases Weber has in mind: to say that one chooses to obey or treat political or legal orders as valid or chooses the ideals one serves is, at least, not inherently paradoxical. The claim that moral requirements *in general* are merely or ultimately the product of one's own choices – to reduce morals to free choice – is much more dubious. It collapses experiences that are, at least phenomenologically, distinct: the experience of deciding and the experience of working under a burden. Weber does not, at least directly, attempt the heroic task of reducing *Sitten* to choice. He deals with *Sitten* under a different heading, as a subcategory within the category of "uniform" actions.[7]

The subcategory in which *Sitten* appear is the category of uniformities of action Weber designates as *Brauch* or usage. The details of Weber's account of the distinctions are pivotal, so it needs to be quoted in full:

> If an orientation toward social action occurs regularly, it will be called "usage" [*Brauch*] insofar as the probability of its existence within a group is based on nothing but actual practice. A usage will be called a "custom" [*Sitte*] if the practice is based on long standing. On the other hand, a uniformity of orientation may be said to be "determined by self-interest," if and insofar as the actors' conduct is instrumentally [*zweckrational*] oriented toward identical expectations.
>
> ([1922] 1978: 29)

Sitten are distinguished from the kinds of uniformities that fall under the heading of "legitimacy-related" uniformities, uniformities that result from obedience to convention or law, in that, in the case of *Sitten*,

> The actor conforms with them of his own free will, whether his motivation lies in the fact that he merely fails to think about it, that it is more comfortable to conform, or whatever else the reason may be. For the same reasons he can consider it likely that other members of the group will adhere to a custom.
>
> ([1922] 1978: 29)

This formulation, in and of itself, hardly appears to be a dramatic refutation of the idea of a commanding social will animating *Sitten*. Indeed, it is presented in a way that even Tönnies or Ihering could not object to. Some *Sitten* presumably have this character. At least it is a coherently conceivable limiting case. So as an ideal-type it is unobjectionable. But it is a very odd model for *Sitte* as a whole. Indeed, taken as a characterization of *Sitte* as a whole it begs the crucial question, the question of the source of the seeming externality and commanding character of *Sitten*.

Ihering, as we saw, was concerned with the distinction between mere practices and obligatory practices. Weber's classification makes a parallel distinction, between *Sitte* and *Brauch* or usage, and we might expect to find an answer to the question of the commanding character of *Sitte* in Weber's account of this distinction. But the account is curiously disappointing. *Sitten* fall into the general category of "usages." They are distinguished by the fact that they are "based on long standing" ([1922] 1978: 29). But the phrase "based on long standing" is blandly misleading. It either means simply "done for a long time," so that *Sitte* would be merely old *Brauch*, or it is an *explanation* which points to the causal basis on which a practice rests. If it is an explanation, it is not much of one, for Weber's statements about the causal basis of practices are not very forthcoming. Although he says that the reasons a person may have for adherence to the practice may vary, he cites only such "reasons" as "that it is more comfortable to conform" ([1922] 1978: 29). This is suggestive: perhaps convenience or comfort rather than "command" is the cause of obedience to customary morality. And indeed, when Weber turns to the question of the "stability of customary action," he is explicit about its "essential" causes: stability "rests essentially on the fact that the person who does not adapt himself to it is subjected to both petty and major inconveniences and annoyances as long as the majority of the people he comes into contact with continue to uphold the custom and conform with it" ([1922] 1978: 30).

One may observe that this curious analysis is an alternative to the account given by Ihering and Tönnies. It supplies an alternative causal explanation for at least some of the facts of conformity which they both found so mysterious. This alternative causal account is presented in an innocuous guise – as a definition of an ideal-type rather than an explanation of the phenomenon generally thought of as *Sitte*. Applied to the ideal-type of *Sitte* that figures in Weber's definition, the analysis is plausible. Uniformities may indeed sometimes be based on comfortable habit and the avoidance of petty annoyance. But we have no reason to accept this characterization of the motives for adherence to *Sitten* in general, to take this kind of *Sitte* as paradigmatic of *Sitten*, or to stop our analysis with these motives, or to conclude that there is nothing in the category of *Sitten* other than these kinds of uniformities.

Sitte is not, as Weber uses the term, a natural category. It is merely a category in his own classification scheme which he is free to define as he wishes. If one considers Ihering's examples, such as the practice of tipping, it is also evident that in some sense the petty annoyances of which Weber speaks are a "lever" and are part of the process of learning and developing the practices which serve reciprocal relations in society. But a counterexample such as tipping, which might be open to another kind of explanation, becomes, from the point of view of Weber's classification, a case which by definition is not pure *Sitten*, but some sort of mixed case. As tipping has, on Ihering's own account, mutual benefits, it might be considered, in Weber's scheme, a mixture of *Sitte* and instrumentally rational material interest. Indeed, this is precisely how Weber might be expected to deal with other examples of "commanding" *Sitten* – as mixed cases. The idea of mixed cases is thus highly absorptive. When one considers these cases and considers types of uniformity of action that are adjacent to *Sitten* in Weber's scheme, something else becomes apparent. The elements of Ihering's and Tönnies's account of *Sitte* begin to reappear – just as the idea of "the custom of custom" reappeared – in slightly different guises and different uses.

The next category in Weber's list of "uniformities of action" includes "orders," in which Weber includes systems of law and convention, both of which involve legitimacy and therefore beliefs about legitimacy. He defined *Sitten* as actual usages which do not involve external sanctions. He defines law and convention as obligations *with* sanctions, but sanctions with distinct sources: in the case of law, it is sanctions by a special group, namely juridical specialists; in the case of convention, it is by individuals acting on their own to compel conformity by the "psychic sanction" of "disapproval" ([1922] 1978: 34). This classificatory distinction closely resembles Ihering's discussions of the "lever" of coercion (though Weber distinguishes psychological coercion from simple disapproval ([1922] 1978: 319)). The category of convention itself, as Weber conceives it, seems to include much of what Tönnies and Ihering classified as *Sitte*. The fact that those who uphold an "order" hold beliefs about the validity of *Sitte* means that the part of the *sittliche* order about which people have opinions with respect to validity are defined as "conventions" rather than *Sitten* by Weber.

One cannot help but notice that Weber's formulation of these distinctions is not only novel but peculiar. The basis on which the categories are divided, it seems, involve only superficial matters. The questions that Ihering or Tönnies wished to ask about the law, such as "What makes law obligatory?," call for a particular kind of answer – a special element or additive (such as the commanding social will or mutual benefit) that distinguishes law or binding *Sitten* from non-obligatory uniformities. Weber does not provide such an additive. Nor, it seems, does he accept the questions that Ihering and Tönnies ask. Their questions are teleological – they end in, or must be answered by, social purposes, such as the purposes of the social will or mutual benefits rooted in the individual purpose of human well-being. Weber asks causal questions, and causal questions of several extremely specific and narrow kinds that make sense only in terms of the specific category scheme he presents. The question that so concerned Ihering and Tönnies, the question of what makes a practice obligatory, simply disappears in Weber's account. But we can treat Weber's discussion as an exercise in slight-of-hand and try to see where in the act the problem disappears – and where, in the end, it reappears.

At the beginning of the section on uniformities, Weber says that the classification would be based on the "typically appropriate subjective meaning attributable to" ([1922] 1964: 120) persons acting in accordance with the uniformities. So one would expect to find a discussion of "obligation." In the case of law and convention, however, as we have seen, he proceeds by distinguishing the *sanctions* employed on their behalf. But in discussing these two cases, Weber adds a consideration that is parallel to the causal problem of the "stability" of customs, the causal problem of how the legitimacy of an order is "upheld." He argues that there are two principal ways in which the legitimacy of an order is "upheld," which is to say there are two kinds of practical guarantees of obedience: disinterested motives, which may be affectual (such as loyalty), value rational or religious in origin, or self-interested motives ([1922] 1978: 33).

Any reference to ethical ideas as an explanation is a sign of trouble. If "commanding" ethical ideas have a large significance, the problem of explaining their provenance and force is also large and "choice" is unlikely to suffice as an explanation. So Weber can concede a role to ethical ideas if and only if he can reduce this role to one which can be made to fit with the notion that one's only obligations are "chosen." Weber freely concedes that ethical ideas may have a profound influence on action even if there is no sort of sanction, and says that they often do "when the interests of others would be little affected by their violation" ([1922] 1978: 36). Thus ethical ideas have a role in a scheme of ideal-types of action as a pure cause of action. But Weber carefully minimizes this role. In fact, he says, "Every system of ethics which has in a sociological sense become validly established is likely to be upheld to a large extent by the probability that disapproval [Ihering's 'psychological pressure'] will result from its violation, that is, by convention" ([1922] 1978: 36). Seen as a causal question, then, the kinds of facts that so concerned Ihering and Tönnies are of little significance. The sanction of disapproval, not the ideas, makes the ethic effective; actual fear of disapproval, not a sense of obligation, is the cause of "ethical" behavior in accordance with systems of ethical ideas. The effect of this reasoning is to collapse ethical action in terms of systems of ideas, *Wertrational* action, into the category of convention, with "convention" defined as "upheld by the sanction of disapproval." Put more precisely, "systems of ethics" are dependent for their effect largely on the same causal processes that Weber identifies as the support of "conventions." Systems of ethics in the sociological sense, that is to say as actually effective historical phenomena, do not, then, rest on free choice exclusively or even principally. Thus the fact that in principle ethical ideas that are "chosen" have a pure effect on action is to be understood as a theoretical possibility and a rarity. Explaining the origin and character of these ethical ideas, for example by showing the social purposes they serve, is thus of little relevance to understanding social life: the inherent force of valuative ideas is simply not of much causal importance in the explanation of uniformities. To account for them in the manner of Ihering and Tönnies is not to account for the main causes of the continuation of the uniformity. It is simply to explain the wrong thing.

Because "ethical systems" and "conventions" are sociological twins, both of which depend for their effects on essentially the same causal process of disapproval, this general lesson about the pure effects of ethical ideas applies to the problem of legitimacy and legitimating beliefs. The continuation of "orders" does not rest causally on the power of validating beliefs, but on the sanction of disapproval, on "psychological pressure," applied against violators of the order. Nevertheless, the content of the validity beliefs upheld by the sanction of disapproval is highly consequential in relation to such things as the form of the state, the form of the economic life of the community, and so forth.

The subject of his next subcategorization is beliefs in legitimacy: the famous scheme of traditional, charismatic, and rational–legal *Herrschaft.* "Tradition" appears here as "belief in the sanctity of tradition," which is described as "the most universal and primitive case" of authority ([1922] 1964: 131). This "primitive case" is of course Tönnies's "custom of custom," a regime of belief in which, as Weber puts it, "The fear of magical evils reinforces the general psychological inhibitions against any sort of change in customary modes of action" ([1922] 1978: 37). Like Tönnies and Nietzsche, Weber suggests that "Conscious departures from tradition in the establishment of a new order" require special kinds of assertions of authority, either prophesies or calls for a return to supposedly earlier and more valid traditions ([1922] 1978: 37).

MORALITY AND BIOLOGY

Categories of belief are ideal-typical constructions which must be applied where they do not fit precisely. This, it will be recalled, provides Weber with the loophole he needed in order to reconcile his highly restrictive rule of not accepting purpose–attributions of the sort Ihering accepted. But different loopholes allow different things to pass. Weber is not very forthcoming about how his loophole works or what it permits. But he tells us a few things. He says, for example, in discussing the application of these conceptual distinctions, that

> In a very large proportion of cases, the actors subject to the order are of course not even aware how far it is a matter of custom, or of convention, or of law. In such cases the sociologist must attempt to formulate the typical basis of validity.
>
> ([1922] 1978: 38)

This is a complex thought with some peculiar implications. The first implication is familiar: this is Weber's way of responding to the problem of loosening the criteria for applying intentional explanations. They may be applied, Weber says, by the sociologist, who constructs a type and applies it to individuals who do not fit it perfectly. This means that the domain of explanation by reference to belief is larger than the domain of conscious adherence to beliefs. As we have seen, this is an important methodological premise for Weber. In the case of much traditional "action," for example, the classification must be applied by attribution to persons who do not consciously hold the beliefs which explain their actions, and that by attributing beliefs we make their conduct into "action." But Weber is careful to say only that a "large proportion" or "great majority" of persons may be handled in terms of this loophole. He never says that there can be a situation in which *all* the people in question are unconscious or only vaguely semi-conscious of the "beliefs" that are the "basis" of their action. Ihering and Tönnies, and notoriously such figures as Freud and Pareto, claimed something quite different – that it was normally the case that the motives of human action were hidden, even from the agent.

This point is the key to Weber's alternative to his predecessors. The compelling *Sitten* of a given society, which Tönnies for one was careful to stress were hidden below the surface of consciousness, disappears in Weber's classification scheme because of this methodological rule about the attribution of "meanings." For Weber, *someone* must be conscious and articulate about given values in order for others to be semi-conscious and inarticulate adherents to these same values. The case where *Sitten* are below the surface of consciousness, but nevertheless strongly felt, is treated, by Weber, as merely a variation of the few cases in which they are the subject of conscious awareness. This means, in effect, that there can be no mysterious category of compelling *Sitten* that are *in general* below the surface of consciousness. Everything that belongs to the category will have a conscious analogue, at least for some people in the relevant group.

Once Weber makes this move, the problem of "command" can be reduced to several distinct problems that arise on the level of conscious belief. Each of them, as we have seen, can be solved differently: in the case of *Sitten*, their force is a matter of petty annoyance or discomfort; in the case of conventions, it is the overt "sanction" of disapproval. Factors other than the "command" element in morality, such as self-interest or mere habit, bear the bulk of the explanatory load: the demands placed on other causes are minimized. If anything is left to explain, or if things are left that can only be explained by appeal to the force of ethical ideas, these things can be explained by collapsing them into the category of *Wertrationalität*, which itself is understood as a matter of choice, or into the category of beliefs which are freely accepted. The problem of what makes *Sitten* compelling thus disappears from

Weber's new conceptual map of the social world along with the phenomenon of unconscious motives with which it is linked.

Many of Weber's contemporaries, of whom Durkheim was the most notable, shared Ihering's and Tönnies's fascination with the problem of the compelling power of *Sitten*, and believed it to be fundamental. Durkheim treated the overt, conscious, forms of traditions as indications and incidental products of the existence of a causally powerful collective mental realm, the *conscience collective*. This conception shared with Tönnies's the idea that consciously upheld ideals cannot be the model for *Sitten*, and, like Tönnies, Durkheim saw the problem as one of distinguishing habits which were mere habits from those which have normative force or reflect the force of society. Their strategies are mirror images of Weber's: where Weber divides the moral world into a long series of conceptually distinct problems, each of which is accounted for differently, Durkheim collects together a variety of apparently disparate phenomena sharing the quality of "constraint" under the heading of "social facts" and, as Tönnies and Ihering did, proposes a univocal account of this novel category. They could do this, however, only because they did not define sociology in the way Weber did, in terms of action.

Even in Weber's classification there is a residue. The obvious residual factor is the sanction of disapproval which plays such a large role in the continuation of the effects of an ethical system. What is the source of the power of disapproval? Ihering, who also placed a considerable amount of weight on this "lever" of action, gave a functional, teleological explanation – disapproval of deviance within a given system conduces to mutual benefit. In the terminology of normative functionalism, it is "functional" for the system. But Weber's sociological definition of action precludes these kinds of explanations because they appeal to hidden motives, motives that have no analogues in conscious meanings. Meanings, or ideology, do not suffice to account for a pheno-menon so fundamental and universal as "disapproval." Indeed, disapproval seems to be an omnipresent fact in the Weberian account of morality, a kind of prime mover unmoved. What entitles Weber to appeal to this mysterious force?

Weber gives an answer to this question, but the answer is best appreciated if it is understood in historical context. The context is Nietzschean. For Nietzsche, "originally . . . everything was custom, and whoever wanted to elevate himself above it had to become lawgiver and medicine man and a kind of demi-god: that is to say he had to *make customs* – a dreadful, mortally dangerous thing!" ([1881] 1982: aph. 9). Weber's variation on this image appears in his commentary on the categories "Law, Convention, and Custom [*Sitte*]," which is devoted to the traditional problem of the relation of custom to law. Weber makes the Nietzschean point that "The further we go back in history, the more we find that conduct, and particularly social action, is determined in an ever more comprehensive sphere exclusively by orientation to what is customary." He adds to this another Nietzschean premise, to the effect that there is a biological basis for conformity – a basis not mentioned in his main exposition of his classification of action. "Deviation from the customary," he says, acts "on the psyche of the average individual like the disturbance of an organic function" ([1922] 1978: 320).

Reactions themselves are quasi-biological responses which demand no sociological accounting. So the force of morality is rooted in biology. Indeed, morality itself appears to be a quasi-biological phenomenon. At one point Weber comments that "Perhaps, a rudimentary conception of 'duty' may be determinative in the behavior of some domestic animals to a greater extent than may be found in aboriginal man, if we may use this highly ambiguous concept in what is in this context a clearly intelligible sense" ([1922] 1978: 321). Of course, this claim opens up the series of methodological puzzles familiar from Ihering's discussions of animals. One problem is attribution. Weber, as we have seen, was restrictive, at least in principle, with respect to the attribution of purposes in the absence of conscious awareness of purposes. He restates this objection here. "It would be," he says, "far-fetched. . . to assume in every . . . case [of human or animal reactions to deviance] the existence of a consensually valid norm, or that the action in question would be directed by a clearly conceived conscious purpose" ([1922] 1978: 321). But here the objection is interpreted to mean that the fact that there are reactions to deviance does not show that there is a hidden *purpose* behind these reactions. The *causal* force behind the reactions that sustain orders is to be found instead in the presumably organic fact of "inhibitions against innovation," the effects of which "can be observed even today by everyone in his daily experiences" ([1922] 1978: 321).

Two things need to be noticed about this claim. The first relates to epistemology. The claim is not, it appears, the sort of claim that is historically relative to or conditioned by the cultural categories of a given epoch. The facts of "inhibition" are presumably universal, and universally observable. However, they might be conceived differently by the people of other cultures or epochs, they are phenomena visible to them – like other phenomena of biology. The second thing that needs to be noticed about the claim relates to explanation. Earlier it was suggested that disapproval was for Weber a kind of prime mover unmoved. We may state this a little differently. The phenomenon of inhibition and reaction is indeed from the point of view of sociology an explanatory asymmetry or dead end. It accounts for sociological facts, yet it cannot be sociologically accounted for. But the reason for this is that they are facts of a different kind – biological causes, which happen to operate at the edge of action and consciousness and mix within conscious and semi-conscious action. Weber is, in effect, compelled to appeal to biology because of his restrictive approach to purposes and his restrictive definition of sociology. He cannot extend the notion of intentions to account for the phenomenon, so he is compelled to appeal to causes outside of sociology.

The genealogical relation between this biologically grounded causal force and conscious belief is this: people come to consciousness of the fact that they share reactions with others, and there is a

> point of transition from the stage of mere custom to the, at first vaguely and dimly experienced, "consensual" character of social action, or, in other words, to the conception of the binding character of certain accustomed modes of conduct.
>
> ([1922] 1978: 320)

The phrasing is revealing. What people come to be "aware of" is a particular kind of conception or belief, a conception that *justifies* the reactions that they already experience to deviations from the normal. Conscious beliefs in binding norms themselves are then given "strong support" by these "inhibitions." So conscious conceptualization strengthens or focuses the force that is already there, typically by sacralizing, in accordance with the generalized belief in the sacredness of custom familiar from Tönnies.

Weber thus does arrive at an answer to the question that puzzled Ihering, the question of how obligations arise. The problem is defined out of sociology – it cannot be solved in terms of "action." But it can be solved by reference to biology. Weber's answer works by inverting the problem. Instead of starting with practices and explaining how they come to be obligatory, as in Ihering's paradigm case of tipping (a paradigm as well of normative functionalism in sociology), Weber starts with the dim sense of consensus and the fact of "reaction" to deviance from it. He does not need to explain how the sense of bindingness first appears, because it is given in the "organic" facts of reaction against innovation. Ihering's model required his tippers to be conscious of mutual benefit. To recognize a mutual benefit is a cognitive or conceptual achievement, parallel to the recognition of the necessity of law, and it is difficult to see how the element of obligation becomes attached. Weber avoids any such complex hypothesis. The empirical recognition and conceptualization of observed common reactions is no more mysterious than any inference from observation and not so different from the inferences discussed by Tönnies. No complex insights involving the recognition of beneficial social consequences are required by Weber's account.

This reasoning places Weber in a specific relation to a tradition of social thought beginning with Hobbes and contractarianism and continued in Parsons. For Weber, there is no normative "problem of order" at the social, much less the "economic," level, because it has already been resolved at the organic level. *Sitten* do not have to be created; they are already there in the nascent form of consistent reactions against behavioral innovation.

EXPLANATORY LEFT-OVERS

Weber's treatment of the domain of morals comes to an end that is strikingly reminiscent of the results of his classification of action. Everything is accounted for – the map is conceptually comprehensive, just as a scheme of classification in a Roman law system should be. But the classification scheme varies drastically from the system of categories used by his competitors. The same terms are used: *Sitten, Mode,* and *Brauch.* But they are conceived very differently. To reiterate, Weber's definitions are definitions in terms of causes – in terms of reasons for the "uniformity" and causes for the "stability" of the uniformity. The phenomena of the moral realm are themselves carefully defined in such a way that in the ideal-typical cases there is no need for an additional "social" explanation of the sort proposed by Ihering and Tönnies. If the ideal-type fits, the uniformity is explained by the particular causes Weber discusses in his commentaries on the categories, none of which involve social purposes or a "social will." Weber admits that the ideal-types may not fit very well, or fit many cases. But he has several devices for assimilating these cases to his scheme. One is to consider some of the ideal-types as conceptual fixed points between which actual cases, which are mixed, fall. Another is to consider semi-conscious reasons to be, for analytical reasons, the equivalent of conscious reasons, and to attribute semi-conscious reasons to actions that are externally similar to actions that are done out of conscious reasons, such as conscious reverence to tradition. A third device is the argument that some mixed cases are partly action and partly biologically determined "reaction." Together, these devices absorb the subject matter that Weber took over from Ihering and Tönnies, who represented for him the tradition of telic social theory.

As with action, Weber does not attempt to systematically describe the distribution of actual uniformities of action on this conceptual map. But he makes a number of comments that make it clear that the actions that make up "uniformities" are rarely cases of action proper, that is to say fully conscious intentional acts in which the intention is the cause. The true causes are such things as the inconveniences that result from failure to conform. The violation of customary morality is not, as Ihering or Tönnies would have it, upheld by some sort of social will that manifests itself in the expression of disapproval of deviant acts. For Weber, the cause of the force of disapproval is not "social" at all. It is rather a blind biological negative reaction to innovation. Weber says that this biological response is easily observed and is part of everyday experience. He treats these causal phenomena not as rare but as ubiquitous, even in modern society.

With this we have a more or less complete picture of the moral domain, a replacement of both the schemes of his competitors and of the explanations they gave of the phenomena as it was conceptualized in their schemes. But the replacement is not entirely complete. Blindly conservative biological reaction to innovation may serve as an explanation of the force of moral ideas. It is unhelpful as an account of moral change. Moral change, the replacement of one customary morality by another, is the major lacuna in Weber's scheme of renovated concepts. Ihering and Tönnies both placed considerable emphasis on this problem, primarily because they believed that they had discerned its historical direction, which was toward the fulfillment of social purposes. Weber, as a consequence of his alternative conceptual map of the moral domain, faced the problem in a different form. He needed to explain how moral change was possible in the absence of "social" forces that in some fashion, such as feedback, produce and direct the change. His answer is to identify two basic processes of innovation: rationalization and charismatic moral prophecy.

Rationalization is more or less equivalent to the process of practices or "uniformities of behavior" coming into conceptual consciousness as practices with purposes and being revised or replaced so that the purposes may be more successfully fulfilled. The latter was Ihering's major mechanism of change. Weber adapts it by observing that an important aspect of the "process of 'rationalization' of action is the substitution for the unthinking acceptance of ancient custom, of deliberate adaptation to situations in terms of self-interest" ([1922] 1978: 30). Other forms of rationalization, including "a deliberate formulation of ultimate values" and a morally skeptical type of rationality are also "conscious" in character ([1922] 1978: 30). If we think of rationalization as "action," the actions that compose the "process" are readily assimilated to the cases of rational decision making or choice discussed in Chapter 2.

The concept of charisma, which we shall examine in the next chapter, accounts for the remaining historical cases of change. It will suffice to note here that Weber's account of charisma deals directly with the problem of novel normative commands by definition: charismatic authority *is* power to command, power to inspire a sense of oughtness ([1922] 1978: 322). In practice, of course, cases are mixed, and the causal power behind the phenomena includes imitation, empathy, contagion, and other organic, sub-social forces, as well as such forces as interest, all of which may serve to reinforce the feeling of oughtness ([1922] 1978: 322).[8] But Weber arrives at the concept of charisma through a complex route, and, as with the moral domain, is compelled to remap the domain of power, authority, and law that was already mapped by his competitors. We have alluded to Ihering's model of legal change. In the next chapter we shall deal with this range of phenomena. Weber's innovations, as we shall see, have similar explanatory effects.

5

AUTHORITY
States, charisma, and *recht*

In the last chapter we dealt with one of Ihering's key rubrics, *Sitten*, and saw how Weber remolded it in his own classificatory scheme. One effect of this remolding was to eliminate any sense of an autonomous force or teleological aim inherent in social life – that is, to eliminate the main *themata* of "social theory" as conceived by Ihering, Durkheim, Tönnies, Parsons, and normative functionalism generally. Weber provided alternatives that fulfilled his purposes. But he never directly considered the claims of social teleology in relation to the purposes for which they were invoked prior to this tradition, which is to say the justificatory purposes of political and legal theory. Because he does not share these justificatory purposes, he makes much of the difference between justification and explanation and of the "error" of confusing them. The error was endemic in "legal science," and is a major theme of his writings on legal theorists. One reason for the ubiquity of the error was historical: putatively "scientific" legal, economic, social and political "theory" had roots in *Naturrecht*, and the concepts from which "scientific" theories were constructed still had theoretical implications or connotations that reflected these origins, or, indeed, were not fully intelligible apart from their teleological basis. Typically the teleological basis was a conception of human flourishing or of human nature which set an evaluative standard for social and legal systems which also constituted their "purpose." Weber's methodological work as a whole was devoted in large part to rooting out these usages and rejecting their normative and teleological implications on the grounds of confusion in the mind of the writers he criticized between factual and normative (or "dogmatic") significance. But inevitably he would meet these same "confusions" in concealed form in the

93

concepts themselves, which had to be reinvented or purged of their problematic implications.

In his long march through the conceptual material of the social sciences he encountered several concepts which posed particularly difficult problems of reinvention and purification. The concept "Man" drew Weber's particular disdain. Any appeal to this concept, he thought, was "an exercise in mystification" ([1907] 1977: 168). "*Sitten*" and "action," in contrast, are terms which are relatively open to reinvention. Legal concepts, however, posed special problems, first because they were entrenched in a highly refined system of concepts defined in terms of one another, so that single concepts could not simply be redefined without consequences for other usages, and second because they were constitutive of the historically developing tradition of the law itself. Many of the constitutive concepts, such as "equity" and "validity," were themselves "normative." It is thus no surprise that the law provided a most fertile ground for confusion and some of the most problematic cases for Weber's project. The "validity" of the law, for example, was, in terms of the philosophy of the time, a legal "fact." Courts routinely decided questions of validity, and decided them on the basis of "rational" principles, principles which professors of law propounded "scientifically." Today we might say that "validity" is a "fact" only relative to certain presuppositions of legal reasoning and not a "fact" as such. For the neo-Kantian, however, this would simply have been naive. *All* "facts," the neo-Kantian would have observed, are "facts" relative to presuppositions, whether these are the presuppositions of natural science, everyday life, or the law. The law is a system of thought and is as much a "science" with its own self-constituted "facts" as any other science. Consequently, "validity" is as much a fact as one can have. This kind of neo-Kantian argument was not only respectable, but conventional, and the status of law as a "science" in the requisite sense was accepted. As noted in Chapter 2, one of the major neo-Kantians, Hermann Cohen, who conceptualized the task of philosophy as one of identifying the presuppositions of natural science and whose views were widely influential, was deeply impressed by law as *Faktum der Wissenschaft*, a fact constituted by legal science, and promoted these views in an important and influential book. His legacy persists. The circular "validation" of law as science reached its fulfillment in legal positivism at the hands of such theorists of the law as Hans Kelsen.

Legal science eagerly grasped neo-Kantianism's philosophical support as an alternative to *Naturrecht*, and this led to a serious problem for Weber. The "facts of science" *he* used in order to avoid appealing to normative, *naturrechtliche* concepts such as legitimacy, were a *different* set of "facts" than legal science operated with, despite the fact that the same terms were often applied to these facts. In cases where the two "concepts" were, to the naive reader, the *same*, there was potential for confusion on a grand scale. Weber was well aware of these problems (cf. [1904, 1905, 1917] 1949: 94). More than confusion, however, was possible: if the construals of the concepts were in some sense competitive, if there were considerations of ultimate validity that could in some sense decide between them, the decision might go against Weber's concepts. The possibility that *each* social science required its own concept of the law and that each might differ aggravated the sense that there was a problem of *ultimate* validity, or at least a problem of conflicting or apparently conflicting claims. So immunizing social science concepts from this kind of competition was a matter of special concern for Weber. Historically, his greatest achievement may indeed have been to perform this conceptual surgery. Yet there is an enduring suspicion that it was an act of conceptual butchery rather than a surgical success, which left political and legal philosophy dead and produced a social "science" the "achievements" of which are empty.

VALIDITY AND THE ORIGIN OF LAW

The problem of the status of alternative schemes of constitutive concepts is multi-faceted. In connection with the social sciences, Weber was concerned primarily to refute "naturalistic monism," the idea that historical events, the subject of social science, could be analyzed without intellectually significant residue into generally valid laws ([1904] 1949: 86). As Weber described it, this position was that

> Only those aspects of phenomena which were involved in the "laws" could be essential from the scientific point of view, and concrete "individual" events could be considered only as "types," i.e., as representative illustrations of laws. An interest in such events in themselves did not seem to be a "scientific" interest.
>
> ([1904] 1949: 86)

This idea, as he put it, "seemed to be the final twilight of all evaluative viewpoints in all the sciences" ([1904] 1949: 86). The same issues did not arise in connection with the law. It was given, in the case of the law, that an interest in "events in themselves" is distinct from a legal interest in events. The issue is rather one of specifying the relation between the legal interest and the legal way of constituting facts and other ways of constituting facts.

Ihering's account of this problem, despite its neo-Kantian elements, had one foot in *Naturrecht*: he attempted to derive the legal interest from the purpose in law, which in turn derived from human purpose. As we have seen, this strategy entangled him in difficulties. Rudolf Stammler, Weber's close contemporary, provided a more sophisticated attempt to do something similar, and it was Stammler's work that drew Weber's most impassioned criticism. Stammler's work itself is now lost in time, superseded by legal positivism. Legal positivism avoided these confusions by accepting the impossibility of grounding the presuppositions of legal thought. But legal positivism is also subject to the suspicion that the baby of a coherent and complete theory of the law was thrown out with the bath water of *Naturrecht*. Stammler's account rejected both *Naturrecht* and Ihering, though in fact the distinctions employed by Stammler, like Weber's own, are taken from Ihering and transformed.

Stammler's major assertion was also similar to both Ihering's and Weber's: volition and ideation were necessary and irreducible presuppositions of the law. Stammler used this result, however, as a refutation of "materialism" in social science.[1] Stammler's negative point is that the material forces that have been taken to explain law are non-existent: "there is no 'system of human wants' as independent *social* magnitudes, which may be determined *a priori* – *concrete* purposes of *absolute* validity" ([1902] 1925: 474). Put differently, this claim simply exposed the problem that Ihering's appeal to "ideal interests" created: because the actual wants found in history are diverse, "wants" cannot serve as an ultimate explanatory category of any power. Thus materialism was not an option in the philosophy of law. One solution to this problem would be to abandon the notion that there was a generic aim to the law. Stammler chose a different solution, "idealism." According to Stammler, the history of law is a history not, *contra* Ihering, of successively greater fulfillments of purposes, but of greater realizations of the legal rightness implicit in all law.

Stammler's reasoning was built up in a conventionally neo-Kantian manner. He identified a series of alleged conceptual dependencies: law forms and is thus conceptually inseparable from society; validity in the sense of the rightness of law is an indispensable part of any concept of law. Because rightness is a developmental immanent, formal idea, it cannot be treated as a mere by-product of other causal processes, such as processes produced by the struggle to realize material interests, but must in some sense be part of the causal processes themselves. Such arguments for the indispensability or inseparability of concepts, of course, were designed to counter attempts to reduce a normative sphere, such as the law, to non-normative facts, or to redescribe a sphere, as Weber does, in a way which eliminates the teleological, normative element. Weber had replies to Stammler's argument: he did not, as for example Tönnies and Ihering did, appeal to the concept of "society" in the first place, and he carefully defined "social action" in terms that did not appeal to a mysterious concept of "the social." But Weber had another argument against Stammler that is more impressive.

Stammler's argument for indispensability produced the following theoretical conundrum: if law evolved, historically, from some sort of pre-legal social existence, how could there have been a moment at which the concept of legal validity, the supposed presupposition of law, "evolved" or otherwise appeared? It would seem that there are only two historical possibilities: societies with such a presupposition and societies without such a presupposition, and hence societies with and without the possibility of law. Ihering at least had an answer to the problem of the origin of "validity," in the form of the idea that law, the binding of norm and force, emerged when the need satisfied by the exercise of *de facto* sovereign force by the exerciser was accepted as valid. Stammler, by claiming that "recognition as valid" presupposed the idea of valid law, and that society itself presupposed it, made the emergence of valid law out of a prior state "inconceivable." Thus, Stammler reasoned, societies without the idea of legal rightness are inconceivable.

Weber argued that the conundrum exposed an error in Stammler's conception. Stammler's reasoning depended on and muddled the question of who decides what is and what is not "law." Stammler simply assumed this to be wholly a present-day problem: we, today, decide whether such and such primitive peoples had law. He did not even consider *their* conceptions of law. Weber's point is that this failure produces the problem of the supposed "transition" between societies with and without a concept of "validity." An empirical approach to this problem would be to see how the idea of legality was produced in history. If we ask this question ethnographically, we see that the distinction between primitive "ethics" and "law" is not precise and that primitive peoples think the law originates in divine decrees ([1907] 1977: 169–70). It is questionable whether Weber's argument here is "empirical" or "conceptual" (whether he is saying that Stammler misapplies his own categories and thus makes false statements or that the categories themselves are inappropriate to the material), but it is clear that there is a historical issue that Stammler's argument does not settle: how does the idea of legal rightness appear and legality begin?

Stammler, who, Weber says, ignores historical reality and adopts "the ludicrous role of the scholastic jurist," fails to see that it is his conceptual imposition of a normative idea of the law that is at the root of the conundrum. Weber's attack is scathing:

> At this point, let us only identify the error which is the source of Stammler's foolish claim about the "inconceivability" of a "transition." Suppose we set up a distinction between the "ideal" *axiological* validity of a "norm," on the one hand, and some purely "empirical" *fact*, on the other – for example, the actual conduct of a real person. This dichotomy does indeed exclude the possibility of any "transition." It is obviously and utterly irreconcilable. Any "mediation" between the two poles of the dichotomy is conceptually "inconceivable." Why? The reason is extremely simple. The two poles of the dichotomy identify two completely different *problematics* and two completely different cognitive purposes. One is concerned with a dogmatic inquiry into the ideal "meaning" of a "precept" and the "*evaluation*" of empirical action by reference to this standard. The other is concerned with the identification of empirical action as a "fact" and the causal "explanation" of this fact. Consider this point of *logic*. There are two different, theoretically possible "problematics" by reference to which an inquiry may be conducted. Stammler projects this property of knowledge onto empirical reality. This is the source of that piece of nonsense about the

"conceptual" impossibility of a "transition" in empirical reality. The confusion that Stammler introduces within the domain of logic is no less serious. Here we find the inverse error. From a *logical* point of view, the two problematics are absolutely different. Yet Stammler constantly conflates them.

([1907] 1977: 171)

Stammler, however, was not without a response to this line of attack. He explicitly rejected this distinction between the two problematics. His grounds were this: it is not just a matter of choice whether one reasons causally or teleologically, as Weber seems to think; purposive reasoning is itself indispensable to a unified explanatory account. A comprehensive explanatory account cannot, Stammler reasons, stop with causes, because there are no "ultimate causes" in history. The only "ultimates" are "ultimate ends." So ends necessarily provide the framework *within which* causal processes in history must be understood and in terms of which historical accounts can be said to be completed. The idea of development, in turn, is necessary to comprehend the evolution of ends ([1902] 1925: 473–84).

Weber's reply to this argument is to again turn the tables – to say that this argument amounts to excluding the possibility of a *causal* investigation of the values that actually "exist" in an empirical sense ([1907] 1977: 174). This is, however, a weak response. Stammler concedes that causal explanations of particular purposes in their origin and genesis "may be appropriate" ([1902] 1925: 479). He simply denies that these accounts can be fundamental or complete.[2]

There is no satisfactory reply to "sufficiency" arguments of the sort employed by Stammler, which perhaps accounts for their enduring popularity. The writings of Habermas attest to this. He employed an analogous kind of reasoning against positivism in *Knowledge and Human Interests* when he claimed that the positivist self-understanding was insufficient, that a full understanding of positivism turned positivism into instrumentalism, and that instrumentalism presupposed purposes, the purposes for which the instrument could be used, and that therefore positivism had purposes, and that positivism would, if it were honest, recognize "purpose" as a necessary category, and thus undermine its own central claims about the meaninglessness of purposive language.

For Weber, the problem took a different form. He could reject

99

particular alternative "social sciences," such as Stammler's, on the grounds of their internal confusions and contradictions. But he could not explicitly or directly argue for the exclusive validity of his own social science or the concepts it employed without invoking grounds other than considerations of "logic" in the Kantian sense, grounds that would themselves be "relative" to some "point of view." So he was forced to identify science itself not with some sort of transcendentally valid purpose such as truth seeking (for to do so would concede the point that there are transcendentally valid purposes), but with a rationally unfounded value choice or "interest", such as the interest contained in the presupposition that the study of a particular subject is valuable. He did, however, have a different rhetorical option: providing an empirically rich alternative cuts the ground from under Stammler-like accounts quite effectively. The "necessary" character of Stammler's immanent notions of legal rightness vanishes in the face of an historically adequate conceptualization of the development of law in which the concept has no role. The effect is to refute Stammler on his own grounds, that is to say the grounds of conceptual necessity or conceivability, by the means of actually supplying workable substitute concepts.

In *Wirtschaft und Gesellschaft*, as we have seen, this strategy of supplying alternative descriptions used as a means of refuting claims about necessity and conceivability is relentlessly extended: one domain of social fact after another is interpreted, in historical detail, in terms of his new categorizations. What Stammler meant by conceivability *was* explanatory necessity: his claim was that the "facts" of law could not be adequately accounted for without appeal to a telic notion of rightness. Of course, adequacy is a matter of philosophical controversy. But by giving an extended account Weber places the burden of proof on Stammler's notion of adequacy, and shows that Stammler's position depends not on the consideration of adequacy as such, but on a disputable *standard* of adequacy.

LEGITIMATE ORDERS

The phenomena of legal order appear first in Weber's categorization scheme under the heading "uniformities of action" as a type of uniformity parallel to "usage." But Weber's classification is itself confusing, precisely because of Weber's attempt to integrate the concept of validity – redefined in "sociological" terms as "legitimacy" – into the scheme. *Sitte*, as we have seen, is a subclassification within the category "usage," which is a subcategory of the category of uniformities of action. Convention and law are also "empirical uniformities of action." *Sitte* (or old usages) are defined in terms of the absence of external sanctions to motivate conformity. This categorization scheme was presented as a set of ideal-types between which many empirical cases fall. Weber says that the transition from usage "to validly enforced convention and to law is gradual" ([1922] 1978: 29). Thus usage, convention, and law are not absolutely distinct categories. Weber also includes uniform responses to similar situations in his list of uniformities of action. The uniformities of the marketplace, which in the ideal case are a matter of pure instrumental rationality, are composed of free acts. *Sitten*, usages which are old, not backed by the sanction of disapproval but followed as a matter of convenience, are also composed of free acts. Weber contrasts these kinds of uniformities with those which involve "a system of norms and duties which were considered binding" ([1922] 1978: 30), which he calls legitimate orders.

One oddity of this classification scheme is that by applying the notion of legitimate order to the categories law and convention, which are themselves "uniformities of action," Weber in effect imposes a new scheme of classification based on a different principle of categorization, which overlaps the scheme with which he had been operating. The old scheme was based on *causes* of action. The new scheme is based on agents' *beliefs about* action – specifically beliefs about the binding character of "orders." One might think that by adding the consideration of beliefs about an order, Weber simply extended his list of uniformities of action but changed the mode of classification from causes of the uniformity to beliefs about the order. In fact he continues to consider cause but suggests that in these cases the causes become mixed in such a way that they do not yield a useful classification. The actions that compose what is, from an "external" point of view, a uniformity, may be variously motivated. So in categorizing uniformities of action according to causes, all that one can do is categorize the variable "contents" of action ([1922] 1978: 31). In the case of legitimate orders, the *distinguishing* content is beliefs about the validity of the order, and not causal contents, which may vary. A legal order may, for example, be causally upheld almost entirely by the same causes that make *Sitten* persist, namely the fact of the inconvenience that results from violations, or almost entirely as a consequence of the rational self-interest of citizens. Beliefs about legitimacy may have a negligible causal role.[3]

The two basic types of order are convention and law. Weber distinguishes them in terms of the causes that *externally guarantee* their legitimacy, meaning the causes that lead an individual to accept the legitimacy of the order. If the guarantee is the "probability that deviation from it within a given social group will result in a relatively general and practically significant reaction of disapproval," it is a case of "convention" ([1922] 1978: 34). If it is externally guaranteed by a probability that deviation will produce a response of psychological or physical coercion by a staff of people, it is "law." Weber's classification of *beliefs about* the legitimacy of orders works differently. The same kind of belief might legitimate either "convention" or "law." The four bases of legitimacy, meaning beliefs contributing causally to the acceptance of the validity of an order, are tradition, meaning the belief that "valid is that which has always been," affectual or emotional faith, value-rational faith, and legality ([1922] 1978: 36). Three of these categories are subsequently reintroduced in Weber's well-known tripartite classification of forms of *Herrschaft* or authority into traditional, charismatic, and rational–legal forms. The relationship between the two classifications is simple. Value-rational faith, meaning natural law, disappears in this later classification because, unlike "revealed, enacted, and traditional law" ([1922] 1978: 37), it can support or fail to support *particular* "positive" orders, but cannot serve as a positive order by itself.[4]

The *negative* significance of Weber's classification is substantial. If there is no sharp line between orientations to orders from different motives, and if motives are usually mixed, there can be no reductive explanation of orders in terms of single motives. This means, for example, that no reductive interest-analysis of the state or legal orders of the sort given by utilitarianism is possible. Weber's classification of legitimating beliefs had other negative consequences as well. The fact that law and convention may each be "legitimized" or accounted "valid" on the basis of tradition, faith, value-rational grounds, and the like, means that "law" does not correspond to one particular type of belief. So if we accept Weber's categories here, an idealist quest for the "distinctive idea" of law would be pointless: the types of ideas that validate the claims of legal orders also may be found to validate non-legal "conventions." There is no "distinctive idea" which is conceptually necessary to law – without which the concept "law" could not be conceived. Indeed, Weber's point, which is implicitly established by the detailed historical descriptive account of the development of legal order in *Wirtschaft und Gesellschaft*, is that a concept of "law" and an explanation of the development of law can be constructed successfully from mundane elements, and that no appeal to ideals developing immanently in history or the like is necessary.

There is, it may be noted, nothing novel about the specific mundane elements Weber selects to make the distinction. Weber's formulation of the distinction between convention and law by reference to the distinctive means employed in maintaining the sanctions they use is borrowed from Ihering's account of the origins of state power, or "organized coercion." Ihering distinguished patriarchal authority ([1877] 1913: 198) from the kind of order in which there is a particular development: specialists in justice emerge within the division of administrative labor. For Ihering, the distinctive specialist is the judge, whose position may or may not be combined with executive functions ([1877] 1913: 291). Weber varies this only slightly by referring to "a *staff* of people" ([1922] 1968: 34).

It would be tedious to detail Weber's borrowings of distinctions from Ihering, but a few of them are instructive. Both Ihering and Weber define the state in terms of its means. The state, for Ihering, is a form of "the organization of purpose" that employs law extensively ([1877] 1913: 32–3). It differs from the Church with respect to the larger and more effective role played by "the purely external element" in achieving its purposes ([1877] 1913: 32). Weber identifies two forms of "ruling organization," the state and the hierocratic organizations (such as the Church), that contrast in means: "psychic coercion" in the form of denials of religious benefits is the key means for hierocratic organizations ([1922] 1978: 54). Ihering defined the state as a territorially limited association with all the properties of compulsive and coercive private associations, such as the patriarchal family ([1877] 1913: 197), plus one special property:

> The state is the only competent as well as the sole owner of social coercive force – the right to coerce forms the *absolute monopoly* of the state. Every association that wishes to realize

its claims upon its members by means of mechanical coercion is dependent upon the cooperation of the State, and the State has it in its power to fix the conditions under which it will grant such aid.

([1877] 1913: 238)

Weber's definition is a variation on this: "A compulsory political organization with continuous operations [*politischer Anstaltsbetrieb*] will be called a 'state' insofar as its administrative staff successfully upholds the claim to the *monopoly* of the *legitimate* use of force" ([1922] 1978: 54).

The main difference between the two definitions resides in the substitution of the term "legitimate" for "social." We shall see that this is a significant difference. But the negative significance of each definition is similar: the state is not defined by the possession of some ideal or mythical property, such as sovereignty, which is simultaneously normative and factual. Thus there is no normative "fact" about the state to explain. There is only the natural fact of the actual possession of a monopoly. In Ihering's definition, it is a monopoly on socially coercive force. In Weber's definition, it is the natural fact of the successful defense of a claim to a monopoly on "legitimate" force. "Legitimacy" is conceived by Weber as a non-dogmatic fact – a fact about the beliefs of the governed. From a normative or "dogmatic" point of view, the claim of legitimacy may be "invalid," but this does not affect its place in Weber's scheme.

Weber's categories of associations and his categorical distinction between legitimate orders and other regularities are another instance of explanatory displacement. The traditional problem addressed by theories of the state, to justify and explain the normative fact of sovereignty, is replaced, in Ihering, by a non-dogmatic explanatory problem, the explanation of the rise of a particular kind of *de facto* monopoly of force. Weber, who was perhaps sensitized by the critics of Ihering to the difficulties in this strategy, includes in his definition the "dogmatic" fact of *claims* to legitimacy. Appealing to the historical fact of claims to legitimacy, however, creates a new explanatory problem for Weber. Many questions of a causal kind about legal orders, notably problems of the transition from a pre-legal to a legal order, cannot be answered without explaining the origins of novel ideas of legitimacy. So the conundrum posed by Stammler about the origin of the idea of legal rightness continues to haunt Weber.

RECOGNITION AND INTEREST

Ihering does not discuss legitimacy *per se*. He discusses the same general subject under two different headings. One is a category with a direct legal analogue: the problem of "recognition" of laws as laws. The other is what he calls "the *moral power* of the idea of the state." These headings parallel Weber's distinction between beliefs about legitimacy and motives for obedience. Ihering considers only the case where there is a conflict between individual interests and the demands of the law, and asks what motivates obedience in this case. He concludes that the "psychological motives which fall into the scale in the cause of the State when we think of the State and the people . . . in . . . conflict," are these: "insight into the necessity of political order; the sense of right and law; anxiety for the danger threatening persons and property incurred in every disturbance of order, and fear of punishment" ([1877] 1913: 239). The difference with Weber's list is striking. Weber considers various forms of self-interest to be crucial guarantees of the legitimacy of an order ([1922] 1978: 33), and the sort of "insight" Ihering stresses might be subsumed under these. But Weber adds a list of means that do not involve material interests: faith, emotion, and conscious value choice ([1922] 1978: 33).

The idea of insight into the necessity of political order plays a central role in Ihering's theory of law as a whole. Indeed, it came to be known as the "reflection theory." To replace the theory Weber would have to provide a substitute for the reflective insight of the necessity of accepting an order as legal. And there are several other matters that Ihering's account explains that Weber cannot easily avoid addressing. As we have suggested, the fact of legal novelty, both in the sense of the creation of a novel legal order out of a pre-legal state and in the sense of the creation of new legal orders by revolutionary means, is a problem for Weber as a historian. Weber does not deny the importance of the problem and, as we have seen, he convicts Stammler of the charge of producing an absurd account of the problem. But what is his alternative?

A brief formulation of Ihering's "reflection theory" is essential to understanding Weber's innovations. The problem of legal novelty, as Ihering conceives it, is a problem of how a particular claim to legal authority comes to be accepted. Since the distinguishing feature of legal authority is the claim to a monopoly

105

of *coercion*, the problem of establishing legal authority, as Ihering puts it, is one of binding norm to force. It is paradoxical to speak of the imposition of law by force, when the specific instances of force in question, such as revolutionary violence, are extra-legal. What must be explained is this: how does extra-legal force *become* law? For Ihering, this was a central philosophical problem, but not a historical mystery. In history, legal orders arose in violence and came to be normative for the societies they governed.

The paradoxical relation between force and right, Ihering argues, is a paradox only for moderns. In earlier times, Ihering says, people regarded force as itself legitimate ([1877] 1913: 192).

> [The] relation between force and law corresponded to the conceptions of people at that stage. They did not look upon force with our eyes; they saw nothing improper or damnable in such a condition . . . but only what was natural and self-evident. . . . They had an instinctive understanding that there is a need for an iron fist in a wild time to force resisting wills to common action, that there needs a lion to tame wolves, and took no offense at it devouring lambs.
>
> ([1877] 1913: 191)

The purpose served by force in these cases was "self-evident": the purpose was peace. This "instinctive understanding" of the basis of law has withered. We have come to think of force as something foreign to law. But this is an error, both historically and philosophically. Force is a precondition for the original establishment of law.

> If force had not prepared the ground for law, if it had not broken the resisting will with [an] iron fist and accustomed man to discipline and obedience, I should like to know how law would have been able to found its kingdom; it would have built on quicksand.
>
> ([1877] 1913: 190)

Weber, as we have seen, rejected the image of early humans as animals needing to be tamed; they were, on the contrary, self-taming, driven by biological forces to react against deviance.

For Ihering, force plays a *continuing* role in the evolution of legal order, for the simple reason that there are always potential conflicts between interests, including the "social" interest, and the law.

Law is not the highest thing in the world, not an end in itself; but merely a means to an end, the final end being the existence of society. . . . . If it appears that society cannot maintain itself under present legal conditions, and if law is unable to render it the proper assistance, then force must step in to do what is demanded.

([1877] 1913: 188)

Law is always adjusting to evolving interests. But the mechanism of adjustment through change in the law through legal means is imperfect. When it fails, force is there to intervene. If we are in a situation where we are forced

to choose either law or life, the decision cannot be doubtful: force sacrifices law and rescues life. These are the *saving deeds* of the power of the government. At the moment when they are committed they spread fear and terror, and are branded by the advocates of law as a criminal outrage against law's sanctity; but they often need only a few years or decades, until the dust which they have raised has settled, to gain vindication by their effects.

([1877] 1913: 189)

The process of the dust settling and of the vindication of force by reflection on its effects is Ihering's answer both to the problem of the original establishment of legal order *and* to the problem of legal novelty. Just as life must be lived forward and understood backward, law must be established by force but recognized retrospectively, and accepted because of its effects.

In revolutionary situations, the same point holds. A legal order which fails to serve the preponderance of interests in society is vulnerable to a revolutionary movement which seeks to establish a novel legal order which can promise to serve a greater preponderance of interests. This kind of conflict is the motor of legal evolution. Ihering's "evolutionary" argument is that the law is a product of struggles between interests which represents the temporary resolution of the fundamental conflicts of interest within a given society. The role of revolution and of the *coup d'etat* are to create new legal orders by force. These new orders embody new compromises between interests, and then allow for the development of other interests, which themselves lead to new conflicts between the legal order and the preponderance of societal interests. Chance always plays a role in situations of struggle, including revolution. But in general, Ihering believed, the tendency of legal evolution through revolutionary change in history was that successive legal orders served wider and wider societal interests.

Weber gives an account of the evolution of law which is parallel to Ihering's, but which replaces the moment of conscious "reflection on purposes" that is a key link in Ihering's account. His thesis, indeed, is directly opposed to Ihering's idea of a primordial situation in which force and norms are bound by the conscious recognition of the necessity for authority. Weber argues that legitimacy and the state evolve separately. The first stage in the formation of political associations is the band of marauders ([1922] 1978: 905). The leader of the marauding fraternal band who is "freely selected" and then legitimated by his personal qualities (charisma) has "authority". There is, of course, an element of Ihering's "reflection-theory" even in this account: the validation of the charismatic leader is a matter of reflection on charismatic success and failure. But Weber claims that legitimacy does not evolve (as Ihering believed) out of force: "'legitimacy' originally had little bearing on violence – in the sense that [violence] was not bound by norms" ([1922] 1978: 905). Even a violent band requires discipline. But Weber suggests that

> Violence acquires legitimacy only in those cases, however – at least initially – in which it is directed against members of the fraternity who have acted treasonably or who have harmed it by disobedience or cowardice.
>
> ([1922] 1978: 906)

Honor among thieves, in short, is the primordial form of "legitimacy."[5]

The primal scene, the origin of legal orders, is thus strikingly different for Weber. As we have seen, there is, for Weber, a quasi-organic reactive basis to responses to deviance, and this is at the base of tradition. But there is nothing in the primitive situation which allowed for the "human enactment" of norms "'valid' for behavior and binding in the resolution of disputes."

> Their "legitimacy" rather rested upon the absolute sacredness of certain usages as such, deviations from which would produce either evil magical effects, the restlessness of

108

the spirits, or the wrath of the gods. As "tradition" they were, in theory at least, immutable. They had to be correctly known and interpreted in accordance with established usage, but they could not be created.

([1922] 1978: 760)

New norms did emerge. But, Weber argues,

this could happen in one way only, viz., through a new charismatic revelation, which could assume two forms. In the older it would indicate what was right in an individual case; in the other, the revelation might also point to a general norm for all future similar cases. Such revelation of law constitutes the primeval revolutionary element which undermines the stability of tradition and is the parent of all types of legal "enactment."

([1922] 1978: 761)

Some of this "law revelation" was "revelation in the literal sense;" usually, however, it was an artificial magical process used "when a change in economic or social conditions had created novel and unsolved problems" ([1922] 1978: 761). Legal formalism, he suggests, is in some sense a residue of the magical element in primitive law.

On the surface, Weber's account looks very different from Ihering's. Revelation, not reflection, is the basis of law. But at a second glance, there are strong similarities. The phrase "problems produced by changed social and economic conditions" is uncomfortably close, especially given Weber's stress on the pervasive importance of material interests, to Ihering's notions about generic social purposes, and indeed to the reflection theory, for the law-giver at least must have some dim notion of the purposes a new law must serve, and more generally of the law as a means to these ends, in order to generate new laws that respond to these "problems." The invisible hand of historical fate perhaps provides feedback in case of errors in charismatic law-giving: the "problems" will not be solved and the conditions will become more difficult if the legal innovation does not succeed.

"Success," as it applies to charismatic leadership or legal enactment generally, is a concept which is both more vague and more flexible than "social purposes." Charismatic revelations may define new purposes as well as new legal means to existing purposes implicit in a situation. But revelations that fail to change the problematic conditions will continue to be threatened by them. Lack of success will mean that the revelators will soon lose their charismatic character. So Weber simply offers a different feedback mechanism and a less rational, less purposive, model of innovation than Ihering's. But the feedback mechanism is no weaker, and no less selective. One advantage of Weber's account, however, is clear: "validity" is intrinsic to charismatic assertion. So Weber need not posit some sort of complex cognitive process, such as "reflection," that leads to acceptance of law as valid law. But the problem of the origin of legal rightness is displaced by this reasoning onto charisma, and charisma is itself a mysterious phenomenon.

SOHM: OBEDIENCE WITHOUT COMPULSION

Weber's source for the idea of charisma was another legal theorist, Rudolph Sohm, a major figure both in Germany and in the history of legal thought. Sohm supplied not only the concept of charisma but also of several of the historical themes of Weber's sociology of religion, including the idea of the important role that asceticism had as a support of the idea that an individual can "set out on his own path" and "work out *his own* salvation" ([1887] 1958: 67).

Sohm's studies of the history of the Church and of Church law, from which these ideas are drawn, are models of Protestant piety and anti-Catholic controversialism, and dealt with what were at the time vital theological issues. The self-constituting theory of the "Reformation" was that it represented a return to true Christianity. The revolution in historiography of the nineteenth century led to a reconsideration of the rather sketchy evidence on the character of the Church before its institutional structures were fully developed. The topic, and more generally the topic of Christianity understood historically as an ancient religion, was a popular one. Even Marx's "orthodox" successor, Karl Kautsky, tried his hand at the subject, finding in the early Church a kind of proto-communistic social welfarism ([1908] 1925).

Sohm's texts on church law are motivated by a problem of legal theory. How can there be a legal order without compulsion? If conscience and faith are not subject to compulsion, if inner assent cannot be caused, how can there be such a thing as "church law" governing such facts? This is a theological or philosophical rather than a purely historical problem. Sohm was well aware of the practical legalism of religious communities, the role of the sanction of excommunication, and the like. What was puzzling to him is the status of Church Law as "law." The difficulty can be seen in terms of the definition of law as a product of a political authority, as commands of the sovereign, as John Austin's famous phrase puts it. The Church is not a political community in the relevant sense. So the only possible legal analysis of church law is that it is an impossibility. "The Church, the people of God, signifies a *spiritual* people; the kingdom which is established in the Church is a *spiritual* kingdom; Christendom forms not a state nor a political union, but is a *spiritual* power. Once for all, a legally constituted Church cannot be" ([1887] 1958: 34).

Nevertheless, there is such a thing as church law. How, Sohm asks, is it possible? What can the term mean? Sohm's answer to this question is given historically, but it is premised on a philosophical anthropology.

> The *natural* man desires to remain under law. He strives against the freedom of the Gospel, and he longs with all his strength for a religion of law and statute. . . . He longs for a legally appointed Church, for a kingdom of Christ which may be seen with the eyes of the natural man, for a temple of God, built with earthly gold and precious stones, that shall take the heart captive through outward sanctities, traditional ceremonies, gorgeous vestments, and a ritual that tunes the soul to the right pitch of devotion.
>
> ([1887] 1958: 35)

The apostolic situation, in which "where two or three are gathered together in Christ's name, there is the *ecclesia*, the Church" in short, is unnatural: "*The natural man is a born Catholic*" ([1887] 1958: 35). "[T]he secret of the enormous power" of the Church "over the masses who are 'babes' [is that] it satisfies these cravings" ([1887] 1958: 35). "Church law" is a solution to a human need for law even in the spiritual domain, despite the fact that the notion is a logical, legal, and theological monstrosity.

A simple historical account can be given of how this monstrosity developed. The ecclesia was turned into a formal legalistic body through the claim to a monopoly over the eucharist by the elected bishops. The claim was consented to because "the community had not seldom to be guarded against robbery by swindlers who went about in the guise of 'prophets,' and knew well how to excite the ready charity of the brethren" ([1887] 1958: 38). The proper theological basis of the concept of charisma is this:

> God, that is, Christ, rules and binds together all the members of Christendom solely through the gifts of grace (charismata) given by Him. To one is given the gift of teaching, to another the gift of interpretation, to a third the gift of comfort. The gift of teaching is at the same time the gift of government. God's people, the *ecclesia*, is to be ruled, not by man's word, but by the Word of God proclaimed by the divinely gifted teacher; and the *ecclesia* obeys the word of the teacher only if, and so far as, it recognizes therein the Word of God.
>
> ([1887] 1958: 33)

In authority, the Apostolic church, in which first the Apostles and then prophets and teachers exercised authority, was purely spiritual; "in point of fact they ruled, but without legal authority" ([1887] 1958: 33). The lack of "legal" authority and the importance of recognition of spiritual gifts by members of the Christendom was a simple reflection of the fact that the Word of God is alive in every *ecclesia*, because all members of the body of Christ, by virtue of the Holy Spirit living within them, are "*priests* and *kings*" ([1887] 1958: 34).

This, Sohm thought, was the theological truth. Any attempt to go beyond this kind of authority was the usurpation of powers. If we interpret the "legal" actions of actual, visible churches in the light of these theological truths, we come to the following conclusions: visible churches are themselves merely associations that come and go in history ([1887] 1958: 66) and rule in the name of God. Sohm sought to deny the genuinely charismatic character of the (highly visible) Catholic Church by denying the link between the invisible Church donated by God and any visible church. The claim of charismatic endowment is a part of the theology of the Catholic church, from which the claim that the law of the church is genuine law follows. The actions taken by the visible church that appear to have a legal character do not actually have a legal character when they traffic in the divine. For example, the power of excommunication is not, as it might appear, a legal power. All the act of excommunication can really be is one of witnessing ([1892] 1923: 178), according to Sohm.

112

Thus the direct authorizing action of the Holy Spirit in relation to the organized Church (as distinct from providing individuals with administrative talent) is always through charismatic *individuals*. The relation of the believer or the religious association to the charismatic teacher can only be one of recognition ([1887] 1958: 33). The visible church is thus a charismatic institution only indirectly, through following the commands of the charismatically endowed teacher, possessing the Holy Spirit. The Holy Spirit speaks prophetically through these persons. Such speech, Sohm says, is always authoritarian ([1887] 1958: 39–41).[6] Such an individual is a "Führer," with authority, but only in the sense that such a person can witness authoritatively ([1887] 1958: 28–9).

Weber appropriates much of this in his discussion of charisma.[7] He of course strips off the overt theology. What he substitutes is the notion of *de facto* recognition, so that for him anything recognized as "charismatic" or anything resembling the ideal-type of charismatic authority and "recognized" *is*, for his purposes, charismatic authority. The purely individual nature of charismatic gifts in Sohm becomes, in Weber, the claim that charismatic power rests "on personal devotion to, and personal authority of, 'natural' leaders" ([1922] 1978: 1117). The two elements of the ideal type, the special properties of the leader and the fact of recognition, fit together in Sohm's account: the spiritual leaders are genuine instruments of the Holy Spirit – for Sohm a real causal force in history – whose real charisma is "recognized." Weber's account does not work so neatly. The fact of "possession of charisma" seems to be nothing more than the fact of "recognition of possession of charisma." But this is not sufficient, even for Weber's purposes. He too needs for charisma to be a force, to be in some sense a prime mover, rather than a force that results from and derives entirely from the phenomenon of recognition. The issues here are complex. But they can be grasped simply in terms of the primordial situation of the pre-legal social herd inhibited by its biological bias against innovation and biologically inclined to "react" to deviance. To overcome this force for stability by "making new *Sitten*," as Nietzsche says, one cannot simply rely on the tendencies of the human herd. Some new force must be added, something which compels "recognition" even in the face of the biological bias against it.

Sohm's *Führer* really are extraordinary. They are, literally, voicing the commands of the spiritual world. Weber defines charisma in terms of extraordinariness, understood as an individual quality of the natural leader which is recognized by others. If extraordinariness is merely a matter of recognition, then the base is pre-established cultural expectations. But if charisma was merely a matter of the coincidence of a person with particular qualities and pre-existing expectations, it is unclear that, or how, charisma is distinguished from traditional authority. If the pre-existing cultural expectations simply take the form of traditional prescriptions for identifying "leaders" or "prophets," it is unclear how the charismatic leader could transform expectations any more than kings and patriarchs whose authority rests on tradition can transform them. In both cases, the expectations would constrain the leader. The relation between ruler and follower in all these cases is like a contract. Violations of expectations will be recognized as punishable deviance. Charisma would be shackled, just as traditional authority is.

One might distinguish two kinds of authority based on cultural expectations: traditional authority, based on fixed traditions, and authority based on cultural expectations that enable "leaders" to be recognized but which enable the leaders to change the rules of the game, change the cultural expectations on which recognition is based. The latter would correspond to "charismatic authority based on cultural expectations." The revelatory power of prophets in the early church might be an instance. But the puzzle of charisma would not be solved by this account.

In the first place, Weber seems to allow for the emergence of charisma directly, that is, apart from a tradition of prophecy of the sort found in the early church. Indeed, charisma supported by tradition would seem by definition to be an impure or mixed form. Second, charisma thus conceived would be useless as an explanation of the original breaks with primal tradition that "make morals" in Nietzsche's sense. If these breaks depended on *prior* prophetic or heroic traditions, the existence and origin of these prior traditions would be a mystery. Third, the model generally shifts the burden of explanation, especially the explanation of novelty, to the problem of the formation of the relevant expectations. In some cases of charisma, those in which the leader fulfills a prophecy, for example, this seems appropriate. But these are precisely those cases in which charisma is mixed with tradition. In cases that are more "pure," it seems that the formation of prior expectations with respect to leadership or prophetic authority is simply a puzzle.

Weber tended to depict the leader as the source of changes in expectations, and to treat the leader–follower relation as quasi-contractual, with the leader in the role of Ihering's creator of artificial interests and user of business eloquence to bring out the follower's interests. But this line of reasoning, taken as an account of charisma, leads to similar difficulties: taken to its logical conclusion it collapses charisma not into tradition but into *zweckrational* action. But Weber wanted to see charisma as an element that could be added to or mixed with rational action to explain extraordinary business dealings, for example. Indeed, in practice, the charismatic "element" in the various situations to which Weber applies the term is the element of faith, hope and trust which is left over or cannot be explained by economic considerations, tradition, coercion, and the like. It is a radically heterogenous residual category – embracing everything from the quasi-magical uses of ordeals as evidence ([1922] 1978: 1116) to the act of faith of granting uncollaterized credit to robber capitalists ([1922] 1978: 1118). Weber's actual use of the concept, then, is this: anything in the domain of authority that is not explained in some other way is attributed to charisma. Weber insists that the "transition is fluid," for example ([1922] 1978: 1122) between cases, and that mixtures of elements are commonplace. Much of his discussion of charisma, indeed, is given over to cases in which charisma combines with something else – discipline, tradition, legal authority, and even money making. This means that the simple model of the individual witnessing in a way that is recognized by others, derived from Sohm, has no obvious relation to most cases of "charisma." All that the various cases of charisma have in common is the element of "extraordinariness." But this is really only another way of saying that these are residual phenomena, unexplained by ordinary considerations.

To have an intelligible concept at all, Weber must unify this category in some fashion, for example by connecting it to the prototype of the witnessing individual and claiming that cases of charisma are genetically connected to charisma in the sense of the prototype of the leader. But the category cannot be unified "genetically" without departing from Weber's usage. Weber does construct a series of genealogical stories in which the charismatic element, for example of the Roman Principate, figures as a remnant of past practices which are presumed to have been more fully based on charisma. In this case, the past practice was the designation of a dictator on the field of battle through acclamation ([1922] 1978: 1125). The "election" of a Pope operates under a similar theology ([1922] 1978: 1126). Weber suggests that there is a "transition" from this kind of "election" to democratic suffrage. Like the Principate, "kingship is normally charismatic war leadership that has become permanent and has developed a repressive apparatus for the domestication of the unarmed subjects" ([1922] 1978: 1135). If all "mixed" cases of charisma had some such lineage, the apparent conflicts in Weber's use of the term charisma might be resolved by dividing cases of charisma into pure, original forms and mixed, routinized, late forms.

But Weber does not say that it is necessary for there to be genealogical stories of remnants of an earlier state of pure charisma, and gives examples where there is no original pure case. Charisma may be attributed, for example, to an office on the basis of a general cultural prejudice that authority is God-given. Weber distinguishes the German attitude to the state from that of the Puritans, for whom "the conduct of an office appeared as a business like all others" ([1922] 1978: 1140), by giving such an account:

> The fundamentally different attitude of the average German toward the *Amt*, toward the "supra-personal" authorities and their "nimbus" is of course conditioned in part by the peculiarities of Lutheranism, but also corresponds to a very general type: the endowment of powerholders with the office charisma of "God-given authority."[8]
>
> ([1922] 1978: 1141)

This is, so to speak, "late" charisma, but late charisma for which there was no earlier stage of new charisma. Weber also suggests that charisma can emerge within more or less developed social forms. The procedures of Hellenic democracy, African palavers, and modern electoral politics themselves reward certain gifts, such as "the charisma of rhetoric" ([1922] 1978: 1129), which are apparently not remnants or routinizations of any case of pure charismatic leadership. Weber seems to have in mind here simply this: these procedural forms rely on persuasion; some people have exceptional gifts of persuasion. The idea that charisma means exceptional gifts is rooted in Sohm's use of the concept. For Sohm, the gifts through which the Holy Spirit works are heterogeneous, and include all the kinds of talents necessary for the work of the Holy Spirit. Weber, it seems, does not remedy this heterogeneity. Charisma simply becomes a secular, rather than a theological, mystery.

Weber stands alone among the major social thinkers of his period in his assiduous avoidance of teleological notions and his caution with respect to notions like "historical forces," interests, human nature, social forces, and the like. But the use of charisma in a crucial point in Weber's account of the origin of the state and law belies all this care. Weber appears not as a disenchanter of the forest of human explanatory usages, but as the source of a new mystification. Is the use of the concept of charisma a descent into mysticism? Does Weber, in the end, simply substitute for the reductive theories of history he attacks yet another reductive theory of history with the same flaws? Is the rhetorical function of the concept of the ideal-type to obscure Weber's purposes: to make what is in essence a mystification and reduction appear dry and scientific? Is the ambiguity between genetic primacy (the type as prototype) and the ideal type (the type as an epistemological tool) a fatal ambiguity?

In the next chapter, these issues will be considered at length. Their importance should now be clear. Weber did not simply appropriate the concept of charisma to describe a few unusual historical facts. The concept played a central role in his strategy of replacing the concepts and categories of traditional social theory. The categories he introduced and defined served to displace explanatory problems and substitute new problems. For the crucial question of the origin of legal validity, charisma is the substitute for what Ihering saw as a cognitive process leading to the acceptance of authority. The character of this process is one of the chief conundrums of social theory, and has been since Hobbes sought to account for the phenomenon of sovereign authority on causal grounds, and remains a problem for present-day con- tractarian game-theorists faced with the free-rider problem. Weber arranged his conceptual scheme in such a way that he was not faced with the problem in either of these forms: unlike Hobbes, he did not attempt to translate the language of human action into a mechanical language; unlike the rational-choice theorists, he did not loosen the criteria for attributing reasons to accommodate unconscious "choices." Did his careful rearrangement of the categories of social description free him from these difficulties, or did he paint himself into a corner? His alternative, as we have seen, was to appeal to facts of biology – the facts of biologically rooted reaction to innovation and deviance. But this appeal forced him to appeal to charisma as an account of the origins of legitimacy. So the argument as a whole comes to rest on the problem of the status of charisma as an explanation.

6

CAUSE

In Weber's methodological writings, he attacked arguments such as those of Marxists on the grounds that Marx had mistakenly treated an ideal-type as a real force. Yet it appears that Weber's own account of historical change suffers from a similar defect. His account too comes to an end in a mysterious phenomenon, charisma, for which there is no further explanation. Did Weber simply fall into the trap that he had pointed out to others? Does his account of history represent no more than a version of such reductive accounts of history as Marx's and Burckhardt's, or for that matter Spencer's, only with a different cast of ultimate explanatory forces? Is his account of law and its history no better than his competitors, such as Ihering and Stammler, with regard to their reliance on real ultimate causes, purposes or forces? These questions can be answered only by a detailed consideration of Weber's methodological writings. Here again, we shall argue, Weber turns to the literature of the law for illumination.

EXPLANATION AND TYPIFICATION

Weber's methodological claims and Weber's strategy of conceptual replacement are parallel. In the latter, he is arguing against the claim that various categories employed by other writers match the essence of a phenomenon. He shows that there are alternative descriptions of some phenomena, such as *Sitten*, by providing examples of alternatives of his own devising that are non-teleological. These alternatives are "ideal-types" that differ from the essentialist, teleological concepts they replace. Weber's point is that each alternative concept is only an ideal-type, and that none of them has any claim to matching the essence of the

119

phenomenon, the ultimate facts about it. But we must ask a difficult question about Weber's alternatives. In what sense do they explain? Have we thrown the baby of explanation out with the bath water of teleology? It is this question that his methodological writings answer.

Consider his comments on "the Marxian theory." Speaking analytically, in terms of the possibly valid meaning of Marxian claims, Weber says that

> naturally all specifically Marxian "laws" and developmental constructs – insofar as they are theoretically sound – are ideal types. The eminent, indeed unique, *heuristic* significance of these ideal types when they are used for the *assessment* of reality is known to everyone who has employed Marxian concepts and hypotheses. Similarly, their perniciousness when they are thought of as empirically valid or real (i.e. truly metaphysical) "effective forces," "tendencies," etc. is likewise known to those who have used them.
>
> ([1904] 1949: 103)

There is, however, an obvious problem here. Unless "charisma," for example, is "real," is an "effective force," can we claim to be explaining anything at all by appealing to it? One is reminded of Ihering's comment on Kant, that "You might as well hope to move a loaded wagon by means of a lecture on the theory of motion as the human will by means of the categorical imperative" ([1877] 1913: 39). Abstractions do not explain, do not have explanatory force, unless they are abstractions *of* forces, such as a theory of motion is an abstraction from the diverse phenomena of physical force. But what are Weber's ideal-types abstractions of? Are they abstractions of more or less diverse groups of actions, each of which is motivated, in which the motivation is typified? Do these abstractions simply serve to summarize patterns of caused or motivated behavior, or do they point to more fundamental causes? Are the single actions of which the pattern is composed self-explanatory? Is each action, so to speak, its own explanatory ultimate? Or are there basic human drives that are the ultimate determinants of behavior? If so, how is their existence to be reconciled with his denunciations of the very idea of such forces in the case of Marx, or his criticism to appeals to the concept "man" in his discussion of Stammler? If not, from whence do his own abstractions derive their explanatory power? If they have no independent explanatory power, if the explanatory power is in the singular instances, in what sense can the singular instances of charismatic submission be said to be intelligible or explicable? Is the mystery displaced from the concept of charisma to the instances?

These are large questions, the implications of which go beyond such things as charisma and to the heart of his whole enterprise as we have reconstructed it in previous chapters. The systematic process of conceptual substitution that Weber undertakes with ideas like legal validity and justice and the externality of obligation and the demands of morality proceeds by replacing these teleologically tinged ideas with categories involving such biological facts as blind, directionless "reactions" to deviance and such things as semi-conscious "decisions" to accept "values" as binding. At the end of this process of conceptual substitution, we have a fully developed alternative to the categories of Ihering and, by extension, the categories of the legal tradition, *Naturrecht*, utilitarianism, and teleological social theory generally. This new scheme of categories ends up with some leftover phenomena that cannot easily be explained in its terms, such as the powerful message of leaders speaking in God's name or in the name of higher justice. But what is left over – the unexplained remainder – is something quite different than what Weber's competitors wished to explain.

For Ihering, as we saw, the basic drive of interest was the source of human action and the interest that arose through association, the social interest, was the source of the law. The social interest was a source ever renewed as new grievances and hurts came into consciousness and inspired calls for justice and the creation of new legal rights. It was the motor of legal development. "Real" forces, namely the forces of "interest," lay behind morality, law, and custom. The concept of charisma is Weber's attempt to deal with these phenomena, or at least what is left of them after he categorizes "uniformities of action." To be sure, it is not an overall substitute for the concept of a supra-individual "moral" force – Weber's new category scheme and his accounts of the causal bases of the various uniformities of action suffice to account for much of the domain that the idea of a supra-individual moral force was constructed to explain. Yet, "charismatic" phenomena clearly cannot be explained in the terms that most "uniformities of action" can be explained, namely self-interest and convenience.

121

Sohm thought of charisma as a real but multifarious causal force in history. Weber, in contrast, makes charisma a "type" to be used for "understanding." To be sure, as is the case with his comments on uniformities of action, he makes "causal" comments about charisma. These suggest that charisma, in actual cases, is a kind of compound of conscious motives that lead a person to "recognize" and become devoted to a leader and quasi-biological phenomena (such as imitation and contagion) ([1922] 1978: 23–4, 242). This reduces the explanatory burden on the concept – in most cases, we do not need to explain the force of the enthusiasm solely by reference to the leader and the leader's message. But charisma in the pure sense, the sense that involves only the conscious element, still needs to be explained.

Here we meet another puzzle. What is a satisfactory account for Weber, and how do such accounts relate to *ideal*-types, such as "charismatic authority?" In Chapter 2 we saw Weber's answer to this foreshadowed in his adaptation of Ihering's notion of the relation between the law of cause and the law of purpose. According to Weber's discussion of the relation between explanation and understanding, an

> interpretation of a coherent course of conduct is "subjec-
> tively adequate" (or "adequate on the level of meaning"),
> insofar as, according to our habitual modes of thought and
> feeling, its component parts taken in their mutual relation
> are recognized to constitute a "typical" complex of meaning.
> It is more common to say "correct."
>
> ([1922] 1978: 11)

A causally adequate interpretation of "a sequence of events" is achieved when "according to established generalizations from experience, there is a probability that it will always occur in the same way" ([1922] 1978: 11). This account serves to separate cause and understanding, but by making them apply to different aspects of action – action itself is a whole, which can be adequately explained only if both aspects are accounted for in such a way that the causal account is consistent with and supports the meaning interpretation. The reasoning one employs in order to "under-stand" and the reasoning one employs to explain causally, however, differ. But both employ abstractions.

Adequacy on the level of meaning requires types – subjective adequacy is defined as recognition as an instance of a type, meaning a type that is already understood. We already possess, through "our habitual modes of thought and feeling," the types we need to in order to understand one another in our ordinary dealings with one another. The sociologist, like the historian, relies on these implicit "habitual mode" types. But the sociologist also *constructs* type concepts for various analytic purposes, and indeed takes the construction of useful type concepts as a goal. These concepts have to be made intelligible, for example by explicating them and showing their logical relations to other types – this, indeed, is the main agenda of *Wirtschaft und Gesellschaft*. But what exactly do these types do? And what do they have to do with cause and the kind of abstraction and application of abstractions to new cases that are part of causal analysis?

In this and the following chapter we shall address these questions. To understand Weber's answers to them we must understand the concepts he uses to replace such notions as "purpose" and "causal forces." Part of the answer is clear. Weber turns to the literature of law for a congenial notion of cause – one that does not depend on the notion of explanatory ultimates. "Adequate cause" is his substitute for the natural science notion of causal law and the notion of cause as a kind of real force. "Meaning," as we have seen, takes the place of "purpose" for Weber. Ideal-types provide access to meaning. The fundamental question we must ask about these substituted concepts is the question of how they fit together. The problem of the character of charisma is a useful case in point. If it is not a "force," what is it? To answer these questions it will be necessary to develop the issues of Weber's concept of causation in detail, and then to examine his ideas about typification, the subject of Chapter 7. Only then can the full significance of his substitutions of novel explanatory concepts be seen.

The form in which Weber attempts to address this group of problems is this question: what is the relation between facts understood in relation to "types" and the facts of causation? We are, he thought, condemned to thinking in terms of types. But scientists and philosophers have ordinarily considered the idea that the facts of causation are relative to the categories one employs to be a monstrosity: science, it has always been thought, is in the business of modifying its categories to match the true relations of causation that hold in the world. Categories are tested by their ability to enable prediction and control. Any mismatch between categories and the world, such as exceptions to general laws, is to be resolved in favor of the world – exceptions disprove laws. In the most common form of this reasoning, natural laws are necessary to causal claims because to explain is to deduce instances from generalizations that are natural laws. Weber's peers, such as Rickert, saw that this model rendered historical "science" a practical impossibility, and went to the other extreme – they denied that the historical "sciences" were "generalizing sciences." But Rickert could not figure out what to do with causality, for he had no alternative to the "deduction from generalization" model of causal explanation.

Weber's answer to these questions has been ill-understood. But if we return the problem to Weber's intellectual roots in the law, we can see the issues more clearly. The best way to understand his answer is to see it in terms of the determination of responsibility in the courtroom. Weber himself regarded the situation of the court and the historian to be analogous. Weber drew the analogy only in terms of causal reasoning proper, that is, in terms of the specific concepts of probabilistic causation, the adequate cause theory of von Kries, that he took to apply to both history and civil liability. But the full significance of the analogy, we shall argue, can be seen only once it is extended to the problem of matching concepts and causes. Weber says many puzzling, even outrageous, things on this subject, the meaning of which becomes clear when the analogy to the courtroom determination of responsibility – the model of practical causal reasoning Weber brought to his thinking about the methodology of the social sciences – is fully developed. Legal determinations of responsibility are a form of decision making about cause in which the concepts are given and fixed, and decisions must be made within the limits of those concepts. This contrasts to the situation of the natural scientist, who is able to revise his or her concepts to fit the results of experiments. "Truth" with respect to legal responsibility is truth in legal terms – responsibility, which is to say causal responsibility in the legal sense, is a finding within the conceptual framework of the law, and not an independent fact against which lawyers' concepts of responsibility are to be held and tested. This, as we shall see, is precisely analogous to the situation which Weber believed the "historical sciences" to be in. The historical scientist, like the lawyer, has concepts fixed in advance by interests. In the case of the historical scientist, of course, the interests are different. Weber sets out to explicate and defend these interests, and to establish the relevance of an alternative to the deductive model of causal explanation.

In this chapter we shall deal with part of this problem, the part relating to the concept of cause. We shall give an account of the concepts of adequate cause and objective possibility, based for the most part on clues and citations which Weber himself provides. These are both precise and profuse, so no ambitious interpretive reconstruction is necessary here. What will be said is more in the way of the explication of a technical device. Unfortunately, this concept has languished in interpretive obscurity, and this obscurity is closely connected to the temptation to read into Weber a notion of causal force he rejected. Parsons is the most egregious and influential offender on this score.

Parsons tells us, in a note to his translation of Part I of *Wirtschaft und Gesellschaft*, that "The concept 'objective possibility' [*objektive Möglichkeit*] plays an important technical role in Weber's methodological studies." Parsons explains that

> a thing *is* "objectively possible" if it "makes sense" to conceive it as an empirically existing entity. It is a question of conforming with the formal logical conditions. The question whether a phenomenon which is in this sense "objectively possible" will actually be found with any significant degree of probability or approximation, is a logically distinct question.
> (Weber [1922] 1978: 61; Parsons [1947] 1964: 149)

"Objective possibility" seems for Parsons to mean "logical possibility" in the Kantian sense of "logic" – so something would be objectively possible if it fits into the possible categories.[1]

A very small part of Parsons' note is correct. The concept and the related concept of adequate cause are important for Weber's methodological argument. Indeed, the subtitle for the crucial second half of "The Logic of the Cultural Sciences" is "Objective Possibility and Adequate Causation in Historical Explanation" ([1905] 1949: 164–88). These terms are also central to the discussion of cause in "Objectivity in Social Science and Social Policy" and in "Roscher and Knies". ([1904] 1949: 79, 80, 92, 93); [1903, 1905, 1906] 1975: 171–2, 175, 190, 266, 273). So important are these uses of the concepts that Weber's primary Russian disciple and friend, Kistiakowskii, regarded these uses as the core of his methodology and especially of his distinction between the social sciences, which use the concept, and the natural sciences, which instead use the concept of law in the sense of law of nature.[2] But no one would come to this conclusion if Parsons' explication of the concept was correct.

Weber simply borrowed the concept from legal science. "The poor condition of the logical analysis of history," Weber tells us, is "shown by the fact that neither historians nor methodologists of history but rather representatives of very unrelated disciplines have conducted the authoritative investigations into this important question" ([1905] 1949: 166). These "authoritative investigations," as he explains, yielded the "theory of the so-called 'objective possibility,'" which rests on the work of the physiologist von Kries and the legal writers Merkel, Rümelin, Liepmann, and Radbruch ([1905] 1949: 166–7). Radbruch, as we have noted, was a friend. The physiologist von Kries, who applied his ideas to the law, was a colleague at Freiburg when Weber was appointed there. Rümelin, an important figure in legal science, was extensively cited by Weber for various legal works.

The theory of adequate cause was a response to the dominant theory of legal causality, formulated by one of Weber's own law professors, von Bar.[3] We shall see that in Weber's famous methodological essays of the 1903–7 period, his remarks on probability, adequate cause, objective possibility, and the place of class concepts and "abstraction" respond to inherent difficulties in the jurisprudential version of the doctrine of adequate cause. So an understanding of these difficulties is essential to an understanding of Weber's solutions.

THE LEGAL BACKGROUND

The dominant jurisprudential theory of cause prior to the theory of adequate cause was the von Buri–von Bar theory. It held that responsibility attached to those actions that were necessary conditions of a harmful result. The difficulty with this theory was that it extended liability too broadly, and the various *ad hoc* restrictions of this tension which were proposed seemed unsatisfactory. The alternative theory, the adequate cause theory, was designed to overcome the difficulties by changes in the structure of the concept of cause rather than *ad hoc* restrictions. The alternative shared many features of the original theory. As Radbruch explains, "the two theories share the assumption that all the necessary conditions are 'equivalent' in the sense that they are all equally necessary for the production of the act. The theories also share the principle that the combination of conditions is the 'cause' of the result" (1902: 9). The difficulty which the adequacy theory sought to correct was that the von Buri–von Bar theory rendered persons liable for results to which their conduct was only a minor contribution. It seemed that there was no way out of this problem without appealing to an anthropomorphic notion of the causal efficacy or potency of an act. Such a concept enables one to limit liability to efficacious acts. But the idea of potency or efficacy was objectionable as "unscientific," meaning objectionable on grounds of the rational inadequacy of the metaphysics that it would presuppose. "Probability," however, seemed to do the work of a notion of potency or efficacy without its objectionable anthropomorphic and metaphysical overtones.[4]

The cases in which the original doctrine got into trouble were cases in which an actor did something which was a necessary condition for the result but which would not ordinarily be regarded as a "cause." The issues are different in civil and criminal contexts. Suppose that Mr Longsuit was a haberdasher who sold a red shirt to Mr Hapless, and that Mr Hapless went to Pamplona and was gored by a bull while wearing the shirt and photographing the running of the bulls. In a criminal context, if the actions of Mr Longsuit *also* met the requirement of intent, that is, if he sold the shirt in order to procure the death of Mr Hapless, Mr Longsuit would be liable for the killing, as his conduct was a necessary condition of the killing. In a civil context where intent is not a test, this would extend liability too far: Mr Longsuit would be liable, under von Bar's theory, if the red shirt was a necessary condition for the harm, apart from intent, in spite of the fact that the act of selling a red shirt was a minor contribution to the outcome – so minor that the notion that one could procure a death by selling a shirt verges on the ludicrous. The problem is this: the odds that this act would produce the result in question are absurdly low – despite the fact that the sale of the shirt was a "necessary condition" of the deadly event as it actually transpired. Of course there are various possible solutions to this problem of legal theory. The solution given by the adequacy theory is that Mr Longsuit's liability depends on the probability that Mr Longsuit's action would result in the harm. Since in this case the probability would be small, the court would conclude that Mr Longsuit is not liable.

More generally, one may say that a certain degree of probability must be reached before a judgment of liability is possible (1902: 17–18).[5]

The intuitive plausibility of the theory rests on the intuitive plausibility of the concept of necessary conditions. An adequate cause is defined as a necessary condition whose probable relation to the result is above a certain quantitative threshold. But this definition is open to serious objections. One is that if probability is defined in a subjectivist fashion, that is, in terms of "expectation," the probability judgment itself becomes "subjective" and therefore not suitable for a court. Von Kries attempts to avoid this result by defining the concept of "objective possibility" in a way which is designed to contrast to "subjective" notions of "probability," or estimates. The difficulty is this: ordinary relative frequency estimates, which are necessarily based on a reference class within which a probability is calculated, differ from what might be described as a "reference-class-free" notion of probability. One may say, for example, that the chance of an American dying of cancer is X where X is a percentage of Americans. The chance of a smoker, or a person with a previous history of cancer, dying of cancer, is of course higher. So each category, "American," "smoker," "person with history of cancer," is a reference class for which statistics can be gathered. Von Kries wishes to contrast such probabilities with the absolute probability of George Smith getting cancer given the unstable myriad of conditions which actually are causally relevant to the outcome. This notion makes some intuitive sense – if George has a probability of getting cancer as an American, as a smoker, and as a person with a history of previous cancer, it seems plausible to say that he has a particular chance of getting cancer as an individual, given the actual causal conditions of his life. Von Kries trades on this by suggesting that the probabilities within a given reference class are no more than "signs" of the true probability of cancer, which inheres in the causal situation of George the individual. Indeed, because there are no clearly valid rules for the selection of a reference class for calculating probabilities, any selection is "subjective," in contrast to the "objective" fact of the inherent or absolute probability of George getting cancer.[6]

Von Kries' theory was developed and elaborated on the intuitive basis of this concept of inherent or absolute probability. An "objective possibility" was the inherent or absolute probability of an individual event. Its numerical values were the same as the probability function, ranging from zero to one. The peculiarity of these single event "objective possibilities" was that they could not be calculated, for no one could state the enormous number of events which were conditional to the outcome events of interest. Yet, as von Kries saw it, there were good reasons for supposing them to exist anyway. His thought was that it is odd to say that a single event can have a variety of true but different probabilities. It is so odd that one might conclude that the fact that different reference classes produced different "probabilities" for the same event showed that these reference-class-based probabilities were not the true probability. On the basis of these considerations, von Kries concluded that the true probability of an event, its "objective possibility," was the *only* "objective"[7] probabilistic fact about a given event, and that, because choices of reference classes were inevitably "subjective," relative frequencies within classes were "probabilities" only in a figurative sense.[8] This, however, was a metaphysical point. Claims about inherent or absolute probability were unverifiable; the only "verifiable" notions of probability either were relative frequency claims which were based on a pre-selected reference class or were "mere estimates" (cf. Nagel, 1939: 20).

The nonempirical or hypothetical character of the notion of "objective possibility" would seem to make it irrelevant to factual determinations, such as those made by a court of law or a historian. Yet the common property of historical and legal inquiry is that the "possibilities" of historians and the legal system are possibilities which have already been realized. So the determination of a numerical probability for a past event will have a "hypothetical" character anyway. The same point holds for the problem of determinations of the necessity of conditions, a problem the adequacy theory shares with the von Buri–von Bar theory. Determinations of the "necessity" of conditions were always handled in these theories by rather vague appeals to "thought" or "past experience," and there is no easy alternative to these vague appeals. One cannot "remove" the conditions of a past event as in an experiment. However, the adequacy theory requires determinations of "necessity" in order to select the list of causes to which its distinctive method of analysis may be applied.

The method of analysis itself proceeds on the following distinctive premises. The first is definitional. All necessary conditions, by virtue of being necessary conditions, are said to contain an objective possibility of the result. The "objective possibility" in this sense is thus a matter of the degree to which particular necessary conditions tend to occur with particular results.[9] Considerations of sufficiency do not play a role in the analysis. There is no question that *some* combination of the conditions which actually obtained prior to a past event were in fact sufficient for the result. As Weber puts it, "historical exposition undoubtedly is governed by the assumption that the 'causes' to which the 'effect' is imputed have to be regarded as unqualifiedly the sufficient conditions for its occurrence" ([1905] 1949: 168). The second premise, then, is that if we are to study causes in history, we must assume it is there: the task is to identify it.

The third distinctive premise is that this is a task governed by interest and cannot be reduced to some sort of mechanical compilation of lists of causes. The reason for this that Weber points out is that "an infinity of conditions which are only summarily referred to as scientifically 'without interest' are associated with the causes which are deemed the efficient conditions of the effect" ([1905] 1949: 168). What is interesting to historians and lawyers is making determinations of responsibility or the extent of the contribution of particular acts to the outcome. This does not mean, however, that the only causes of interest are intentions. The fourth distinctive premise is that one can make an estimate of causal contribution or responsibility by comparing the probability of an outcome given a particular set of conditions with the probability of the outcome absent the condition one is interested in assessing. These sets of conditions are what Radbruch calls "concrete condition complexes" (cf. Turner 1986; Hart and Honoré 1959: 411–39). These "complexes," however, are not given. They must be constructed by the analyst. And they may be constructed differently – that is to say made to include different conditions – for different analytic purposes.

An actual adequate cause analysis would proceed in the following manner. The analyst would select a set of relevant conditions that were necessary for the event. These would ordinarily include, in a legal setting, conditions that might have had an effect on the actual outcome, that is to say conditions that would have increased the probability of the outcome or that would ordinarily be understood to mitigate or cancel the responsibility of the agent. The analyst could first estimate the probability of the outcome if the entire "condition complex" obtained. Next, the analyst would estimate the probability of the event had all the conditions in the complex besides the one in question obtained. The difference in the degree of probability would be the causal effect. A negligible difference would not count as an "adequate cause."

To get any estimate of the dependent probability of an event on a given prior event or set of prior conditions, one must "abstract" in two major ways. To use Weber's terms, drawn from the Roman law tradition (cf. Schulz [1934] 1936: 39), one must "isolate" and "generalize" ([1905] 1949: 175). To isolate, in the Roman law tradition, is to exclude non-legal considerations from consideration in matters of law – a primary conceptual skill of lawyers. In this context, to "isolate" means to consider a causal relation in terms of some particular, specified set of conditions, thus isolating these conditions from the remaining "infinity of conditions" which must be left unstated. To "generalize" is to describe in general terms or to place the case within some particular reference class. Both types of abstraction are necessary in making judgments of objective possibility. One must consider the case as a member of a class of factually equivalent cases in order to calculate the dependent probability (understood here as a relative frequency within this class), and one's estimate of the dependent probability will be the relative frequency of the outcome event in the class of events with equivalent conditions. The class is an abstraction produced by first treating cases as equivalent that are in fact equivalent only in selected relevant respects. The selection is "isolation." And one must "generalize" by treating an actual case as a member of this class.

These acts of abstraction may be done differently, and done differently may produce different outcomes. More simply, events may be described in different ways: described in one way, they will be part of one class; described in another way, they will be part of another. If one considers the liability of a person who strikes another person and describes his action as "striking another person" and calculates the probability of the outcome of death, one will get a relatively low probability, perhaps one below the threshold of adequacy. However, if one describes the same act as "a 250-pound man striking a 95-pound man in the windpipe with full force" one will calculate a far higher probability of death as an outcome. Yet both descriptions may be "true" of the event. Each probabilistic causal attribution made according to the kind of

131

reasoning used in Weber's sources among the legal probabilists depends on placing an event in a class of events which must be treated, analytically, as equivalent. Thus if one were to sue alleging that cigarettes caused the death of a person and to attempt to hold a tobacco company responsible, on the basis of actual probabilistic evidence of frequencies, the evidence would be of probabilities that held for some class of events which were treated as equivalent for the purpose of computing the frequencies. While the calculation is "objective," the selection of the description, and therefore of the pertinent equivalence class, is not. It is a matter, to use the language both of Weber and his jurisprudential sources, of "interest."

The problem of explanatory ultimacy, of how far to push into the causal web, is illustrative of the problem of the interest relativity of isolation and generalization. Consider the causal argument assigning responsibility to the tobacco company. One of the causal "conditions" for the event was the discovery of America, which was a condition for the spread of tobacco use and its industrialization. Is Columbus rather than the company responsible? Or is perhaps the stress of modern life responsible? Or since "modern life" is not a legally culpable entity, is it, as a San Francisco jury decided in a criminal case, that "we are all responsible?" If so, if indeed any necessary condition is equally a source of responsibility, the liability of the tobacco company pales into causal insignificance.

Lawyers can ignore these considerations in part because they "isolate" by excluding non-legal elements from consideration. Doing so reflects something they do not share with non-lawyers, namely a "juridical interest" which developed historically in a particular setting and which is itself reflective of a particular path and stage of social development. Ihering argued that psychology did not and could not supplant the vocabulary and concepts of the law, despite the fact that they appear to be about the same thing and transform the same ordinary concepts of responsibility and action, on this ground. The same "interest" lets us ignore the role of Columbus in the causal background to a cancer suit, however much this might be of interest to historians, who might today, for example, make it part of the "Columbian Exchange" and thus an element of this pivotal causal event in world environmental history. Historians may be said to have a different interest than lawyers, and indeed, as we shall see, the historians of one epoch may have different interests from those of another.

132

Weber does not attempt to give a positive or normative account of what historians ought to be interested in, just as Radbruch does not presume to tell the courts what they ought to be interested in. He makes a polemical case against historians who suppose that history can ignore questions of cause, and in this sense does make the claim that identifying causes is part of the historian's "interest." But in Weber's writings and in a crucial work by Weber's friend, Emil Lask, to be discussed at greater length in the next chapter, the interests of the historian were considered to be analogous to the lawyers' interest, and the one kind of interest was explained in terms of the other kind: legal science was both a model and a case of social science. The key difference between Weber and Lask is in something Weber does *not* say. When Lask discussed sociology, he followed his teacher Rickert by treating it as a systematic discipline which is open to being organized around a key concept, namely "the social," just as the systematic study of legal science may be said to be organized around the concept of law or legal validity. Weber, it is important to note, never accepts the idea that sociology is organized around the master concept of "the social." Georg Simmel did precisely this. In this respect Weber was, as others have noted, of a later generation than Simmel (Lichtblau 1991). Weber's account of the interest of the historian is concerned instead with the historical variation of value concepts and the inevitable changes in our historical interest that result from the continuous transformation of the cultural ideas that inform it. This too will be discussed in the next chapter.

If we proceed from the idea of the historian's interest as analogous but not identical to the lawyer's interest, we can reconstruct Weber's argument as follows:

1 The interest of both the lawyer and the historian is in causal explanation.
2 This interest cannot be satisfied by causal explanations formulated in the abstract vocabulary of the natural sciences, but can be satisfied by probabilistic causal analysis in which the vocabulary of use in contemporary society (which may of course be further abstracted by the historian or lawyer) can be employed.
3 The selection of concepts for use in the formulation of causal questions in each domain is purpose relative (teleological in the language of Lask, or interest relative in Weber's). There is no

external justification for the historian's interest, or for the interest of the historian in these types of causal explanations which is practically entailed by this interest – the historian's purpose is just a choice which others may not share.

4 The realization of this interest is governed by certain logical limits which result from the specific problems of abstraction contained in the problem of equivalence classes dictated by the probabilistic form of causal analysis the historian is compelled to employ if he wants to answer his causal questions.

This reconstruction of Weber's argument allows us to answer a few of the questions with which this chapter began. The idea of causal force, which led to such puzzling results in connection with the concept of charisma, turns out simply not to be an element of Weber's concept of historical causation. In the von Kriesian picture of the world, causality or rather probabilistic propensities inhere in particulars. Generalizations are not approximations of underlying causal forces, as a physicist might say. They are merely collections of particulars, each with its own probability. Similarly for Weber. Thus in the case of charisma, there is no "force." But we may collect similar particular cases, treat them as a type, and calculate probable outcomes for cases of that type. Weber in fact does not do this. But the possibility of doing this makes the construction of ideal-types with causal properties a meaningful strategy.

The benefit Weber receives as a result of the substitution of the concept of adequate cause for the idea of causal forces is substantial. Weber gets the free use of the everyday notion of single event causality without incurring any obligation to refine causal claims into "laws" or to ground them in laws. By conceiving of probabilistic causes as the broad category and nomic causes as a special case of the aggregation of ordinary single event causalities, he is able to avoid the appeal to general laws and forces. Cause in this sense requires no tracing of the causal chain down to its initiation, to ultimate forces, or to ultimate human purposes. The price Weber pays is also steep. To employ this concept of cause he must accept a certain amount of arbitrariness, simply because of the problems of selecting a reference class. His response to these problems is to deny that any historical analyst can escape them, and to argue that historical problems are necessarily constituted by our interests, interests which change as cultural ideas change. This is a "solution" to the problem of the nature of historical explanation that raises problems about objectivity that his predecessors would not only have regarded as serious but as fatal. To say, for example, that the causal analysis of the evolution of the law given by Ihering was the product of an interest-relative conceptualization would mean that Ihering's purpose, which was in part at least to validate certain legal claims (for example, rights claims) as historically inevitable and therefore correct, would have been fatally undermined. Rather than accounting for rights, his results would be the products of conceptual choices which were not open to further justification or, worse, were themselves the expression of, rather than the justification of, an interest.

7

ABSTRACTION

Weber was, by his own account, not a philosopher, and this has tempted interpreters into a search for the philosophical authority on which Weber's arguments might have relied. The possible sources have now been surveyed repeatedly, with widely divergent results. The obvious candidate is neo-Kantianism, and the primary means by which interpretations of Weber's approach to questions about abstraction have been constructed is to see Weber as a neo-Kantian – or simply as a pupil of Heinrich Rickert, whose terminology he partly employed. As was suggested in Chapter 2, the pervasive though diffuse influence of neo-Kantian themes in German (and indeed Continental) intellectual life in the last half of the nineteenth century was such that it would be difficult to separate the neo-Kantian elements of the arguments from those with other sources. Weber would have imbibed neo-Kantian ideas and this vocabulary apart from any of these specific sources, simply because the whole of the discussion of the major intellectual figures of the nineteenth century, exemplified by such texts as Simmel's *Schopenhauer and Nietzsche* ([1907] 1986), which Weber apparently knew,[1] was conducted in these terms.

Weber read this literature and took it seriously. He would have been unable to escape it. His friends, such as Radbruch, absorbed and reproduced its central ideas and terms in works he not only read but engaged and agreed with. The salon he and Marianne Weber ran in Heidelberg was attended by persons who were intensely concerned with these topics. His analyst, admirer, and friend Karl Jaspers was one of these. Jaspers, of course, developed these ideas in an existentialist direction; Lukács developed them in another – a direction which led to a kind of *Lebensphilosophie* affirmation of the vital historical force of the

136

proletariat. Emil Lask, Rickert's student, was also concerned with these ideas.

Lask's testimony on the subject, contained in his *Habilitations-schrift* published in a *Festschrift* for Kuno Fischer, is perhaps the best source we have on the connection between Weber's understanding of legal science and his understanding of social science. The text displays the history of the problem of abstraction in a different light: one in which the legal problem of abstraction is prior to, and influenced, such neo-Kantian contemporaries of Weber's as Rickert. The evidence Lask provides about Weber is largely indirect. But the work is useful in ways that Weber's own texts are not, for it gives us insight into the way that the works in question were read in Weber's circle, and indeed by Weber himself, for Lask was a frequent visitor to Weber's home at the time and engaged in intense scholarly discussions with him.[2] But to understand Lask's work, the larger legal science setting and the role of the problem of abstraction in it must be appreciated.

ISOLATION AND GENERALIZATION IN LEGAL SCIENCE

The problems of abstraction in the law were distinctive, and had a distinctive history quite unlike that of natural science. At the root of the discipline of legal science itself was the practice of abstraction that was distinctive to civil law. It is sometimes said that there are three great systems of law, the law of Rome itself, the common law, and the modern "Roman law" tradition. The modern Roman tradition, the "civil law," is an anomaly: the basis of the civil law is not a local legal tradition which developed into a systematic body of legal concepts and practices, but is a product of scholarly inquiry into a dead system known only through legal textbooks. As we noted in Chapter 2, the central originating fact of the civil law was the "reception" of the legal theory of Rome, that is to say the rediscovery of Roman legal texts and their creation of a university subject matter based upon them. The centrality of legal scholarship in this tradition rests on the historical fact that the teaching of law in the Continental universities, such as Bologna, was oriented to the demands of students who often came from other regions of Europe, but who could be taught the most general conceptual building blocks, the abstract principles, of the available codifications of the Roman law.

The historical connection between legal scholarship and the

practice of the law was perpetuated by the preference for codification as against judge-made law in the civil law world: the place of law finding through supreme courts or Law Lords which decide cases in which the legal aspects of the case are in dispute and establish authoritative precedents, central to the common law, is largely taken, in the civil law world, by successive codifications of the law and by "legal scientists" who construct conceptual solutions to problems in the codes that leave apparent gaps. These solutions have the character and force of legal reason, and a judge who failed to follow an accepted understanding of the principles and concepts at stake would err legally by doing so. This meant that law professors and the consensus of expert opinion took the place of Law Lords and Supreme Court Justices as the arbiters of legal questions. Not surprisingly, professors played a large role in the recurrent tasks of codification as well. The German legal system was undergoing this process, as a consequence of the unification of Germany, during Weber's early career as a lawyer, but he was too young to be a participant. The great practical product of German legal scholarship was thus completed – another reason why Weber might have seen the law as a domain of diminished opportunity for national service.

The ancient Roman law that was "received" was a body of texts which were themselves the product of attempts to make a coherent system out of actual Roman practice. Perhaps the most famous of these attempts was the work commissioned and made authoritative by Justinian, the *Institutes*. After the reception, schools of legal interpretation arose with different approaches to these texts, each of which contributed to systematization and abstraction. This produced a curious discrepancy. As Fritz Schulz points out, the Romans themselves were "extremely reserved" when "it came to abstraction . . . compared with the jurisprudence of the eighteenth century (law of Nature) or with German legal science in the nineteenth, Roman jurisprudence on the whole shows a disinclination to the process" ([1934] 1936: 41). With the adoption of civil-law-based codes in the various countries of the Continent, however, the status of the study of the Roman law changed. The code actually in force, not the ancient legal system which inspired it, was legally valid. So the study of Roman law became a matter of purely historical interest.

For the Germans, who were latecomers to the process of codification, the decline of scholarship in Roman law came late.

One of the major national tasks after unification was the creation of a new uniform code, which went into effect only in 1900. The massive effort of codification and reconciling codes placed legal science at the core of national consciousness, and placed legal scholars in the position of nation builders. It is thus not surprising that the law and the historical study of the law attracted an array of scholars of extraordinary talent during this period.

One of the puzzles that faced the German law professoriate of the nineteenth century was set by Savigny, the nobleman who raised the status of the professoriate at the beginning of the century by joining it. Savigny posed the problem of the relevance and authority of the Roman law for a people which already had a legal tradition of customary law which matched their character as a people. What claim, exactly, does the rationality of the Roman law have against law that is rooted in the life of the people? The long dispute that arose from the combination of Savigny's text on this subject and the Romantic reaction to the French Revolution need not be examined here. Suffice it to say that by the time Ihering began his career as a legal scholar, it was possible to ask the question of the roots of the law in the social life of a people about the law of Ancient Rome itself. Ihering's great work on the history and spirit of the Roman law was devoted to this question. Weber himself retraces this history in *Wirtschaft und Gesellschaft*, and in a sense this work is a complex response to Savigny's question. What Weber shows in this text is the way in which the process of rationalization – in the law and in other domains of life – is fed and entangled by other historical processes and interests.

Weber had a great deal to say about the processes of legal rationalization, about the role of maxims and casuistics, and about abstraction in the law. His discussions of abstraction relate broadly, but not in detail, to the claims he makes in his methodological writing.

As we saw in Chapter 2, Weber knew from the history of law that even the most fundamental concepts of human agency have varied historically, that the everyday concepts of agency and the legal concept do not match, and that there is no fact of the matter to decide between them – so he would have said that to decide on "scientific" grounds, for example by reference to the findings of psychology, is simply to decide to accept the concepts of a variant tradition, and not to settle the "scientific" issue. This realization, in this form, depends on neo-Kantianism of the variety promulgated by Kuno Fischer, but it is powerfully reinforced by, and perhaps is a simple inference from, the prosaic fact of the difference between legal conceptualizations of everyday matters and "folk" conceptions, a relation as familiar to the workaday lawyer as it is to the legal theorist. As we noted in the last chapter, Weber knew this contrast from the legal literature, under the heading "isolation," meaning the legal point of view rooted in the concepts of the Roman jurists (cf. Schulz [1934] 1936: 19–39).

"Generalization" is a closely connected conceptual phenomenon which appears both in the legal literature and in Weber's methodology. How do cases add up to maxims or legal principles, and how do maxims and principles inform decisions about cases? Weber was fascinated, as Ihering had been, by the history of this process, not only in the case of Rome but in other legal systems. Typification, one-sided selectivity, idealization (especially in the context of instruction), rationalization, and codification were central to the law-forming process in civil law, as they were to the process of applying precedent in the common law. Indeed, application and generalization are part of the development of the law in both traditions, with the application of precedent being the mode of choice in the common law world and the formation of general rules open to mechanical application being the mode favored in the civil law tradition.

Isolation and generalization play an explicit role both in the legal literature and in Weber's thought. The third concept, application, does not play an explicit role, but is the key to the parallel between the two problematics. "Application" is a problem with a special historical importance in the countries that "received" the Roman law. As we have noted, legal categories of Roman law were alien to the social life and commercial practice of these countries, and the discrepancies were evident. But the advantages of the Roman law in conceptual clarity and precision, as well as the greater generality of its categories, meant that it was far better than customary law for the purpose of erecting novel legal structures, especially in such domains as the creation of forms of contract for which customary law had few provisions. These advantages meant that its dominance on the Continent was assured. Its fetishization by scholars, who mastered it literally and metaphorically as a foreign language into which the needs for contractual forms in their own societies had to be translated, followed from its alien character. The problem of the application of conceptualizations to other epochs or other cultures was part of the experience of the civil lawyers and law scholars. But they experienced it as an everyday problem: the legal categories they employed *were* those of an alien culture.

Weber saw problems of conceptualization in the social (or, as he put it, the "historical") sciences in very similar terms to these, and his unusual conclusions with respect to problems of objectivity may be the best understood in terms of the similarities between civil law conceptualization and social science concept formation. The problem of historical variation in cultural concepts, and thus the problem of the eternal youth of the social sciences (and the problem of the application of our concepts, which are always changing, to the social life of other times), he saw in a way which fits this experience. He saw the discrepancies between "our" cultural categories and those of our historical subjects not as absolutes that defeat historical understanding, but rather as a mundane or practical problem which cannot be eliminated but which can be ameliorated on a piecemeal basis: not as a "problem of other cultures" in which social totalities must be grasped as spiritual or functional wholes, but as cases in which the concepts that make sense to us and our audiences, our habitual modes, simply may not apply very well to the historical material we wish to address. We may deal with this problem in the manner of legal construction, by refining our concepts, or by producing novel ideal-types,[3] such as "charisma," that can be made meaningful to our audiences.

The fact that we as historical scientists are constrained by what we and our audiences can understand and assess as significant is fundamental, and it is the source of a problem of objectivity. But the problem is inescapable, because it is based on an even more fundamental problem – the problem of selectivity with respect to the facts that are significant for us. Selectivity is the price of all conceptual understanding and causal knowledge. The promise of "objectivity" in the sense either of completeness ([1904] 1949: 72) or finality ([1904] 1949: 85) is an illusion. One-sidedness of the sort that lawyers practice on life must also be practiced by any causal analyst, both for the reasons given in the last chapter, the technical need for the selection of reference classes in order to form causal expectations, and because of the complexity of social life, which must be reduced for social life to be mastered intellectually ([1904] 1949: 87). Conceptual schemes, consciously constructed, are indispensable for this. Conceptual schemes aim for clarity, but the construction of these schemes and their evaluation is governed by pragmatic considerations as well: they are purpose relative, relative to our purposes as historians and to our culturally pre-given sense of significance ([1904] 1949: 80–90).

This, *in nuce*, is Weber's account of concept formation (or abstraction) and objectivity in the historical sciences. Once we are attuned to the similarities to the experience of the lawyer, the relationship is obvious. The lessons of the indispensability of conceptual schemes, the inevitability of problems of application, especially to other cultures, the inevitability of one-sidedness, but also the possibility of "objectivity," in an internal sense, within a discipline and for an audience which shares the pre-given sense of significance, are each lessons that flow from the ordinary daily experience of the civil lawyer. Yet Weber did not claim legal science sources as his epistemic authority for his discussion of abstraction in the 1904 "Objectivity" essay, as he did for his discussion of cause in "The Logic of the Cultural Sciences." Why? One may identify a variety of possible answers to this question. The very quotidian character of this aspect of a lawyer's life, the business of explaining to clients the difference between what is true in their own terms and what is true in law once non-legal considerations have been excluded, is one explanation. There *is* no authority for such a basic fact of the lawyer's life, and therefore no one to cite. Another answer might be that in a sense Weber does appeal to legal science in "Objectivity": the text uses the law, the problem of legal validity, and the possibility of purely formal "legal history" as points of contrast to social science and history as he envisions them. But perhaps Weber had other good reasons for not asserting the centrality of the law as a model as he did in the case of the theory of objective possibility. The "influences" in question were sufficiently diffuse that there was no point in doing so: this was Weber's distillation of his own reading and thinking, not something derived from these sources in any direct way. Nor was the text of "Objectivity" the same kind of document as the "Logic" essay. "Objectivity" was an editorial: it is devoid of references and all of its discussions of other positions are masked and indirect. Perhaps Weber also sought to pay his respects to his new profession and to the needs of his new audience by referring to its traditions. As "Objectivity" was an introduction to a journal of social science and social policy rather than a law journal, it would have been an understandable attempt at ecumenism to have spoken in the most general language possible about the broadest range of problems, especially given the explicit message of the editorial, that the pages of the *Archiv für Sozialwissenschaft und Sozialpolitik* were to be open to all viewpoints that fulfilled the rules of scientific discourse. All of this, however, is speculation. We do not need to speculate about how the intellectual genealogy of the problems he raises was understood in Weber's circle. Lask's work provides direct evidence on this point.

LASK ON RICKERT AND IHERING

Lask's essay both illuminates and illustrates the complexity of the context. Oakes, in his recent studies of the relationship between Rickert and Weber, makes much of Lask's significance for Weber, especially as a promoter of the idea of the *hiatus irrationalis* between concept and reality (1988: 42, 169–70), and also for his "reconstruction of the analytic and emanationist theories of concept formation" (1988: 42). The latter is precisely Lask's theme in his study in the philosophy of law. Lask's purpose in this text is to pursue the implications of the then new Rickertian understanding of the nature of the cultural sciences for legal science if legal science is understood as a cultural science. He thus parallels Weber's own discussions. Both Lask and Weber explicitly and implicitly rely on the literature of legal science. The direction of the discussion, however, is the reverse: Lask starts from a model of the cultural sciences, under which he subsumes legal science. But Lask, writing after Weber's "Objectivity" essay and citing it, as well as such texts as Simmel's *Philosophy of Money*, relies in part on the model Weber constructs.

What is instructive about Lask's approach is how much, and what specifically, of the problem-structure of the philosophy of social science is attributed, by Lask himself, to sources in the philosophy of law, *rather than* to Rickert. Lask uses Rickert's distinctive jargon of individual and typical values ([1905] 1950: 5), and insists that while empirical reality is "the only kind of reality, . . . at the same time [it is] . . . the scene or the substratum of transempirical values or meanings of general validity" ([1905] 1950: 4). In this respect he was a more faithful Rickertian than Weber, who rejected the idea of the existence of generally valid transempirical values. Lask also takes from the other neo-Kantians a concern with "a systematic consideration of how absolutely to justify causal events" ([1905] 1950: 9). But he applies these considerations to an already formed set of problems in legal science, problems with their own structure and history.

Many of these preformed problems may be found in the writings of Ihering. One of these is the problem of the abstract character of the law. Lask summarizes Hegel as saying that "The mission of Romanism in world history was to bend the concrete individuality under the power of abstract freedom and the abstract state" ([1905] 1950: 19). Lask accepts, similarly, that the transformation of what Rickert called "prescientific thought" into systematic abstractions is central both to science and to the law. Lask pointed out that this way of thinking had long since become the conventional wisdom. "All attempts at a theory of juridical method so far, from Ihering to the present, have recognized this concept-forming spirit inherent in the law" ([1905] 1950: 30). Ihering's account of "symbolic generalizing of concrete sensible environments," it may be noted, deals with the subject at the most basic epistemological level, the point at which meanings are attached to the world. He argues that complicated expectation associations, which can be discerned in concrete associations only with difficulty, become thematically accessible through symbolic generalization and unified under a symbol. By symbol, Ihering means "an object or process that at the same time is something and means something. The object of the symbol has an independent existence from the thought it serves" (quoted in Gromitsaris 1989: 251). So Ihering's account gives rise to the question discussed in Chapter 2, of whether the law is a world forming paradigm or a fundamental ideology.

The "concept forming spirit inherent in the law," Lask argues, echoing Ihering, is teleological or purposive, as it operates according to the purposes implicit in the law.[4] The main contribution of modern legal theorizing has been "to render conscious and explicit . . . the teleological principle which jurisprudence has always applied" in the course of its abstractive transformations. This general lesson can be elaborated in various ways. Lask notes that "Rickert, applying Ihering's ideas, has characterized the purpose of the law as the principle determining the legally 'relevant' conceptual elements" ([1905] 1950: 30). This was a lesson Weber repeated and applied to social science. Legal scientists said the same sorts of things as Rickert did. Thus "G. Rümelin[5] and Zitelmann have pointed out that here as always it is the task of science to overcome the indefinite generality of prescientific thought" ([1905] 1950: 30).

For Lask, then, the law was an exemplary case of interested concept formation.

> Its methodological significance is this: the juridical pattern of the world makes possible wholly different articulations, which are unheard of in the epistemological and naturalistic views and often even in the common-sense view of life; it offers new syntheses, new principles of unification and individualization. What is continuous in the naturalistic view may be discrete in the juridical view; what is but a collective plurality, naturalistically speaking, may legally be a unit distinct from any mere sum.
>
> ([1905] 1950: 31)

The figures who preceded Lask and Rickert were struck by the conflicts between other standpoints and that of the law, conflicts that were especially troublesome where the law shared concepts with science or common sense. Of these, the concepts of will and causation, shared with psychology and science respectively, were the source of the most trouble.

The problem over "will," at the time a characteristically psychologistic concept, was "made famous by Ihering," as Lask says ([1905] 1950: 34). The solution to the conflict was to see that the causal concepts employed by lawyers and psychologists were of different kinds, motivated by different world forming purposes. Lask gives the example of "Liepmann [yet another jurisprudential causal probabilist who] has expressed the view that the solution of the problem of causation in criminal law depends on the recognition of specifically juridical selective principles" ([1905] 1950: 34–5). Lask simply endorses this as a contribution to

> the correct view that the legally relevant "adequacy" of causation can be determined only by practical criteria which rest on considerations of expediency and justice; for instance, by the "foreseeability" or "calculability" of a result which must be ascertained by "objective prognosis after the event," as pointed out frequently in the literature of civil and criminal law.
>
> ([1905] 1950: 35)

Lask points to Ihering as the source of the key idea of the special legal interest that dictates the irreducibly legal form of description of caused actions.

For Lask, specifically Rickertian ideas on general concepts bear on this issue through their connection with the thesis that "Legal science is a branch of the empirical 'cultural sciences'" and therefore subject to its conceptual limitations ([1905] 1950: 24). To understand this link we must, he says, distinguish between "historical" and "systematic" tendencies in the cultural sciences.

> From the complexity of given facts, typical cultural elements are selected by the systematic disciplines. In history, these typical cultural elements are submerged in individual events of unique and indivisible significance. In the systematical disciplines, on the contrary, they remain explicitly isolated in their formal structure and are elevated to become guiding concepts of the several disciplines. To avoid misunderstanding, it may be added that these sciences of general concepts are sufficiently distinguished from the natural sciences by the complete disregard of cultural meanings in the abstractive and systematizing principle of the natural sciences.
>
> ([1905] 1950: 24)

"Systematical" disciplines, such as the law, have guiding concepts which are cultural or value oriented. The world these concepts form to create the subject matter of these disciplines is a kind of amalgam. The systematizing conceptual work of these disciplines consists in molding the "prescientifically" conceived world into the distinctive selective forms appropriate to that discipline. But this operation is not performed directly on some sort of unformed reality. The "prescientific" is "a world already related to cultural meanings, comparable to a half-product; and this complex cultural reality, and not the original reality which is free of any kind of value relation, becomes the material of the cultural sciences proper" ([1905] 1950: 26). For Lask, then, the law is not a world creating ideology. It operates on a world already created by culture.

Weber's argument with respect to the initial disciplinary transformations of this already formed world is identical to Lask's. In "Marginal Utility Theory and 'The Fundamental Law of Psychophysics,'" published in 1908, Weber rejects the idea that

146

psychology is "fundamental" to economics by making a general claim:

> The "everyday experience" from which [economic] theory takes its departure . . . is of course the common point of departure of *all* particular empirical disciplines. Each of them aspires beyond everyday experience and must so aspire, for thereon rests its right to existence as a science. But each of them in its aspirations "goes beyond" or "sublimates" everyday experience in a different way and in a different direction.
>
> ([1908] 1975: 31)

This is both a crucial point of similarity and a crucial extension of the argument: all disciplines, it appears from this quotation, transform everyday experience in a manner parallel to the transformation exemplified by legal conceptualization. So economic conceptualization, in particular, must be understood in the same terms as legal conceptualization.

But here the similarities between Lask's and Weber's accounts of the process of the conceptual transformation of the world end. Lask points out that beyond the transformation of everyday experience is another step, the ascent to a systematic concept that "serves as the selective principle of a particular science" ([1905] 1950: 25). In the case of the law, this step was the step taken by Stammler, who wished to identify the teleological abstractive principle of validity in the law. Something analogous might be found in the case of economics, which might be supposed to have an organizing idea such as value or the pursuit of wealth. Lask points out that the task of abstraction toward a higher-order systematizing science fits Simmel's conception of sociology. He comments that

> all cultural types may well involve the element of the social, which in its complete isolation and unadulterated purity could be grasped only by an ultimate, most abstract analysis. That analysis would then be the "sociology" postulated by Simmel, which would start from the final results of the other disciplines and constitute their "general part."
>
> ([1905] 1950: 26)

Obviously this generalizing conception is not the conception Weber adhered to, either in his sociological or his methodological writings.

There is nevertheless a relation between this conception of

sociology and Weber's. The first step, the idea that the material of the cultural sciences is a "half-product" related to cultural meanings, he of course did accept. The last step, the idea of a discipline constituted by the general concept of "the social," he rejected. But he substituted something for it. In his methodological writings of 1904–7 he wrote not as a sociologist but as a "historian" in the broad sense and as a practitioner of *Nationalökonomie*. His 1904 "Objectivity" essay appears to rely on Carl Menger's distinctions between historical sciences, theoretical sciences, and practical sciences. The latter is the category that includes *Nationalökonomie* ([1883] 1985: 38–9). Weber accepts the notion that these sciences are ultimately tied to practical purposes. The selection of concepts in these sciences is governed by these purposes and not by any higher-order systematizing concept. Legal science in the strict sense falls outside Menger's scheme. It is a dogmatic science. The line between the dogmatic science of the law and history runs through the category of legal history. Weber illustrates his point about the difference between the two by distinguishing their purposes: "The universe of legal norms is naturally clearly definable and is valid (in the *legal* sense!) for historical reality. But social science in our sense is concerned with practical *significance*" ([1904] 1949: 94). By this, as he explains at length, he means significance for us as members of a particular cultural epoch. Legal history done as history, accordingly, abstracts differently than legal history done with an eye to the dogmatic question of legal validity.

"Practical significance" is an elusive concept. Weber means it very broadly. If social science aspires to say something about the world that is useful for the sophisticated politician or policy maker, however, it is evident that a great deal is included beyond mere data or technical knowledge. But the idea that the kind of social science Weber practices is "practical" does tie this "science" to a particular audience of practitioners, the audience of Weber's own time, with its values and habitual modes of assessing what is significant. Weber was well aware that the kinds of causal questions we ask, and what we regard as acceptable answers to them, are also governed by audience-relative criteria. Reconciling the relativizing consequences of this recognition with the idea of causal facts as in some sense genuinely hard or objective presented Weber with his most difficult problems, and provides his readers with his most confusing arguments.

148

IDEAL-TYPES AND CAUSATION

Weber approached these problems through a broader argument about the indispensability of abstract concepts in social science. The background to his arguments is complex: both the history of neo-Kantianism and the *Methodenstreit* in German economics bear on Weber's formulation of the problems. The basic ground for Weber's arguments is the *Faktum der Wissenschaft* of historical knowledge. Consider a few of these arguments. Weber says that "if the historian (in the widest sense of the word)" imagines that explicit abstractions are "useless or dispensable for his concrete heuristic purposes, the inevitable consequence is either that he consciously or unconsciously uses other similar concepts without formulating them verbally and elaborating them logically or that he remains stuck in the realm of the vaguely 'felt'" ([1904] 1949: 94). His advice to those who dispute the particular concepts of economic theory, such as "historical school" critics of classical economics, is this:

> Those who are so contemptuous of the "Robinsonades" of classical theory should restrain themselves if they are unable to replace them with better concepts, which in this context means clearer concepts.
>
> ([1904] 1949: 95)

The error of these critics is that they have misunderstood the purpose – the practical purpose – of their own disciplines, or misunderstood their own practice. But these arguments are curiously weak – the latter is a *tu quoque* argument that applies only to those who actually fail to clarify their concepts. The former rests on the valorization of "clarity" as a methodological ideal. Weber has other arguments along these lines as well, all of which have similar defects.

Many of these arguments are primarily prudential methodological arguments or generalizations from practice. No argument of either kind can establish the broader claim that abstraction is a precondition for social scientific knowledge. Weber appears to argue for this more significant claim. The weakness of the arguments becomes apparent at a specific point. What Weber would like to be able to claim is that causal analysis is essential to historical understanding, and that abstraction is essential to causal analysis. This would make "ideal-types" a necessity: the only

149

"objection" to them would be an objection to clarifying what is "vaguely felt." But he could not have made this claim stick. Some historians explicitly reject causal analysis. They are easily disposed of through *tu quoque* responses, showing that they implicitly rely on causal analysis nevertheless. But another kind of social science is not so easily disposed of: the kind that conceives itself naturalistically and rejects abstraction on naturalistic grounds.

Weber was well aware of the power of what he called the "will-to-believe of naturalistic monism" ([1904] 1949: 86), and explained its basis in the following comment on Darwinism, portions of which have already been quoted:

> When modern biology subsumed those aspects of reality which interest us *historically*, i.e., in all their concreteness, under a universally valid evolutionary principle, which at least had the appearance – but not the actuality – of embracing everything essential about the subject in a scheme of universally valid laws, this seemed to be the final twilight of all evaluative viewpoints in all the sciences. For since the so-called historical event was a segment of the totality of reality, since the principle of causality which was the presupposition of all scientific work, seemed to require the analysis of all events into scientifically valid "laws," and in view of the overwhelming success of the natural sciences which took this idea seriously, it appeared as if there was in general no conceivable meaning of scientific work than the discovery of the *laws* of events. Only those aspects of phenomena which were involved in the "laws" could be essential from the scientific point of view, and concrete "individual" events could be considered only as "types," i.e., as representative illustrations of laws. An interest in such events in themselves did not seem to be a "scientific" interest.
>
> ([1904] 1949: 86)

He saw that "despite the powerful resistance" to this "dogma" by "German Idealism since Fichte . . . the naturalistic viewpoint in certain decisive problems has not yet been overcome" ([1904] 1949: 86–7).

One area in which it had "not yet been overcome" was the status of economic theory. Weber disposes of this problem, inherited from Menger, by assimilating economic theory to the concept of ideal-type, which is to say by understanding it as a case similar to legal abstraction rather than natural scientific abstraction. "Isolation," in this case of a psychological impulse to enrich oneself ([1904] 1949: 88), is a method as essential to economics as it is to the law. But economics, in Menger's terms, is a pure science. The historian's task (and that of the "National Economist," such as Weber, who is a "practical" and a "historical" scientist) is to assess the divergence between ideal-types and reality. For this kind of scientist, ideal-types are not hypotheses, nor are they descriptions; they are, rather, heuristic aids to the construction of descriptions ([1904] 1949: 90–1). The justification for their employment is that they do provide aid. The naturalistically inclined, however, challenge the employment of abstractions as such, and Weber himself concedes that social science often employs "classifications" that are not abstractions, that is to say "mere classifications" that can be conceived naturalistically.

Weber's account of causation, curiously, leaves him especially open to the naturalistic challenge. He might have been satisfied with the reply that there are no known exceptionless laws of a natural science kind in social science, and that all the known laws are partly conceptual and abstract in character. He could then argue pragmatically, and say that we would simply have no causal knowledge of the social world if we accepted the methodological implications of naturalism. But the "objective possibility" theory precludes this response: the making of judgments of causal adequacy in terms of this theory of causation *is* possible using naturalistic classifications, that is to say mere classifications with no degree of abstraction, and indeed this use is commonplace in legal settings. If one is identifying the persons present at a crime, for example, no additional step of abstraction beyond mere classification is required.[6] According to the "objective possibility" account of cause, all that is needed to make a causal judgment are the probabilities of a given outcome for two reference classes: one defined by a particular set of conditions, the other by these conditions minus the condition in question. If the difference in the probabilities is sufficiently large, the causal contribution is in the technical sense "adequate" and is sufficient to be noticed by the courts. Consequently, if the classifications one employs are "mere" classifications, one has cause without abstraction.

Weber sees that he must respond to the argument that the additional step of abstraction is not required, and he does so at length. The issues are at the core of Weber's argument, for it is at

151

the core of his account to the problem of audience relativity. A member of another culture, a "Chinese," to use Weber's phrase, could, presumably, employ purely classificatory means. So the Chinese could, in principle, construct classifications of a naturalistic sort, apply them to Western society, and produce causal results. Weber's response to this is to try to show that purely classificatory distinctions are not adequate for the purposes of the historian. The arguments, however, are murky:

> Let us take for instance the concepts "church" and "sect." They may be broken down purely classificatorily into complexes of characteristics whereby not only the distinction between them but also the content of the concept must constantly remain fluid.
>
> ([1904] 1949: 93)

This means that once one has selected a list of classificatory characteristics, the concepts of "church" and "sect" lose their original meaning, for example their meaning in past cultures or in contemporary cultures. They acquire no new fixed conceptual significance, and they cannot: the content of the classes depends on what falls within the criteria (which is to say that it is a matter of historical contingency), rather than on the boundaries of the category depending on the concept themselves.

Yet it is not clear, *a priori*, why this should be, in general, a defect rather than an improvement. A "positivist" methodologist would reason that if a "concept" is dispensable in favor of something more precise, for example through "operationalization," perhaps it should be dispensed with. Weber's response to this kind of consideration is to claim that we cannot explain the things that are significant to us if we proceed in this fashion:

> If however I wish to formulate the concept of "sect" genetically, e.g., with reference to certain important cultural significances which the "sectarian spirit" has had for modern culture, certain characteristics of both become *essential* because they stand in an adequate causal relation to those influences.
>
> ([1904] 1949: 93–4)

If we are concerned with the particular "genetic" relation that produced the thing we want explained, we cannot settle for a list of classificatory characteristics. From this it follows that the ideal-type as distinct from mere classification is essential to "genetic" explanation, because "the concepts [in question] thereupon become ideal-typical in the sense that they appear in full conceptual *integrity* either not at all or only in individual instances" ([1904] 1949: 94). In short, "genetic" explanations, which are the kind we seek, are fully instantiated only by a few instances at best. Hence they are ideal-typical abstractions.

As Weber concedes, at the moment of going beyond mere classification to something more abstract one loses direct contact with reality. There is no middle ground: "every concept which is not purely classificatory diverges from reality" ([1904] 1949: 94). The choice is thus between using abstract concepts which diverge, which may not be instantiated by any particular cases, and settling for mere classifications. For Weber, this is no choice at all. But there are at least two different and potentially conflicting justifications for choosing to employ abstractions. The first is purpose relativity, and the supposed fact that a purely classificatory list of characteristics cannot satisfy the historian's interest. The second is the general epistemological consideration that we comprehend reality through a "chain of intellectual modifications"[7] and therefore are compelled to abstract if we are to "know" at all.

The second – and along with it such issues as the *hiatus irrationalis* between concept and reality – may be readily dispensed with. It does not apply to the problem at hand, the role of purely classificatory distinctions, which by definition are not "conceptual." The first is more subtle. The implication of the argument is that the purposes of the historian, the desire to explain "genetically" something in its "significances," requires going beyond mere classification. In a sense this is trivially true, if we define "significances" to exclude "mere classifications." But to do this would make the argument circular. It also would raise the question of whether the historian might better attach significance directly to mere classifications and dispense with abstractions. It is evident, for example, that classifications that have predictive value *acquire* "significance" for us, and that our scheme of concepts is always open to revision on such grounds as greater predictive utility, or to being discarded if it serves no such purposes. However, if we assume that the concepts defining the things to be explained are themselves fixed in some manner, and not open to this sort of revision, they cannot be discarded.

Weber does assume them to be fixed in the sense that they belong not to the historian but to the historian's audience. And he assumes, following Menger's classification, that the social sciences generally have purposes fixed externally by "significances" or purposes outside of science, and that the social scientist is bound to constitute his or her problems, or formulate his or her conclusions, by reference to them. This "constitutivity" consideration applies to the *objects* of explanation, however, and not to the explanations themselves. Why suppose that abstract concepts are necessary for explanation? As we have seen, Weber's own account of causal explanation implies that they are not necessary for the making of judgments of causal adequacy. When, in "Objectivity," Weber uses the term "genetic" for the causal relations of primary interest to the argument, this is a clue to an important distinction that Weber never elaborates: the distinction between genetic and causal explanations. The reason why the relation between genetic explanations and adequate cause explanations is never explained by Weber in detail will soon be apparent: the key implication of his argument is quite odd and quite radical.

Weber says that genetic ideal-types "are constructs in terms of which we formulate relationships by application of the category of objective possibility." And he goes on to say that "by means of [the category of objective possibility] the adequacy of our imagination [in constructing genetic ideal-types] . . . is *judged*" ([1904] 1949: 93). This suggests that the term "genetic" means more than "causal," but also that there is a kind of causal knowledge at the core of a genetic ideal-type. Perhaps the use of ideal-typifications of human action are an instance of this same relation: to be a causally valid imputation of a motive there must be some probabilistic relationship between outcome and motive, as well as a "meaning" relationship of the sort Ihering had in mind with his "law of purpose."

The closest Weber comes to giving an account of the distinction is in connection with the concept of exchange, which he suggests is open to interpretation either as a purely classificatory concept or as a genetic concept. As a class concept (*Gattungsbegriff*) it is "a complex of traits which are common to many phenomena, as long as we disregard the *meaning* of the component parts of the concept, and simply analyze the term in its everyday usage." The dividing line between the purely classificatory sense of the concept of exchange and its "genetic" sense is marked by the use of the non-classificatory concept "typical."

154

If however we relate this concept to the concept of "marginal utility" for instance, and construct the concept of "economic exchange" as an economically rational event, this then contains as every concept of "economic exchange" does which is fully elaborated logically, a judgment containing the "typical" *conditions* of exchange. It assumes a *genetic* character and becomes therewith ideal-typical in the logical sense, i.e., it removes itself from empirical reality which can only be compared or related to it.

([1904] 1949: 100)

Weber stresses that by this term he does not mean typical in the purely statistical sense of a mere average, but something more.

So we are back where we began: Weber needs an argument that would establish the necessity or indispensability of abstraction or ideal-types as distinct from classifications. But he can do no better than *defining* the concepts he appeals to, such as "typification," in terms of their essentially "conceptual" character, and then arguing for the audience relativity of concepts. The appeal to the term "genetic" is precisely parallel. The "genetic" relation itself is a case of audience-relative "conceptualization": it is "genetic" only for us, that is, only for those who share the added genetic concept. A "Chinese" would be able to apply purely classificatory concepts of church and sect, for example, and would be able to calculate the probabilities needed to estimate causal adequacy. These classifications would not be sufficient from the point of view of *our* sense of their cultural significance. But more intriguingly, the "genetic" relation itself might be inaccessible to the "Chinese." There is no assurance that a person from another culture could master the concepts necessary for our conceptualization of the "genetic," as distinct from the causal relation. So Weber's argument is this: a causal relation is a quantitative matter of subtracting one probabilistic expectation from another. A genetic explanation is something more. But, like abstractions generally, it is subject to the problems of objectivity with which the last chapter closed.

Weber was not, of course, compelled to defend his view of social science against an actual "naturalistic" competitor. None of his competitors – Marx, Spencer, Tönnies – employed purely classificatory concepts in constructing their analyses. At most, they misinterpreted themselves "naturalistically," or were misinterpreted thus by their audiences. To them, Weber may say that the very fact that they employed non-classificatory concepts in constituting problems and giving explanations meant that they could not "naturalistically" appeal to the "reality" of causal forces, for these "forces" were the product of their constructions rather than an independent reality to which their constructions directly corresponded.

This argument, which is central to "Objectivity," places the whole of Weber's elaborate "explanatory displacement" in perspective. Taken as an alternative to the conceptual schemes of his competitors which purport to correspond to underlying causal realities, Weber's systematic set of distinctions, which admits to diverging from reality, is not impressive. But if all of the causal and explanatory devices of social theory are seen as "ideal-typical" constructions with no special claim to reality, the playing field is levelled. It becomes apparent that the *competitors'* schemes are one-sided and selective – as all ideal-types are. Worse, it becomes apparent that their appeal rests largely on their (spurious) claims to correspond to reality. Weber admits the one-sidedness and selectivity of his own typifications. Because he uses them "heuristically," he avoids any spurious appeal to "reality." And in fact the typifications, because they are developed from the rich historical literature on the law and religion, are more useful in understanding the phenomena than are the abstractions of utilitarianism or Marxism into which this rich historical literature must be rendered.

WEBER'S SKEPTICISM

Weber's undermining of the claim of various social theorists to have constructed categories that correspond to the essence of social life, as we have seen throughout this book, is systematically, indeed unrelentingly, developed. But the positive picture is full of puzzles that Weber himself does not explore. The major puzzle with which we began the last chapter is the question of what ideal-types do – of how they contribute to explanation. Much of Weber's discussion, as explicated here, was devoted to the establishing of the necessity for typification and the value of self-conscious clarification of typifications. In the last section this issue was met with in the contrast Weber makes between causal classifications and genetic ideal-types. The claim to be made for genetic ideal-types is that they are, unlike mere causal classifications, intelligible to us in relation to our interests. And they are intelligible in relation to our interests because they have been constructed with those interests in mind. Where this claim became obscure was the point at which the explanatory concepts themselves, rather than merely the concepts that define the object of explanations, were claimed to be interest relative or culturally relative. What might Weber have had in mind?

Weber does not say that the legal concept of responsibility is the paradigm of an interest-relative explanatory concept that in the courtroom we are not interested in cause but in a very special conceptualization of cause, and that in the historical sciences we are similarly interested in a specially restricted notion of cause. He thus does not conceive of the causal concepts that figure in "genetic" explanations in the social sciences as causal concepts distinctive to various social sciences. He does not say, for example, that economic causation, social causation, and legal causation are distinct conceptualizations of causation. Indeed, the analogy would be imprecise. For Weber, social science is in the business of making up novel "genetic" models, just as it is in the business of inventing ideal-types. In each case the goal is the same – greater intelligibility. But in social science – perhaps with the exception of pure economics – neither the interests or the concepts are fixed in the way that they are in the law.

The "eternal youth" of the social sciences derives from the fact that the interests of the audience change, and therefore what is intelligible to them changes. Moreover, the production of novel genetic ideal-types is one of the intermediate aims of the social sciences in their pursuit of greater intelligibility. Fixing them in advance would be like producing the kind of ossification of intellectual life that occurred in the history of China ([1904] 1949: 84). It would

> render mankind incapable of setting new questions to the
> eternally inexhaustible flow of life. A systematic science of
> culture, even only in the sense of a definitive, objectively
> valid, systematic fixation of the problems which it should
> treat, would be senseless in itself. Such an attempt could only
> produce a collection of numerous, specifically particularized
> heterogenous and disparate viewpoints in the light of which
> reality becomes "culture" through being significant in its
> unique character.
>
> ([1904] 1949: 84–5)

157

Legal science, and its conceptual schemes, do represent an attempt to produce a "definitive, objectively valid, systematic fixation of the problems." But they operate under a quite different imperative than social science – like theology, law is a "dogmatic" science, in Weber's terms. To practice the same strategy in a practical science would simply produce a multiplicity of academic dogmas.[8]

The guiding principle of the construction of ideal-types and genetic ideal-types is practical value. Different historical disciplines serve different practical aims. Audiences have different explanatory needs in different periods, and grant different significances to historical phenomena. Consequently, explanations vary between disciplines and audiences. This is Weber's argument. But it leads in puzzling directions.

In the case in which genetic concepts are close to classificatory concepts and our intuitive sense of causal genesis is close to the results of a numerical judgment of adequate causation, his reasoning appears to work. The adequate cause relation is the rational kernel; the genetic ideal-type is the intelligible husk. We need to clothe the one with the other to answer the questions of interest to us – and "interest to us" involves not only the constitution of the objects of explanation but the form of the explanation itself. "Practical" relevance, in the extended sense (in which knowledge of economic history may be said to contain lessons for economic policy) is the source of our interest in both objects and forms of explanation. The "adequate cause" theory minimizes such conflicts. If all that is required for an interpretation to be causally adequate is, as Weber says, some degree of objective possibility, few if any interpretations of action would fail to meet this standard. Like Ihering's law of purpose, it is a minimal requirement. All that is needed to satisfy it is that a reference class of persons with the intention actually act in the way indicated by the intention some of the time.

With genetic explanations of a more elaborate sort, such as Weber himself proposes in *The Protestant Ethic and the Spirit of Capitalism*, matters are not so simple. A model of the genetic process of the development of the spirit of capitalism out of Protestant theology might be made very convincing as an ideal-type: it may be made very clear, and it may be constructed in a way that corresponds to such things as our own habitual feelings about religion and capitalism and to our desire for an intellectually satisfying sense of "why" the one followed from the other. But when we compare this "ideal-type" to actual historical cases, we see immediately that no cases, or virtually no cases, correspond to the "ideal-type." Should we discard the genetic ideal-type at this point? What if there are no alternatives? What if the only explanation that serves our cognitive purposes diverges from reality quite substantially? Weber's advice seems clear: we should not discard genetic ideal-types that diverge from reality. Is this advice valid?

With this question we get to the heart of the problem of the relation between explanation and understanding. Categorizing in terms of types, however "unrealistic," may serve nicely to help us make sense of the "meaning" of an action. But making sense of meaning in cases where there is a gap between our concepts and the actions requires us to perform some sort of gap-filling operation. We must do something to make the relevance of the concept to the reality from which it diverges clear. In the case of the law, the gap filling is done by casuistry, and this is Weber's model of what the social scientist must do ([1922] 1978: 20). This model is the source, as we shall see, of some serious problems. Casuistic thinking is rooted deeply in the Roman law, and necessitated by it. To decide a Roman case is to decide what legal category something, such as an act, belongs in. And one must decide between certain limited alternatives. How one decides is highly consequential, even where the cases do not fit either alternative very well. The casuistic method is to identify a paradigm case. In the case of a moral question, similarly, a theological casuist would begin with a paradigm case, a case in which an action was unambiguously a moral offense, and assimilate the problematic case in question to this paradigm case by introducing intermediate cases with "various combinations of circumstances and motives that made the offense in question less apparent" (Jonsen and Toulmin 1988: 252).[9] By reasoning by analogy, and applying the paradigm step by step to cases with varying circumstances, it becomes possible to build up grounds for placing a problem case in a given category. The grounds may become tenuous, but in the case of legal casuistry, as with moral casuistry, we know in advance that the case has to fall someplace – moral or immoral, legal or illegal. The probative weight behind the categorization may be greater or smaller, as the casuists recognized. The similarities in question were not demonstrative but cumulative, so that several arguments that tended to support a given categorization added to the weight of the argument.

Weber uses the term *Kasuistik* to describe his own use of ideal-types of action for the purposes of attributing *meanings*, and meanings in sociology, like moral meanings or meanings in the law, cannot be attributed in any other way. We do not have a set of typified meanings that is sufficiently extensive to match all cases perfectly, nor would that be a realistic goal. We are forced to apply our meaning-granting types to cases where they do not fit perfectly, but fit only approximately. But recognizing this leads directly to troubles over causality. Causal relations presumably *cannot* be attributed analogically. Even the adequate cause theory requires that estimates come from a reference class assumed to be homogenous. This assumption is known to be false. But even if we consider individual (but inestimable) probabilities to be the basic causal facts, we cannot generalize to other individual cases except by assuming they are in the same reference class.

We cannot apply causal conclusions analogically. The reason for this is simple. Even in terms of the adequate cause theory, the operative causes, those that increase the probability of an event, are a subset of the necessary conditions of an event. Analogies to other cases will be analogies to cases with different necessary conditions. A difference of a single condition can make a radical difference in results. So "similar causes, similar effects" is not, in general, a valid rule of inference. The question of cause, unlike the question of meaning, arises anew for every case with even slightly different conditions. In the case of action, the bad consequences of causal reasoning by analogy are usually slight. Slight differences in intention in connection with simple actions will often under similar circumstances produce similar acts. But in the case of subtle or complex actions, slight differences in intention may produce quite different acts. When we scale up to ideal-types of masses of action, such as those that compose the genetic model of the *Protestant Ethic*, the problem becomes severe. A causal model, involving actions or events which consist of a sequence of events in which each event is a condition for a successive event in the sequence, can only work if all the links in the chain are present. To apply such a causal model analogically, so that the model "explains" cases in which one of the links in the chain is missing, is simply an error.

Weber's reasoning in *The Protestant Ethic* seems to make precisely this mistake. No Protestants, it seems, or very few of them, fit the entire sequence that Weber outlines, from the acceptance of a specific combination of religious doctrines through the complex series of psychological steps he describes to the "spirit of capitalism." Many Protestants, however, fit the model to some extent, and it is a compellingly "meaningful" picture of a form of life that was still practiced in Weber's own time. It would be plausible to conclude that the hypothesis – the genetic ideal-type presented in *The Protestant Ethic* – is an intelligible husk without the rational kernel of a classificatory adequate cause probabilistic relationship.

But in fact there is a statistical relationship: Weber begins the work with a statistical presentation that makes clear that there is a statistical association between Protestantism and involvement in the kinds of economic activities traditionally associated with modern capitalism. The statistical relationship, however, is not exactly a "kernel," because it does not correspond precisely to the ideal-type. It is a kernel that the husk does not fit. So Weber's analysis might be better interpreted as an attempt to provide a meaningful interpretation of a statistical relationship, a type of analysis he briefly discusses in *Wirtschaft und Gesellschaft* ([1922] 1978: 12). The logic of causation would be the same: one would have to believe that the genetic ideal-type one proposes would prove to correspond to an adequate cause relationship.

Has Weber simply erred here? Perhaps not. But to repair the discrepancy, the traditional picture of Weber's methodological views must be revised. In the next few pages, we propose a radical reconsideration of his ideas about the character of action explanations. The difficulties with his Protestant ethic explanation, as well as the difficulties with the concept of charisma discussed in Chapter 5, need to be understood in the light of a far more extreme skepticism about historical explanation than previously has been attributed to him. Weber, we shall argue, believed that the kinds of explanations that could be constructed within his definition of sociology were subject to serious general doubts with respect to causality, and that the criteria of causal adequacy that one could construct within sociology could not resolve these doubts. Weber simply did not believe that any sort of sociological evidence or reasoning could overcome a fundamental question: whether the purposes we can attribute to people are the real causes of their actions. "Real causes" is a peculiar phrase to use in connection with Weber. But it is nevertheless apt, for Weber's concern is that "meaningful" explanations may often merely mask biological, psychophysical, and other causes, the "reality" of which he makes no attempt to deny (cf. [1922] 1978: 321).

To begin to understand Weber's skepticism, it is necessary to reconsider Weber's highly skeptical comments about the possibility of understanding action in terms of intentions and quasi-intentions, that is to say of using meaningful ideal-types to make sense of the social world. In connection with the problem of understanding animal behavior, as we saw in Chapter 2, Weber was a pronounced skeptic, extending his skepticism about understanding animals in intentional terms to a deep skepticism about understanding primitive peoples, understanding the conduct of persons in crowds under the sway of charismatic enthusiasm, and understanding the adherents of various exotic "ideals." The nature of this skepticism, however, is somewhat unusual. He does not deny that we can attribute clear and plausible intended purposes to people. Nor does he deny that these attributed intentions are admissible as causes. The adequate cause theory can show that such intentions do have such consequences at least some of the time. But what is difficult to show is that the intended purposes that are attributed are the real causes of the action. Consequently, even a meaning-interpretation of action that achieves a high degree of "certainty" and clarity can be "only a peculiarly plausible hypothesis" ([1922] 1978: 9).

Weber says that real "verification [of motives, that is to say cases where we know that these motives produced these consequences] is feasible with relative accuracy only in the few very special cases susceptible of psychological experimentation" ([1922] 1978: 10). This is a peculiar claim for Weber to make. It amounts to an acknowledgement of the relevance in principle of the experimental method to questions in the human sciences, but its irrelevance in practice. Sociology cannot make causal attributions without making claims that the attributed motives are the actual causes. But the means of "verifying" these claims, psychological experiments, are out of reach. There are some substitute means, but these are very weak. They include quasi-experiments such as "comparing the largest possible number of historical or contemporary processes which, while otherwise similar, differ in the one decisive point of their relation to the particular motive or factor the role of which is being investigated" or imaginary experiments which do the same things, or comparing to a large number of cases ([1922] 1978: 10).[10]

The example he gives of an "entirely satisfactory" verification is this: in history, bad money repeatedly drives out good; Gresham's ideal-typical model enabled this to be understood; the consistent statistical evidence enables us to say that this model actually holds. In these respects it meets the sociological criteria for an adequate causal interpretation of action. There are no plausible alternative hypotheses. Saving one form of specie and spending another is a fully conscious act. The degree of "clarity" is maximal. The evidence is consistent – there are no exceptions. But conditions are quite different in the situations the sociologist normally encounters. In most cases of action, including charisma, biological causes play a large if not predominant role, and therefore the motives attributed to the agent are questionable and at best partial. In these cases there is no question of whether the ideal-type of action entirely captures the real causes – it is freely admitted that it does not.

Weber could have used such skeptical considerations to deny the possibility of sociology. He does not. Nor does he hold his explanation in *The Protestant Ethic* to especially high "scientific" standards of proof. One reason seems to be that he did not operate with either the model of scientific precision of the physical sciences that so many sociologists before and since have operated with, or a philosopher's model of certitude. Instead, he seems to have thought about evidence as a lawyer would: he considered some kinds of evidence to be better than others, but considered weak evidence and weak interpretations to be better than none at all. The picture he develops is thus a modified skepticism: the historical sciences are practical sciences, not pure sciences; they have tasks to perform that must be performed regardless of the conditions under which they must work.

General skepticism and purism is as out of place for practical sciences as it is in the courtroom when decisions must be rendered. Lawyers are compelled to proceed by applying concepts that are the product of a dogmatic form of learning to actual cases. Sociologists as sociologists are compelled to see whether they can interpret whatever facts are presented to them (such as racial differences, historical events, and statistical uniformities) in terms of intended meanings ([1922] 1978: 8, 11–12). Many of the most important relationships "are not 'understandable'" ([1922] 1978: 12) and are thus beyond the realm of sociology. Some are partially understandable. But the sociologist's powers of understanding, in

163

general, are limited. What is limited, however, is not so much the sociologist's (or historian's) ability to provide meaningful interpretations, but their ability to verify them, in the sense of showing that the interpretation in question identifies the true cause. The main tools with which the sociologist must work are extremely weak – not weak so much with respect to their rational clarity but with respect to the extent to which they can be shown to represent the real causes of the actual course of events.

The usual response to these difficulties has been to turn sociology in a "positivistic" direction. But Weber had some important technical reasons why he could not have taken this option seriously. The reasons derive from the "adequate cause" theory of causation itself. Classifications, in this account, do not have the same status as the kinds of classifications that correspond to the terms of laws of nature. In the case of laws of nature, the "correctness" of the classification is assured by the exception-lessness of the laws themselves. In the case of adequate cause explanations, however, the classifications merely correspond to, and define, a reference class within which calculations of dependent probability may be made. A given event may be placed in various reference classes, using various classifications, each of which will typically produce different dependent probabilities. The "real" probability, however, is something that inheres in the event as conditioned by its actual necessary conditions. Thus classifications in social science have no special status in relation to cause – they are not so much rational kernels as alternative "abstractions" from the "real" but unknowable probabilities. The classifications that are used to estimate an "objective possibility" have no special claim to reality. The only classifications for which such a claim might be seriously made, those involving the laws of physics and chemistry, do not yield descriptions that have any hope of serving our purposes.

Our purposes thus play the crucial role in determining what kind of answers to causal questions we want. We may imagine Weber arguing thus: Where the lawyer is constrained by the dogmatic conceptual framework of the law, the sociologist is constrained by the conceptual framework of the audience – a shifting "eternally young" framework, but one which limits the sociologist nevertheless. The sociologist, like the economist as a practical scientist, is compelled to use ideal-types that are known to be false because they are best for the purposes of the science of sociology or economics as a practical science. To serve these purposes the ideal-type must be intelligible to the audience. The economist has a pure theory which supplies a conceptual framework and the dogmatic legal science supplies a conceptual framework for the law; the sociologist has some general categories of action. But to explain historical phenomena the sociologist is obliged to invent "local" ideal-types, such as the genetic ideal-type of *The Protestant Ethic*. The adequacy of these types is relative to the practical purposes of the science. Explanatory constructions that do not serve these purposes are simply of no interest. "Nothing," Weber says,

> should be more strongly emphasized than the proposition that the knowledge of the *cultural significance* of *concrete historical events and patterns* is exclusively and solely the final end which, among other means, concept-construction and the criticism of constructs also seek to serve.
>
> ([1904] 1949: 111)

The genetic ideal-type of *The Protestant Ethic* is, under the circumstances, the best solution possible to the practical need to make sense of how we became what we are as cultural "modern capitalists." It fits more or less with the statistical patterns and thus makes them intelligible – again, as well as they can be made intelligible under the circumstances, the circumstances being our particular, culturally determined "practical" need for an explanation. Similarly for the ideal-type of "charisma," with which Weber's complex scheme of explanatory displacements concluded in Chapter 5.

The sociologist has an advantage over the lawyer: the sociologist may invent, within the limits of the practical purpose of sociology, novel concepts. But in the face of the "infinite richness of events" ([1904] 1949: 111) the sociologist cannot shirk the task of deciding between explanations, however poor, any more than the lawyer can, simply because sociology is a practical science rather than a pure one. The sociologist is thus condemned to make sense of a complex reality with tools that do not fit that reality very well – to impose intentional models of action on quasi-intentional acts and to reduce complex historical processes to "intelligible" genetic simplifications.

8

EPILOGUE

Bacon "wrote philosophy like a Lord Chancellor," in Harvey's famous phrase. Weber, we have argued here, thought of social science like a lawyer. His academic contemporaries in Germany, France, and the United States sought, in various ways, to make social theory scientific and to make sociology a science. The ideas they had about what sort of "science" of society was possible were diverse. Some simply identified science with the elimination of superstitious and theological elements. Others saw in the relationships that had been established by the social statisticians of the nineteenth century the basis of a hope that laws, like the laws of physics, could be discovered underlying social life. Others thought of "science" on the model of philosophy, and sought first principles or organizing concepts, such as "the social," on which a science could be founded. Still others thought that the analogy between the organism of society and biological organisms made biology a model for sociology. Others thought that reducing social facts to other, "harder," facts, such as the supposedly determining facts of race and physical environment, would make social life scientifically comprehensible.

Weber was free of these ambitions. He gave "sociological" historical explanations and constructed sociological categories, and wrote critically on questions of "methodology." But he did not erect an ideal social science to which he urged others to aspire. He considered the limitations and prospects of the social science he himself practiced to coincide with the limitations of the possibility of social science, and sought in his methodological writings to understand these limits. What he understood was that social science is not a special heightened form of knowledge, but a cognitive enterprise with much in common with the sorts of

166

cognitive enterprises that already existed, notably jurisprudence and the legal determination of responsibility.

THE EPISTEMOLOGY OF THE COURTROOM

If we see that Weber's model for conceptualization in social science was the model provided by Roman legal concepts, a number of puzzles about Weber's use of the concept of ideal-type can be resolved. In its simplest form, the neo-Kantian model of the relation between concepts and a conceptually unformed reality is this: Facts are constituted as facts by, and only by, concepts. This "constitutivity" model leads to a series of problems. In the case of ordinary physical objects it is evident that there are variant sets of constitutive concepts. Ordinary language provides one. The technical language of physical science provides another. And variant fundamental physical conceptions and cultures may also constitute objects in different ways.

The physicist may insist that the facts as constituted by physical science are the fundamental or most fundamental facts, and dismiss the "facts" constituted by the variant languages and cultures of the world as "pre-scientific" and ignore them for serious purposes – such as science and metaphysics. The concepts of social science cannot be readily handled in this manner. The difficulty here is captured by Anthony Giddens' claim that sociology necessarily employs a "double hermeneutic." The "facts" that are constituted by sociology are not "constituted" directly by the conceptual structures of sociology being placed on a meaningless chaos of undifferentiated experience. Sociological concepts are instead meta-concepts, that is, they are reconceptualizations of material, such as actions, which have been conceptualized already in some sort of primary language or form of description by the agents who perform the actions.

This primary language has a continuing significance. Sociological descriptions depend on correct descriptions in this primary language. When the description in the primary language is shown to be erroneous, the sociological conceptualization is deprived of its main evidentiary support. The situation of the courtroom is analogous. The case discussed in Chapter 2 of the trial by Austin is characteristic. The business of the lawyers and the judge is to determine whether the primary descriptions of the facts – in the language of the ordinary, legally untutored person – are correct. Once this is determined, the lawyers engage in the activity of placing the already described act into legally relevant categories, in this case categories of culpability. This activity, which Austin characterizes as bad argument, bad analogy and mischievous misclassification, is central to this second step. If this lawyerly discursive activity leads to the act being classified by the court in one way, the finding may be radically different than if it is classified in another way. It is, to employ the term Weber uses both for the sociologist's classifications of actions and the lawyer's, casuistry.[1] The relation of dependence between legal classification and ordinary language – between the primary and secondary form of description – is the crucial conceptual feature of legal casuistry and shapes legal discourse throughout.

By applying the term "casuistic" to both, Weber indicates clearly that he understands the conceptual activity of the social scientist to be parallel. Like the lawyer, who applies notions of culpability within a given framework of legal concepts to primary descriptions of actions that are non-legal, the social scientist applies social science concepts to material that is already described, or constituted, by a primary language of description. Thus the social scientist in possession of a concept, such as charisma, is obliged to apply it, not to the material of behavior itself, but to the pre-conceptualized actions of individuals who are party to the relationships that the concept of charisma is designed to make intelligible.

The social scientist, as understood by Weber, has different classification schemes than the lawyer, and they are not held "dogmatically," as are legal conceptualization schemes. The social scientist's schemes have different cognitive purposes and a different relationship to the primary language of description. We may consider this last difference first. The social scientist is typically concerned, as the practicing lawyer almost never is, with the application of second order abstractions to a wide variety of "primary" languages of description. Thus when we apply our social science concepts to alien cultures, we are engaged in an even more complex operation than the courtroom lawyer, one which encompasses the kind of casuistic reclassification that is central to the law, but includes some other steps. Consider the historian whose subject is other cultures. The activities of the dervishes, holymen and warriors of these cultures are initially constituted for the historian by reference to the historian's own "ordinary language," our primary, culturally given, modes of description of the historian's audience. Cognitive concerns that arise from and are conditioned by this background are important in two ways that are not typically found in the courtroom. The audience's cognitive concerns constitute the objects of cognitive concern to the historian in the first place – they define the things that our culture constitutes as historically significant. The second way is this: our "primary" culture decides in the last analysis what constitutes for us an *answer* to the questions posed by the facts of history. Thus the work of the historian, and the social scientist more generally, is controlled both at the beginning, in the act of constituting objects, and at the end, in the acts of judging accounts to be acceptable, by his or her culture.

Once a given historical fact, such as the emergence of the kinds of conduct that we as members of a capitalistic culture recognize as characteristically "capitalistic," is constituted for us as a historical puzzle, the social scientist steps in and performs his or her characteristic work of "rendering intelligible" its causes. But before explaining this conduct, the social scientist must make sense of the ways in which the historical personages involved themselves made sense of their own conduct. This, as Weber saw, was an activity fraught with difficulties. The main difficulty is this. The activities of most individuals most of the time are only quasi-actions: people are largely not motivated by intentions that are fully conscious and accessible to analysis in terms of intelligible reasons; there are almost always additional motives which are not conscious and perhaps not articulable. This situation is, of course, typical of courtroom determinations of culpability as well.

The social scientist and the lawyer are thus ordinarily not as fortunate as the lawyers in Austin's example, in which the facts, that the attendant "made a mistake in the taps," are clear and need only to be redescribed, for example in the "dogmatic" categorical language of the law. But even in the face of uncertainty about motivation, the lawyer nevertheless must provide reasons for deciding cases one way or another, and must do so within the framework of these categories. In doing so, the lawyer may need to construct a "theory" or narrative of the case which accords with the evidence and provides an explanation of the intentions of the persons involved which can be used as the basis of a classification in terms of "dogmatic" legal categories of culpable action. The social scientist is in a similar position with regard to motivation, and Weber's recommendation is that the social scientist engage in a similar kind of narrative activity. The social scientist may construct a set of ideal-types, such as the ideal-type of the Protestant motivated by anxiety over damnation to rationally order life in a way congenial to what subsequently was recognized as a capitalistic spirit, or employ ideal-types that have already been constructed for the purpose of enabling the creation of causal historical accounts or narratives, such as the concept of charisma.

Just as a lawyer's theory of a case is constructed with an eye both to the facts and to the need to describe these facts in a way that makes judgments in terms of legal categories possible, the social scientist constructs ideal-types with an eye both to the facts and to the purposes of historical social science. These ideal-typical constructions are thus purposive abstractions, artistic representations from the historical material. In court cases, the way in which the material must be tortured to yield a legal decision is often extreme, and the "facts" that are taken account of are typically taken account of in a way that the participants in the trial will regard as distorted. The court operates, so to speak, with epistemic blinders in the form of procedures of evidence and exclusion that are unlike those employed in the fact finding and judging of ordinary moral life. But the purposes of the law require a decision and, consequently, a great deal of "legally irrelevant" fact and fact which is very difficult to establish may be discarded.

One consequence of this is a tension between the ordinary moral agent and the court. What is a wrong in the eyes of the wronged party may not be a wrong in the eyes of the court, blinkered by its own rules of evidence and procedure and compelled to decide right and wrong in terms of its own distinctive legal concepts of such things as culpability. Indeed, the fact that there is a distinctive legal concept of culpability shows how deeply variant the sense making activities of the court and the sense making activities of the ordinary moral agent may be. The same discrepancy arises for the social scientist. But the social scientist's ultimate purpose is bound to a different need for an intelligible world – a need that exists in the lay audience of the social scientist. The lawyer is bound in a different manner. The "audience" to which the court speaks is the higher court in which the justifications and thinking of the court can be tested. In a sense, of course, there is a court of public opinion without which legal systems cannot endure. But the operation of this court is, especially in civil law jurisdictions, remote. The social scientist, in contrast, is bound more directly to the audience whose needs for sense making it aims to satisfy.

The kind of sense making that is exemplified by the ideal-type presented in the Protestant ethic, however, is only one step in the social scientist's work. The fundamental categories of Roman law lend conceptual order to the law. There is a similar need in the social sciences. Weber's categories of action, which this book has concentrated on, are an attempt to provide a kind of conceptual order. The scheme cannot be "dogmatically" enforced, as it can in the law, but must be accepted, as Weber puts it, on the grounds of its utility. So Weber offers his own scheme as a potentially useful classification. Its usefulness, of course, is ultimately controlled by the purposes of social science. But, like the categories of the Roman law themselves, these categories might continue to be useful to persons in epochs in which the cultural concerns and standards of intelligibility that were characteristic of Weber's epoch have changed.

Today, it would be perhaps more characteristic of the inquiring mind to ask about the history of sexism or racism than to ask the questions Weber found compelling, and, one suspects, the answers Weber provided in *The Protestant Ethic* to the questions of his own epoch may well seem less than adequate today. The actions of the early Protestants were alien to Weber's readers. But they could be rendered intelligible in terms of the ideas and sentiments of Weber's audience through Weber's ideal-typical construction. Today this may no longer be possible. Weber was able to speak to an audience that was still capable of seeing the world in the Calvinistic manner of Weber's early Protestants. This audience is likely to disappear, if it has not disappeared already. Weber's explanation will thus in the future be as much an artifact of history as the lives of the Protestant capitalists themselves. Weber's categories of action, however, may find uses far into the future.

PLURALISM

Weber did not accept an image of the social sciences as divided into various paradigms, each of which represented a soup-to-nuts creation of a "world." He assigned the primary task of constituting objects to the culture of the audience and claimed that the culture of the audience, and its practical purposes, controlled the purposes of social science. He also was untroubled by the claim that the world as conceived juridically was a different world from the world conceived by social science or by the idea that within the social sciences the fundamental methodological devices were theory relative. In his criticisms of other social scientists, such as Marxist materialists, he considered that they shared a common interest in causal explanation and consequently were bound by the conceptual limits that a methodological investigation of social science causal explanation would reveal. He is scathing about "intuitionist" historians but similarly argues that they too are in the business of causal analysis and are bound by its conceptual limitations as well. He believed, in short, that there was both common conceptual ground and a common cognitive interest – in causal explanation – among "historical scientists."

After Weber, under the influence of legal positivism, it was generally understood in legal theory that the law as discussed by legal theorists was simply a different object than the law as discussed by social scientists, and that Weber's arguments with respect to the law did not undermine legal science claims about the law but were simply irrelevant to them, to legal theory, and to the philosophy of the law. Weber would perhaps have reasoned that legal theories of the law or philosophies of law have as their ultimate audience not lawyers but the laity and consequently must first conceive the law in the language of the laity. The "separate world" of the law is thus for him a different abstraction from a shared world. There is no primary juridical world, just as there is no primary world of social science. The primary world in both cases is the world preconstituted by the culture of the lawyer and the social scientist and their lay audiences.

Ihering, as we saw, became entangled in the difficulties of speaking legalistically to a general audience. Later philosophies of law, notably Kelsen's, sought to avoid these difficulties by viewing the world of the law as one constituted by axioms which were not claimed to have extra-legal foundations in history or human nature. Weber understood the process of "positivization" of the law as an adjunct to the historical process of rationalization, or rather as a form of this process. But one suspects that, like purely instrumental action, Weber considered that a purely positive conception of the law was a self-contradictory ideal, for precisely the reasons discussed here: the concept of the law is a concept not just for lawyers but for an audience that expects non-legal justifications for the law or finds purely legal justifications insufficiently intelligible. What positivism inadvertently produces is a conception of the law that can be grounded only in a kind of "faith."

The distinction between legitimacy and legality, which has been a continual source of controversy among interpreters of Weber's writings on law, may be interpreted as a distinction between two audiences. The audience of professional specialists in the law is concerned with legality. Those who are non-specialists, the laity (or lawyers in their capacities as citizens), are concerned not merely with technical questions of legality but with legitimacy, and they are forced to be so concerned with respect to the question of the status of the legal system as a whole. Stammler made the mistake of thinking that considerations of legal validity that were, properly, internal to the profession of the legally trained could be turned into an immanent principle inhering in and animating the development of law itself. Legal positivism makes a similar error, not by failing to distinguish internal and external questions about the law, but in denying that there are questions about the law that require extra-legal answers.

The Critical Legal Studies movement, feminist jurisprudence, and a good bit of the commentary on the issues that these movements have raised have concerned themselves with the nature of the distinction between law and society and legal and extra-legal discourse. Whether the distinction between audiences imputed here to Weber provides a solution to these difficulties or merely reinforces them is an issue that cannot be adequately addressed here. However, it is clear that attempts to overcome these distinctions have typically collapsed into one or the other side. In the case of Critical Legal Studies, it is clear that the arguments rest on a particular, essentialist, theory of society, and are not meaningful to audiences who do not share a Marxisant view of present social life. The case of feminist jurisprudence is considerably more complex, reflecting the complexities of feminist thought generally and the peculiarities of feminist epistemology.

One form of feminist jurisprudence, that of Catherine MacKinnon, seems to exemplify the kind of strategy observed in Stammler. MacKinnon argues that the "legal" concept of equality cannot be fulfilled – fulfilled in its proper legal sense – unless it is conceived in a way which is equal with respect to its fidelity to

173

women's experience. The criteria of fidelity to women's experience is obviously imported from feminist theory generally and is problematic in its own right. The question in part is a question of authority: who is the "we" that authoritative assertions about women's experiences rest on? Yet the construction of the requirement of fidelity to women's experience proceeds within the framework of legal construction and extends the notion of equal protection in a recognizable way within the American Supreme Court tradition of finding novel meanings of the Fourteenth Amendment. So the notion of equality is, so to speak, "dogmatically" fixed, and MacKinnon does not challenge it, rethink it historically, or ground it. Thus, hers is not a social theory of the law of the sort which allows egalitarianism to be problematized. It is an extension of egalitarianism into novel legal domains.

What Weber would have most decisively rejected from the movements of critical legal studies and feminist jurisprudence is their acceptance of a kind of social teleology in which some sort of essential direction for history is derived from a consideration of unalienated nature. MacKinnon's extension of the notion of equality rests directly on the notion of "women's experience." But her claim to be able to speak univocally for women rests implicitly on a notion of women's experience undistorted by sexism. These are examples of the kind of social teleology that Weber disdained.

BIOLOGY WITHOUT BIOLOGICAL REDUCTIONISM

The focus of much of the literature on Weber as a value thinker has been on the idea of meaning and the associated idea that the seeking of meaning is a fundamental, quasi-telic, human property. But as we have seen, Weber's image of human nature is altogether less flattering. The conscious strivings of individuals are for Weber a small portion of conduct. This is not to say that the effects of ideas and the like are not important, but that for the most part conduct is governed by biology. Indeed, Weber may be usefully regarded as one of the irrationalists of the late nineteenth century, along with Pareto, Gabriel Tarde, and LeBon. The denials that Weber issues about the possibility of making the behavior of primitive peoples intelligible, and the grounds he gives for this, namely that they are governed primarily by biological forces, are indicative, as are his assertions about the mixed causal character of daily action in more advanced eras. What Weber believed was that the paradigm of fully intelligible intentional action with which sociologists were compelled by his definition of the field to work was, in fact, largely inapplicable to human conduct, yet partly applicable to a significant portion of human conduct. The concepts of sociology, consequently, were fated to be like ill-fitting shoes, owing to the shape of the material on which they were to be fit.

Parsons, who interpreted Weber as another teleological thinker like himself who had somehow failed to grasp such things as the inevitably telic "normative" character of social action, was compelled to ignore or suppress Weber's remarks on the preponderance of biological causality in human action. In his own translation of this material on action at the beginning of *Wirtschaft and Gesellschaft*, Parsons adds a note to the effect that Weber, not having the benefit of the advances of modern anthropology, was simply empirically wrong about the character of the mental lives of primitive peoples. But, as we have seen in comparing Weber with Ihering with respect to the explanation of the conduct of animals, what Weber believed was that it was a mistake to attribute purposes in many of the realms in which thinkers like Ihering and Parsons freely attributed purposes, and indeed that it was an "imposition" to attribute purposes to the kinds of quasi-actions that make up the bulk of human conduct. It was an "imposition" because the causes were mixed, and the attributed intention represented only part of the cause.

The major concepts that Weber introduced in place of the concepts of telic social theory rely on the idea that in most if not all actual cases the causes of social action were mixed. In the case of charisma, the causes are familiar from the crowd psychology of the time and are interpreted by Weber as biological rather than "sociological." They include such things as "contagion." The same holds for the basis of "morality," which rests in large part on biologically rooted "reaction." Order, for Weber, was assured by the biological fact of the reactive repression of "deviant" conduct. The mold-breaking actions of the heroic charismatic leader could transform morality and standards of legitimacy. But even the phenomenon of charisma was largely rooted in the quasi-biological processes of crowd psychology. Material interests, of course, are largely rooted in biology as well.

But Weber was very far from being a biological determinist. Though he carefully circumscribed his claims about their causal importance, he gave a considerable role in historical development to fully conscious intentional actions and their semi-conscious counterparts. In the realm of values, this led not to the rational recognition of a single good, as in Ihering, but to the recognition of the rational necessity of arbitrary choice or faith. The instrumental rationalization of one domain of thought after another was a central theme in Weber's historical account of Western civilization, and the impediments that prevented this process were a central focus of his studies of non-Western civilization. But rationalization was not and could not be a new *telos*. The concept of instrumental rationality had an inherent limitation: the selection of goals could not be rationalized. So the goals pursued by instrumental rationalizers were necessarily supplied in non-rational ways. Weber's great dread was that these purposes would be supplied authoritatively by state socialism or by the needs of large capitalistic enterprises rather than by free individual choice. But he did not believe they could be supplied by reason.

WEBER TRANSFORMED

We began this book with the promise to consider three transformations. The first, which we discussed very briefly, was biographical: Weber's own self-transformation from lawyer to social scientist. This transformation, as we observed, has been lightly regarded in the Weber literature. We have established, in our discussions of the other two transformations, some substantial grounds for taking the facts of Weber's intellectual biography more seriously. Some additional grounds might be added. It is clear, though we did not discuss the point in this book, that the writings on the history of Christianity and church law of Rudolf Sohm provided Weber with much more than the concept of charisma. They provided a model for the examination of the interplay between interests and religious ideas and the conflicts that religious ideology helped sustain that was extremely useful to his own studies of the economic ethics of the world religions. A full account of Weber's sources in the law and in legal history would analyze these connections. Fully analyzed, we suspect, they would establish a new Weber, Weber as a lawyer-intellectual, to be placed alongside and perhaps above Weber as a founder of sociology, Weber as a political man, and Weber as a cultural analyst.

Our focus in this book has been on the two other transformations: Weber's transformation of legal science concepts into sociological concepts, and the intent that is revealed by Weber's strategy in transforming legal science concepts. As we suggested, Weber's rethinking of these concepts was an assault on traditional telic social theory. The source of many of Weber's sociological terms and of his fundamental categories of explanation was in Ihering's *Zweck im Recht*. But he carefully reconstructed these concepts to eliminate the teleological element. By providing a non-teleological alternative to the terms employed by his competitors, and by providing non-teleological accounts of the phenomena that the terms, such as *Sitten*, described, he undermined the basic argument on which they rested: that some sort of collective or telic force was necessary to explain social life. But his argument raised questions about explanation and causality.

The sources for Weber's concept of causality and its associated notions of abstraction were, we suggested, in the analogy to legal abstraction in the Roman law tradition and the specific theory of legal causality that was dominant in tort law in the German jurisprudence of Weber's own time. The evidence of Weber's reliance on legal notions of abstraction is largely circumstantial. But the hypothesis serves to account for some of the complexities of Weber's methodological thinking in a way that the hypothesis that Weber was merely an applier and adapter of neo-Kantian philosophy does not. With respect to the concept of causality and the operations of abstraction necessary for its application, the evidence is overwhelming. Weber's sources were directly in the legal tradition.

We have hoped in this book to open a window on Weber as a social thinker that has long remained largely closed. Weber deserves to be read in terms of the intellectual tradition in which he was trained, and to be read not just as a user of the conceptual tools of legal science and legal history, but as a sophisticated subverter of the kind of social thinking that flourished in the law and in the nascent discipline of sociology in his time – and continues, in various guises, to flourish today.

APPENDIX

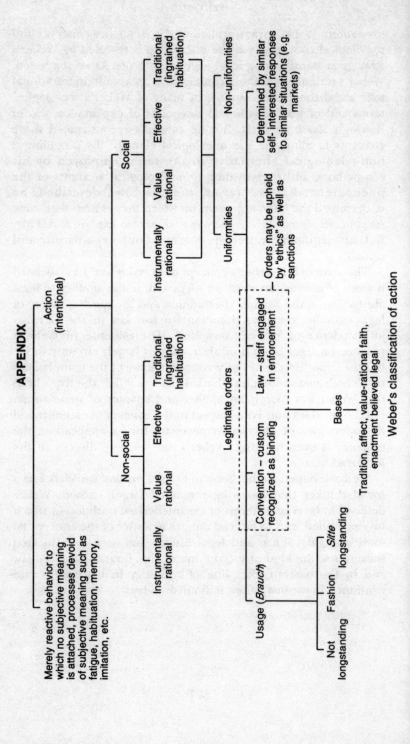

Weber's classification of action

NOTES

1 INTRODUCTION

1   The lack of discussion in the English language universe is somewhat less mysterious: this universe is more or less coterminous with a different legal system, that of the common law, so that a series of difficult obstacles, beginning with fundamental differences in the structure of the law, separates the Anglo-American interpreter from the German sources. For German interpreters and others from countries under the civil law, there are other obstacles, such as the limitations that arise from early academic specialization, and the fact that the law has a more limited role in public debate and consciousness. One must also note the decline of the traditions of history and philosophy of law in German universities since Weber's time, when they were at the apex of the greatest academic hierarchy in the world. The leading legal scholars of the time produced a massive and daunting body of scholarship on the Roman Empire and the reception and transformation of Roman law in Europe. The many changes in fashion in both historical writing and philosophy between their time and ours mean that this context can be mustered and reconstructed only through considerable historical effort, and that the concerns of these older thinkers cannot be readily explained.

2   This claim should be read carefully. Weber's specific sources for many of his most important analyses have been identified. So there is no shortage of *direct* connections to texts that influenced Weber, or that Weber drew heavily from. There is also no shortage of connections to traditions. But direct connections *to traditions* are much harder to come by, especially in Weber's "social thought". The influence of Kant epitomizes the problem. Martin Albrow, in a chapter in his *Max Weber's Construction of Social Theory*, the best attempt to provide an overview of Weber's context, provides a very useful account of the Kantian background to Weber's thought (1990: 29–45). But the *direct* connection is tenuous. Weber obviously knew something of Kant from his student days, and from the neo-Kantian philosophers and theologians who surrounded him. But there is little evidence of reading Kant. Indeed, the best personal testimony we have comes

from Karl Jaspers, who recalled a discussion with Weber after the speech "Science as a Vocation." Jaspers recalls that "I spoke about Kant's 'ideas' and the fact that each science only preserves its meaning, which itself proceeds beyond science, through an idea. Max Weber hardly knew anything about Kantian ideas and did not react to them. Finally I said, facing Thoma: 'He himself, does not know what meaning science has and why he is pursuing it'. Max Weber winced visibly: 'Well, we see what we can withstand, but we'd better not talk about it' " (Jaspers 1989: 188–9). This discussion refers to only a part, though an important one, of Kant, but there is no evidence of any systematic study of Kant on Weber's part. In this book, our strategy has been to seek out sources of Weber's thought for which there is such evidence, and this has proved illuminating. We do not propose to erect this as some sort of novel interpretive standard. But it is an enterprise of a fundamentally different kind than speculation on influences based on comparing Weber's texts with texts he never read.

3 The specific Weber and Ihering texts are quoted in Chapter 5.

4 Mayer goes on to "express the hope that a lawyer who happens to read this book may feel encouraged to criticize Weber from the point of view of a universal sociology of jurisprudence" (1956: 147). He notes the then recent publication of Max Rheinstein's lucid and still useful introduction to Shils and Rheinstein's graceful translation (and abridgement) of selections from Weber's sociology of law, a text originally designed to be the first volume in the Harvard "20th Century Legal Philosophy" series. Mayer's wish may be said to be fulfilled, in a fashion, by the large German literature on Weber's sociology of law, exemplified by Rehbinder (1987) as well as by the writings of American law professors, such as Kronman (1983), Trubeck (1972), and Feldman (1991), and by a still valuable article by Albrow (1975). But the focus of these authors has been on Weber's sociology of law and its implications for the evaluation of legal systems. The present volume, it should be stressed, is concerned only indirectly with these topics.

5 Collini, Winch, and Burrow are illuminating about the influence of Henry Sumner Maine's comparative historical method – essentially an approach to legal history – on political science in Britain (1983: 209–46). Maine was of course influential in the United States, as was Freeman. Tracing Anglo-American political institutions to their Teutonic roots was a vogue in the nineteenth century. But the influence of Continental legal thought on American social science was also great. Many of the early social scientists in the United States, encouraged by such Germanophiles as Burgess, attended the same lectures as Weber himself did, and were exposed to the same influences. For example, E. A. Ross, economist and sociologist, found Ihering to be a revelation. Ihering's ideas on interests clearly influenced such works as Beard's *Economic Interpretation of the Constitution (1913)* and Beard's thesis on the *Justice of the Peace in England* ([1904] 1967), as well as Bentley's interest theory of politics (1908).

6 No monograph on Ihering exists in English. Stone (1950) in many
respects remains the most useful treatment, but there are several
useful law review articles, including Seagle (1945) and Jenkins (1960).
The German literature is more substantial, including Gromitsaris
(1989), Klemann (1989), Losano (1984), Pleister (1982), and
Wieacker (1968, 1969). A useful source in relation to Nietzsche is
Kerger (1988).

7 The same change in views of British liberalism, and indeed of the
central political and economic issues of the century, may also be
observed in the historical study of Rome, the area of most of Weber's
early scholarship. Agrarian Roman history, far from being an
academic backwater, was a major political battleground. In a century
which began with the final abolition of serfdom in parts of North
Central Europe and closed with the bitter disputes over the
preservation of the peasantry and agrarian estates which Weber
himself participated in, the question of the nature of Roman property
rights was crucial. Britain provided a controversial standard: the
model of a yeoman peasantry with private property broadly
distributed. Disputes over the origin of private property, the existence
of primitive village communism, and the nature of Roman ownership
were crucial to the arguments for socialism of the time.

Momigliano gave a charming account of these issues, and Weber's
contribution to them, in which he observes that the striking
difference in Weber's approach to Rome is that he focused not on the
small private plots of an acre or so but on the public lands, available
for exploitation through the payment of a fee, on which the
subsistence of the community largely depended. The decline of
Rome, Weber argued, coincided with the exploitation of public lands
by large slave-holders who displaced the yeoman peasantry. The
parallel to the Junkers was unmistakable. Momigliano emphasizes the
centrality of Weber's legal training to this work. He notes that
Theodor Mommsen, who devoted a fifty-page article to Weber's
habilitation dissertation on these subjects, was clearly "pleased that
the study of Roman agrarian problems was passing from the hands of
philologists into those of economists and lawyers" (1982: 29–30).

2 COMMON STARTING POINTS: THE WORLD CREATED
BY PURPOSE AND THE CONCEPT OF ACTION

1 Logical positivism is sometimes described as terminal neo-Kantianism,
and one can see how the problematics follow from one another. The
next question one must ask is "what counts as 'science'?" The Logical
Positivists answered this, of course, but in a way that distinguished law,
theology and other non-empirical "Sciences" from the natural
sciences.

2 The idea that the lawyer is necessarily involved in, and indeed that the
pursuit of justice consists in, the activity of translation is much more
fully developed by James Boyd White in his *Justice as Translation* with

reference not only to common law examples but to the human pursuits other than the law (1990: 229–69).

3 The change from "purpose" to "meaning" changes the character of the ideal types. Consider the notion of objectivity as it applies to "meanings" and to "purposes." To claim that there are objective meanings, as some of Weber's contemporaries did, is to claim that there is a kind of ideal to which actual usage approximates, and that deviation is intellectual error or unclarity on the part of the user. To claim there are objective *purposes* is to claim something about the actual consequences of an act or practice, misunderstanding of which would be an intellectual error on the part of the agent. If Malinowski's Argonauts of the Western Pacific engaged in rituals whose objective purpose or "function" was to reduce anxiety about sea travel, the purpose is something that must be discerned from the actual, rather than "ideal," conduct of the ritual actions. In the case of purpose, then, objectivity is the business of the observer, not the agent. In the case of meaning, however, the same cannot be true. If we are to ask what the "objective" *meaning* of these same rituals is, we are asking what it means in a "pure" sense *as distinct from* what it means for various individuals. Weber declines to embrace Simmel's notion of objective meanings.

4 The philosopher Alexander Rosenberg has made this point recently in his critique of the explanatory pretensions of economics (1992). As we shall see, Weber, by considering economically rational action to be a very small subset of action, avoids such criticisms, but opens himself up to other objections, for example to the claim that this classificatory analysis requires a theory of human motivation to serve any explanatory purposes.

5 Some of the subsequent history of these ideas of reason, specifically in relation to "value," is discussed in Turner and Factor (1984). The sociological side of the reception history is discussed in Sica (1988).

6 See Tönnies's discussion of the drunkard ([1909] 1961: 32–3).

3 INTERESTS AND IDEALS

1 Mill's difficulties were not, of course, purely theoretical. In 1905 Dicey opened the published form of his *Lectures on the Relation between Law and Public Opinion in England during the Nineteenth Century* ([1905] 1962) by quoting the same passage in Mill, with the purpose of showing how far public opinion had gone towards a recognition of collective interests in the preceding fifty years.

2 It was difficult to give an account of this process in terms of individualistic egoism, and many other social theorists took a simpler route. They abandoned egoism, solving the problem of the insufficiency of the Kantian "will" to explain such collective phenomena as the law by inventing new, social, "wills" that such institutions could be conceived as the servant of. This was the solution proposed by Tönnies, as well as by Durkheim.

3 Weber's definitions of power parallel this, and Weber also uses the term psychological coercion ([1922] 1978: 35).
4 Ihering was an expert on contract law, and contributed to the law himself with an article which identified a gap in the law of contract and suggested a solution, which was subsequently written into the code. The issue had to do with responsibility for the actions of agents during the preliminary steps toward making a contract that is never properly concluded (Watson 1981: 174).
5 Today, to take a familiar example, it is considered ignoble, and is illegal, to pay for certain sexual services.
6 Ihering discusses money in this section in a manner akin to Simmel's in the *Philosophy of Money* ([1877] 1913: 91).
7 Ihering might have dodged these difficulties, as Kelsen later did, by restricting himself to a pure theory of the law that treated the law as a separate object, a system, to be studied as such.
8 Again, this is reminiscent of Durkheim, particularly his advice to seek the social functions of each social fact.
9 In the early pages of his 1917 essay "The Meaning of 'Ethical Neutrality,'" Weber commented, in a footnote, that "As to the 'irreconcilability' of certain ultimate evaluations in a certain sphere of problems, cf. G. Radbruch's *Einführung in die Rechtswissenschaft* I diverge from him on certain points but these are of no significance for the problem discussed here" ([1917] 1949: 11). Radbruch's views on these issues in this text were consistent with other of his works quoted in this chapter (cf. also Chroust 1944).
10 In 'presenting . . . exhaustively the possibilities of decision' (Radbruch [1914] 1950: 57) he lists three categories of possible choices, and the personal hierarchy of values they imply:

> In the individualistic view, work values and collective values are subservient to personality values. Culture is but a means to cultivate the person; the state and the law are but institutions to secure and promote individuals.
> In the transindividualistic view, personality values and work values are subservient to collective values, morality and culture to the state and the law.
> In the transpersonal view, personality values and collective values are subservient to work values, morality as well as law and the state to culture.
> The ultimate ends may be summarized by the slogans of freedom, for the individualistic view; nation, for the transindividualistic view; and culture, for the transpersonal view.
> ([1914] (1950: 94)

It may be noted that the same scheme of categories is found in Heinrich Rickert, who does not, however, accept the claim that there is no objective solution to conflicts between them.

4 THE COMMANDS OF MORALITY

1 Margaret Gilbert has recently provided a massive defense of collective descriptions which establishes their legitimacy in terms of the problem of reference (1989; cf. Udehn 1987). This is a persuasive response to Weber's ontological arguments. But it leaves the issue of cause untouched. Weber could concede her point with no consequences for his own substantive explanatory claims, if he could establish the argument examined in this chapter. The issue is the status of collective facts as explanations: if they are gratuitous, unnecessary for explanation, and if appeals to collective fact have bad explanatory consequences, there is no reason for the sociologist to appeal to them.

2 The text discusses, for example, such figures as the theorist of matriarchy, Bachofen, who was influenced by Savigny.

3 Durkheim thought that there were moments of "collective fusion" in which novel moral ideas were formed charged with collective force (cf. Turner 1993: 11) and perhaps these correspond to moments of recognition. The fact that Durkheim, who was well aware of and much influenced by Ihering, proposed this alternative solution indicates some of the reasons he did not find Ihering's account satisfactory. The main difference is with respect to the *force* of feelings of obligation, which Ihering's account is poorly equipped to explain.

4 Cf. Nietzsche, who speaks of "fear in the presence of a higher intellect which here commands, of an incomprehensible, indefinite power, of something more than personal – there is *superstition* in this fear" ([1881] 1982: aph. 9).

5 In the case of religion, like the case of learning from parents, "reverence" derives from the manner of learning. In the case of the learning of ritual practices, "the natural sentiments, feelings of servility, of humility and diffidence, all of them expressions of reverence, are expressed strongly and distinctly through the performance" (Tönnies [1909] 1961: 49).

6 We have not discussed every detail of these different classifications. Suffice it to say that Ihering, Tönnies and Weber, and to a great extent Nietzsche, each provide parallel classifications with roughly similar elements, and employ a similar strategy of accounting for each category *Sitte* and *Mode*, for example, in different ways.

7 To understand Weber's procedure in this discussion, it is essential to understand his method of classification. The case of action proper, discussed in Chapter 2, is quite strange, but *not*, as we shall see, exceptional. The categories of action are, with one exception, limiting or borderline cases: virtually all actions fall someplace in between the limits or on the borders. The categorization is thus a conceptual one, a mapping of a space in which actual cases may be located by placing them along continua in multiple dimensions. At the next level of classification (see the Appendix) the method of categorization changes: Weber divides action into the categories of "uniform" and "nonuniform." These are classes, not regions on a continuum. The

category of "uniformities" is then divided into subcategories and subsubcategories which match, more or less closely, those familiar from Tönnies and Ihering. The level of uniformities includes four basic types: usages, uniformities of action involving legitimate orders, uniformities that are value rational, and self-interestedly rational responses which are uniform because they are similar rational responses to similar situations. The first two are subdivided in turn into *Sitte* and *Brauch*, that is, custom with moral force and mere custom, and into law and convention. But the first subcategorization is treated as a continuum. Thus we are told that the "transition from this [mere practice] to validly enforced convention and to law is gradual" ([1922] 1978: 29). The issues become further confused by Weber's commentaries on the categories, which discuss causes. The causes often apply to more than one category. Interest, for example, is an occasional causal element in the upholding of all uniformities of action.

8   "Reinforce," however, means reinforce a sense of "oughtness" that is already there in another form.

5 AUTHORITY: STATES, CHARISMA, AND *RECHT*

1   The historical impact of this refutation was great. It influenced the "revisionists" of the Social Democratic party in their "return to Kant." Lenin's philosophical writings on science were motivated by his rejection of these tendencies. The style of reasoning is not, however, entirely lost to the distant past. The issues that arise in connection with it, indeed, are similar to issues that arise with present "critical" social theory. Stammler's mode of argument has, for example, a certain similarity to that of Habermas's theory of communicative action. Both arguments depend on turning explanatory usages established as "indispensable" into normative concepts. In Habermas, the normative concept of undistorted communication is discovered to be immanent in, and inseparable from, the explanatory idea of communication itself.

2   Stammler's final statement on this issue takes an ontological turn. He rejects Weber's claim that he is presenting a "partial" view of historical development and argues that only Stammler's own account can apprehend the character of the evolving human community as a whole (1925: 671–3).

3   There is a puzzling discussion of "orders" that is not included in the diagram in the Appendix. Weber defines "order" separately from legitimacy as follows: "the content of a social relationship [will] be called an order if the conduct is, approximately or on the average, oriented toward determinable 'maxims'" ([1922] 1978: 31). The category of orders in general thus seems to include something other than "legitimate" orders. But he gives no examples of orders other than legitimate ones. Yet only where the maxims are seen as obligatory or exemplary is there a claim to validity for the order.

4   There is a large literature on this classification of forms of *Herrschaft*, much of which concentrates on the apparent anomaly of the exclusion of democratic legitimacy. Neither the classification nor the topic of democracy will be discussed in this book. However, it might be suggested, on the basis of Weber's placement of value-rational faith in this scheme, that Weber did not consider democracy as an administrative form of rule but as contributory value-rational legitimating belief that could potentially support various forms of administrative rule.

5   Blood vengeance by kin, Weber acknowledged, is a primitive case of legitimated violence. But it is anomalous among primitive uses of violence, and largely irrelevant to police and military action, which have stronger bases.

6   This is a sufficiently muddy point that it deserves some emphasis, especially in the light of the stress placed in the notion of the charisma of central institutions by Edward Shils. Shils solves the problem of reconciling the diverse uses of the notion of charisma in Weber by rejecting his (and Sohm's) account of it. His strategy is to invert the idea of routinization, or rather to eliminate the unidirectional implications of the term. The term itself is problematic, for reasons to be discussed shortly. Shils argues that charisma is *normally* distributed through the routines of society, or "dispersed." The special case is the case of "concentrated" charisma, in which an individual or office has an unusual amount of it. This requires a change in the notion of charisma itself, which Shils provides by appealing to Rudolf Otto's concept of the "numinous" in his *The Idea of the Holy* ([1917] 1923). Shils' discussion criticizes Weber for his "failure to acknowledge in a systematic and explicit manner that traditional and rational–legal authority both contain charismatic elements." He notes that Weber's "treatment of the transformation of charisma leaves unsettled the question whether charisma 'evaporates' or becomes attenuated in the course of its transformation" (1975: 407). The problem derives in part from the terms that Weber employs. The German term translated as "extraordinary" is "*ausseralltäglich.*" The term translated as "routinization" is "*Veralltäglichung.*" The literal reading would thus clearly imply "evaporation" rather than dispersion and infusion into procedures, which is Shils' model. But as we have seen, Weber is unable to supply origin stories that lead back to charismatic individuals for phenomena he himself describes as charismatic. As Charles Turner has pointed out to us, there is a whole set of uses of the term in Weber's writings on China in which charismatic elements are taken to be associated uniquely with the education of members of status groups. The theory behind this education, both in its primal and ideal-typical form, Weber stresses, is that charismata, meaning heroic or magical qualities, are "awakened" in a person through this education. Tests become tests of the presence of the quality. But the same ambiguity between "primal" and "ideal-typical" that occurs with political charisma recurs here. There are grades between this ideal-typical form and the very diverse historical forms of education.

In these mixed cases, there is no reason to believe that there was some primal charismatic theory of education from which present ideas degenerated or were produced by transformation (cf. Weber [1915] 1951: 121–3).

7 There are many more themes in Sohm that reappear in Weber that are not discussed here: the Church–Sect distinction, the individualizing effects of the doctrine of predestination and its class affinities, the idea that the importance of Protestantism is in its remolding of practical life, and the paradoxical worldly/other worldly character of monasticism and its ideals, to name a few. There are also striking historiographic similarities between Sohm and Weber with respect to their treatment of the relation between ideologies and material interests.

8 Weber notes that this kind of attribution of charisma is not the product of theories of the state so much as a cause. He speaks of "purely emotive state metaphysics" as "flourishing on this ground" ([1922] 1978: 1141).

6 CAUSE

1 Weber ([1922] 1978: 61). The presence of this remark in the notes to the translation of *Wirtschaft und Gesellschaft* is curious in the first place, for the term "objective" does not appear in either the English or German texts in conjunction with "possibility" (Weber [1922] 1978: 51). This absence is a point we shall remark on further. Parsons' more elaborate discussion of the concept in *The Structure of Social Action* is no improvement over this note; perhaps because it is premised on the strange notion that *Weber* "developed the categories of objective possibility and adequate explanation" (Parsons ([1937] 1968: 610).

2 Cf. Vucinich (1976: 136–7).

3 One reason for the prominence of theories of causality in German legal usage is that the judge in German civil cases must justify his substantive findings and this justification may be appealed (cf. Fletcher 1978: 195–6). No such justification is needed in American courts, where the appeals process is based on procedural considerations.

4 This was obviously part of the attraction for Weber as well: Marx, Spencer, and Tönnies (as well as Durkheim) each were committed to highly dubious figurative notions of ultimate social forces, and the notion of social forces was a source of difficulty for sociologists of the era *tout court*.

5 Radbruch makes the point (against von Kries, who wished to apply the adequacy theory in both criminal and civil contexts) that the adequacy theory alone does not account for ordinary legal practice in cases of criminal liability. Weber endorses this point, but suggests that the historian is not concerned with cause in the sense of criminal liability but in the sense of civil liability. The criminal law, as Radbruch notes and Weber agrees, is concerned to punish the actor with the bad

will or criminal intent who acts on this intent or will (Radbruch 1902: 30; M. Weber [1905] 1949: 169). Civil liability does not involve the question of "the bad will." Civil liability is concerned instead with responsibility, and the main legal distinction which is analogous to the historian's concern arises in connection with responsibility, between intended and unintended damages. Subjective guilt is not an issue in these cases. The subjective fact of intent is an issue, however, especially in connection with the distinction between actually foreseen and unforeseen consequences of an action: a judgment of intent depends in part on whether or not the actor did in fact foresee a particular consequence. This fact, however, is a subjective fact, in the sense that it is an assertion about the subjective standpoint of the actor.

6 von Kries' use of "objective" is discussed in slightly different terms by Hart and Honoré (1959: 413–15). A standard discussion of the problem of selecting a reference class may be found in Salmon (1971: 40).

7 The Kantian background of this notion of "objectivity" is evident.

8 Cf. Radbruch (1902: 10).

9 Cf. Hart and Honoré (1959: 403–4).

7 ABSTRACTION

1 Weber's actual familiarity with various authors is a matter of scholarly dispute. The significance of this particular text and the annotations to the copy in Weber's library is an example of this. Suffice to say that arguments relating to "influence" in this volume do not rest on graphical analysis, but on the existence of specific citations, or the personal connection of scholar and student. These are not foolproof criteria either, unfortunately, so these established connections must be treated as only a first cut, and supplemented by additional internal textual evidence. Redundancy – different kinds of evidence pointing in the same direction – is perhaps the best assurance of interpretative adequacy under the circumstances created by the state of the Weberian textual corpus and by our historical knowledge of the man and his working procedures. Nothing in this volume depends on an argument to the effect that Weber was in a dialogue with figures for whom there is no strong evidence that he ever read or took seriously. But no methodological rule can exclude the possibility that such an unattested influence was in fact operative.

2 Wolfgang Mommsen writes that "As far as we know, Max Weber clarified his own methodological position by means of a constant dialogue with Emil Lask, who himself occupied an intermediate position between neo-Kantianism and a *Lebensphilosophie* following Nietzsche and Simmel . . . . [Lask] was very close to Max Weber and had been a frequent guest in Weber's house in Heidelberg" (Mommsen 1987: 15–16).

3 There is a large literature on Weber's concept of ideal-types. The origins of the concept are nevertheless not entirely clear. Weber

NOTES

obviously had in mind Menger's writings on types, but wished to
correct them, and for good reason: they confused several issues,
including the problem of the nature of economic laws, the logic of
ceteris paribus conditionality, and the "reality" of what Menger calls
"exact types" and the relation between exact types, such as Menger
took to be the subject of economic laws, and particular situations and
actions. This topic has recently been addressed in a series of papers by
Uskali Mäki, one of which (1991) compares Weber and Menger.

The term is found in contemporary *Rechtswissenschaft* and
Staatswissenschaft, notably in the writings of Georg Jellinek. His
Allgemeine Staatslehre used the term before Weber's 1904 essay, and in
subsequent editions he commented on Weber's usage. It is evident
from his comments that there was no precise understanding of the
concept extant at the time Weber wrote. Jellinek wrote that the
concept of type had changed greatly in recent times, primarily in the
context of political thought, owing to the separation of normative
from scientific usages. The idea that a type is exemplified fully in its
"best" case is the casualty of this change. Yet the concept, even in its
"scientific" uses, retained an essentialist, even teleological character.
Jellinek points to an article by Windelband on criminal psychology
which contrasted the ideal-type to the empirical type ([1900] 1914:
36). Windelband, like Jellinek, claimed that the development of
typifications – which was a kind of natural tendency of the mind – is a
human rather than a strictly scientific capacity (1907: 2).

The empirical type was thought by Jellinek to be distinguished from
the ideal-type by the fact that the empirical type was developed
through a self-conscious kind of abstraction in which the researcher
accentuates particular marks of phenomena and brings together
classes based on these orderings ([1900] 1914: 36). These types are set
into the flow of historical happening and change over time ([1900]
1914: 39). This is a point Weber will take up. But Weber divides the
categories somewhat differently, more sharply distinguishing what he
considers purely classificatory categorizations from those with
conceptual content. In his notes Jellinek concedes the general
epistemic point that all abstraction from individual facts gives us only
pictures which can never fully coincide with reality, and that
consequently all sciences that employ concepts face disputes over the
reality of their concepts ([1900] 1914: 36).

4 Rickert was concerned with the ascent from the pre-scientific to the
scientific, from "the primitive disciplining of the materials which [the
scholar] encounters at the start" to the special technical concepts of
the various disciplines (Lask [1905] 1950: 25). This is the common
problem of the whole Kantian tradition.

5 Rümelin we have already encountered as a legal scientist and theorist
of probabilistic causation repeatedly cited by Weber. Zitelmann was
cited for his work on the legal meaning of customary law ([1922]
1978: 753).

6 The problem of the status of ordinary classifications which do not
involve "abstraction" and its attendant problems of resemblance

189

derives from the problem of specifying the point at which the world constituting work of concepts begins. It is one of the hoary problems of neo-Kantianism, dating back to Trendelenburg's polemics with Kuno Fischer (cf. Fischer 1870; and Trendelenburg 1869).

7 "But the discursive nature of our knowledge, i.e., the fact that we comprehend reality only through a chain of intellectual modifications, postulates such a conceptual shorthand" ([1904] 1949: 94).

8 Parsons, of course, made the attempt, with precisely the effect Weber anticipated.

9 Among the other features of casuistic thinking is the reliance on maxims, such as the Ten Commandments in the case of moral casuistry, considerations of circumstances, of "who, what, where, when, why, how and by what means" (Jonsen and Toulmin 1988: 253), probability, i.e. the degree to which cases fit the paradigm, and cumulative arguments, in which additional arguments with the same conclusion are treated as adding probative force to the conclusion and resolution (Jonsen and Toulmin 1988: 254–7). Weber, it may be observed, was fascinated with the role of such things as abstraction and maxims in the development of legal thinking, and well aware of the character of casuistic reasoning in its legal forms.

10 The question of whether a motive was a cause is a question that can be addressed within the adequate cause theory, and Weber is ambiguous as to whether he thinks he has departed from the adequate cause model in discussing "verification." His mention of experimentation suggests that he has. His discussion of "thinking away certain elements of a chain of motivation" and his appeal to large bodies of statistical evidence suggests that he has not, except in the case of experimentation. In earlier writings on this passage we have interpreted the claims in different ways: first as a return to the classic Millian model (Turner and Factor 1981: 20), later as a continuation of the adequate cause theory (Turner 1986). The issue is undecidable on the basis of the texts. The key issue, however, is this: the specific problem to which these notions are applied in this passage is an unusual one – not a question of the causal structure of the genetic model being applied, which is still "adequate" rather than Millian causality, but of whether the genetic model is relevant to the phenomena to which it is applied, that is to say captures the true causes.

8 EPILOGUE

1 The disappearance of the notion of casuistry is another quirk of the English translation of *Wirtschaft and Gesellschaft*. In the opening section, Parsons translates "Kasuistik" as "theoretical differentiation" ([1922] 1978: 20), which is a serious distortion – casuistical reasoning is usually understood in *contrast* to theoretical reasoning. The elaborate index to the English edition includes no entry on the topic. The German edition includes twenty-eight ([1922] 1976: 902).

BIBLIOGRAPHY

Albrow, M. (1975) "Legal Positivism and Bourgeois Materialism: Max Weber's View of the Sociology of Law," *British Journal of Law and Society*, 2: 14–31.
—— (1990) *Max Weber's Construction of Social Theory*, New York: St Martin's Press.
Austin, J. L. ([1961] 1970) *Philosophical Papers*, 2nd edn, Oxford: Clarendon Press.
Beard, C. ([1904] 1967) *The Office of the Justice of the Peace in England, in its Origin and Development*, New York: B. Franklin.
—— (1913) *Economic Interpretation of the Constitution*, New York: MacMillan.
Bentley, A. F. (1908) *The Process of Government: A Study of Social Pressures*, Chicago, IL: University of Chicago Press.
Brunet, R. ([1921] 1922) *The New German Constitution*, trans. J. Gollomb, New York: Alfred A. Knopf.
Chroust, A. H. (1944) "The Philosophy of Law of Gustav Radbruch," *Philosophical Review*, 53: 23–45.
Coase, R. H. (1988) *The Firm, the Market, and the Law*, Chicago, IL: University of Chicago Press.
Cohen, H. (1877) *Kants Begründung der Ethik*, Berlin: Harrwitz and Gossmann.
Collini, S., Winch, D. and Burrow, J. (1983) *That Noble Science of Politics. A Study in Nineteenth-Century Intellectual History*, Cambridge: Cambridge University Press.
Dicey, A. V. ([1905] 1962) *Lectures on the Relation between Law and Public Opinion in England during the Nineteenth Century*, 2nd edn, London: Macmillan.
Feldman, S. M. (1991) "An Interpretation of Max Weber's Theory of Law: Metaphysics, Economics, and the Iron Cage of Constitutional Law," *Law and Social Inquiry*, 16: 205–48.
Fischer, K. (1854) *Geschichte der neuern Philosophie*, vol. IV, Mannheim: Bassermann & Mathy.
—— ([1866] 1976) *A Commentary on Kant's Critick of the Pure Reason*, trans. J. P. Mahaffey, London: Longmans Green.
—— (1870) *Anti-Trendelenburg. Eine Gegenschrift*, 2nd edn, Jena: H. Dabis.

Fletcher, G. P. (1978) *Rethinking Criminal Law*, Boston, MA: Little, Brown.
Fouillée, A. *et al.* ([1878] 1916) *Modern French Legal Philosophy*, trans. Mrs F. W. Scott and J. P. Chamberlain, South Hackensack, NJ: Rothman Reprints.
Gilbert, M. (1989) *On Social Facts*, Princeton, NJ: Princeton University Press.
Gneist, R. ([1882] 1986) *The History of the English Constitution*, trans. P. A. Ashworth, 2 vols, New York: G. P. Putnam.
Gottfried, P. (1990) *Carl Schmitt, Politics and Theory*, Westport, Ct: Greenwood.
Gromitsaris, A. (1989) *Theorie der Rechtsnormen bei Rudolph von Ihering. Eine Untersuchung der Grundlagen des deutschen Rechtsrealismus*, Berlin: Duncker & Humblot.
Habermas, J. ([1968] 1971) *Knowledge and Human Interests*, trans. J. Shapiro, Boston, MA: Beacon Press.
Hart, H. L. A. and Honoré, A. M. (1959) *Causation in the Law*, Oxford: Clarendon Press.
Hennis, W. (1987) "A Science of Man: Max Weber and the Political Economy of the German Historical School," in W. J. Mommsen and J. Osterhammel (eds) *Max Weber and His Contemporaries*, London: Allen & Unwin.
—— (1988) *Max Weber: Essays in Reconstruction*, trans. K. Tribe, London: Allen & Unwin.
Ihering, R. von (1852–63) *Der Geist des römischen Rechts auf den verschiedenen Stufen seiner Entwickung*, 4 vols, Leipzig: Breitkopf & Härtel.
—— ([1872] 1979) *The Struggle for Law*, 5th edn, trans. J. Lalor, Westport, CT: Hyperion Press.
—— ([1877] 1913) *Law as a Means to an End*, vol. I, 4th edn, trans. I. Husik, New York: Macmillan.
—— ([1877] 1884) *Der Zweck im Recht*, vol. I, 2nd edn, Leipzig: Breitkopf & Härtel.
—— ([1883] 1886) *Der Zweck in Recht*, vol. II, 2nd edn, Leipzig: Breitkopf & Härtel.
Jaspers, K. (1989) *On Max Weber*, New York: Paragon.
Jellinek, G. ([1900] 1914) *Allgemeine Staatslehre*, 3rd edn, expanded by W. Jellinek, Berlin: O. Häring.
Jenkins, I. (1960) "Rudolf von Ihering," *Vanderbilt Law Review*, 14: 169–90.
Jonsen, A. R. and Toulmin, S. (1988) *The Abuse of Casuistry. A History of Moral Reasoning*, Berkeley, CA: University of California Press.
Kant, I. ([1781] 1965) *The Critique of Pure Reason*, trans. N. K. Smith, New York: St Martin's Press.
Käsler, D. ([1979] 1988) *Max Weber. An Introduction to His Life and Work*, trans. P. Hurd, Cambridge: Polity Press.
—— (1985) *Soziologische Abenteuer: Earl Edward Eubank besucht europäische Soziologen im Sommer 1934*, Opladen: Westdeutscher Verlag.
Kautsky, K. ([1908] 1925) *Foundations of Christianity. A Study in Christian Origins*, London: International Publishers.
Kelly, R. F. (1979) "Historical and Political Interpretations of Jurisprudence and the Social Action Perspective in Sociology," *Journal of the History of the Behavioral Sciences*, 15: 47–62.

Kerger, H. (1988) *Autorität und Recht im Denken Nietzsches*, Berlin: Duncker & Humblot.
Klemann, B. (1989) *Rudolf von Ihering und die Historische Rechtsschule*, Frankfurt am Main: Peter Lang.
Kronman, A. T. (1983) *Max Weber*, Stanford, CA: Stanford University Press.
Lask, E. (1902) *Fichtes Idealismus und die Geschichte*, Tübingen: J.C.B. Mohr.
—— ([1905] 1907) "Rechtsphilosophie," in W. Windelband (ed.) *Die Philosophie im Beginn des zwanzigsten Jahrhunderts. Festschrift für Kuno Fischer*, 2nd expanded edn, Heidelberg: Carl Winter's Universitäts-buchhandlung.
—— ([1905] 1950) "Legal Philosophy," in *The Legal Philosophies of Lask, Radbruch, and Dabin*, trans. K. Wilk, Cambridge, MA: Harvard University Press, pp. 4–42.
Lichtblau, K. (1991) "Causality or Interaction? Simmel, Weber and Interpretive Sociology," *Theory, Culture and Society*, 8: 33–62.
Losano, M. G. (1984) *Studien zu Ihering und Gerber*, vol. 2, Ebelsbach: Rolf Gremer.
Mäki, U. (1991) "Universals and the Methodenstreit: Carl Menger's Conception of Economics as an Exact Science," paper presented at the International Congress of Logic, Methodology and Philosophy of Science, Uppsala, August.
Mayer, J. P. (1956) *Max Weber and German Politics: a Study in Political Sociology*, 2nd edn, rev. and enl., London: Faber & Faber.
Menger, C. ([1883] 1985) *Investigations into the Method of the Social Sciences with Special Reference to Economics*, formerly published under the title: *Problems of Economics and Sociology*, trans. F. J. Nock, ed. L. Schneider, New York: New York University Press.
Momigliano, A. (1982) "New Paths of Classicism in the Nineteenth Century," *History and Theory* 21: 1–64.
Mommsen, W. J. ([1959] 1984) *Max Weber and German Politics, 1890–1920*, trans. M. S. Steinberg, Chicago, IL: University of Chicago Press.
—— (1987) "Introduction" in W. J. Mommsen and J. Osterhammel (eds) *Max Weber and His Contemporaries*, London: Allen & Unwin.
Mommsen, W. J. and Osterhammel, J. (eds) (1987) *Max Weber and His Contemporaries*, London: Allen & Unwin.
Nagel, E. (1939) "Principles of the Theory of Probability," *International Encyclopedia of Unified Science*, 1(6), Chicago, IL: University of Chicago Press.
Nietzsche, F. ([1881] 1982) *Daybreak: Thoughts on the Prejudices of Morality*, trans. R. J. Hollingdale, Cambridge: Cambridge University Press.
—— ([1887] 1969) *On the Genealogy of Morals*, 8th edn, trans. W. Kaufmann and R. J. Hollingdale, New York: Vintage Books.
Nozick, R. (1974) *Anarchy, State, and Utopia*, New York: Basic Books.
Oakes, G. (1988) *Weber and Rickert: Concept Formation in the Cultural Sciences*, Cambridge, MA: MIT Press.
Otto, Rudolf ([1917] 1923) *The Idea of the Holy: an Inquiry into the Non-Rational Factor in the Idea of the Divine and its Relation to the Rational*, trans. J. W. Harvey, London: Oxford University Press.

Parsons, T. ([1937] 1968) *The Structure of Social Action: A Study in Social Theory with Special Reference to a Group of Recent European Writers*, 2nd edn, Glencoe: Free Press.
—— ([1947] 1964) "Introduction and editorial comments," in M. Weber, *The Theory of Social and Economic Organization*, New York: Free Press.
Pipes, R. (1955) "Max Weber and Russia," *World Politics*, 7: 370–401.
Pleister, W. (1982) *Persönlichkeit, Wille und Freiheit im Werke Iherings*, Ebelsbach: Rolf Gremer.
Posner, R. A. (1991) *Sex and Reason*, Cambridge, MA: Harvard University Press.
Radbruch, G. (1902) *Die Lehre von der adäquaten Verursachung*, Berlin: J. Guttentag.
—— ([1914] 1950) "Legal Philosophy," in *The Legal Philosophies of Lask, Radbruch, and Dabin*, 3rd edn, trans. K. Wilk, Cambridge, MA: Harvard University Press, 43–224.
Rawls, J. (1971) *A Theory of Justice*, Cambridge, MA: Harvard University Press.
Rehbinder, M. (1987) "Max Weber und Die Rechtswissenschaft," in M. Rehbinder and K. P. Tieck (eds) *Max Weber als Rechtssoziologe*, Berlin: Duncker & Humblot.
Rosenberg, A. (1992) *Economics–Mathematical Politics or Science of Diminishing Returns?* Chicago, IL: University of Chicago Press.
Salmon, W. C. (1971) *Statistical Explanation and Statistical Relevance*, Pittsburgh, PA: University of Pittsburgh Press.
Schulz, F. ([1934] 1936) *Principles of Roman Law*, trans. M. Wolff, Oxford: Clarendon Press.
Seagle, W. (1945) "Rudolf von Ihering: or Law as a Means to an End," *The University of Chicago Law Review*, 13: 71–89.
Shils, E. (1958) "Tradition and Liberty: Antinomy and Interdependence," *Ethics*, 68: 155–7.
—— (1975) *Center and Periphery: Essays in Macrosociology*, Chicago, IL: University of Chicago Press.
Sica, A. (1988) *Weber, Irrationality, and Social Order*, Berkeley, CA: University of California Press.
Simmel, G. ([1900] 1978) *Philosophy of Money*, trans. T. Bottomore and D. Frisby, Boston, MA: Routledge & Kegan Paul.
—— ([1907] 1986) *Schopenhauer and Nietzsche*, trans. H. Loiskand, L., D. Weinstein and M. Weinstein, Amherst, MA: University of Massachusetts Press.
Sohm, R. ([1883] 1940) *The Institutes. A Textbook of the History and System of Roman Private Law*, trans. J. C. Ledlie, London: Clarendon Press.
—— ([1887] 1958) *Outlines of Church History*, trans. M. Sinclair, Beacon Hill: Beacon Press.
—— ([1892] 1923) *Kirchenrecht*, 2 vols, Berlin: Duncker & Humblot.
Stammler, R. von ([1896] 1906) *Wirtschaft und Recht nach der materialistischen Geschichtsauffassung. Eine sozialphilosophische Untersuchung*, 2nd edn, Leipzig: Viet & Comp.
—— ([1902] 1925) *The Theory of Justice*, trans. I. Husik, New York: Macmillan.

—— (1925) *Wirtschaft und Recht nach der materialistischen Geschichtsauffassung. Eine sozialphilosophische Untersuchung*, 4th edn, Berlin: Walter de Gruyter.

Stone, J. (1950) *The Province and Function of Law: Law as Logic, Justice, and Social Control*, Cambridge, MA: Harvard University Press.

Taylor, C. (1964) *The Explanation of Behavior*, New York: Humanities Press.

Tenbruck, F. (1987) "Max Weber and Eduard Meyer," in W. J. Mommsen and J. Osterhammel (eds) *Max Weber and His Contemporaries*, London: Allen & Unwin.

Tönnies, F. (1887) *Gemeinschaft und Gesellschaft Abhandlung des Kommunismus und des Sozialismus als empirischer Kulturformen*, Leipzig: R. Reisland.

—— ([1909] 1961) *Custom: An Essay on Social Codes*, trans. A. F. Borenstein, New York: Free Press of Glencoe.

Trendelenburg, A. (1869) *Kuno Fischer und Sein Kant. Eine Entgegnung*, Leipzig: S. Hirzel.

Trubeck, D. (1972) "Max Weber on Law and the Rise of Capitalism," *Wisconsin Law Review*, 720–53.

Turner, S. (1985) "Explaining Capitalism: Weber on and against Marx," in R. Antonio and R. Glassman (eds) *A Weber–Marx Dialogue*, Lawrence, KS: University Press of Kansas.

—— (1986) *The Search for a Methodology of Social Science*, Dordrecht: D. Reidel.

—— (1990) "Weber and his Philosophers", *International Journal of Politics, Culture and Society*, 3: 539–53.

—— (1993) "Introduction," in S. Turner (ed.) *Emile Durkheim. Sociologist and Moralist*, London: Routledge.

Turner, S. and Factor, R. (1981) "Objective Possibility and Adequate Causation in Weber's Methodological Writings," *The Sociological Review*, 29: 5–25.

—— and —— (1984) *Max Weber and the Dispute Over Reason and Value. A Study of Philosophy, Ethics and Politics*, London: Routledge & Kegan Paul.

—— and —— (1990) "Weber and the End of Tradition," in P. A. French, T. E. Uehling, Jr. and H. K. Wettstein (eds) *Midwest Studies in Philosophy*, vol. XV, Notre Dame: University of Notre Dame Press, pp. 400–24.

Udehn, L. (1987) *Methodological Individualism, A Critical Appraisal*, Uppsala: Uppsala Universitet.

Ulmen, G. L. (1991) *Politischer Mehrwert. Eine Studie über Max Weber und Carl Schmitt*, trans. Ursula Ludz, Weinheim: VCH, Acta Humaniora.

Vucinich, A. (1976) *Social Thought in Tsarist Russia: The Quest for a General Science of Society, 1861–1919*, Chicago, IL: University of Chicago Press.

Watson, A. (1981) *The Making of the Civil Law*, Cambridge, MA: Harvard University Press.

Weber, Marianne ([1926] 1975) *Max Weber: A Biography*, trans. and ed. H. Zohn, New York: Wiley.

Weber, Max, ([1895] 1971) "Der Nationalstaat und die Volkswirtschaftspolitik," in *Gesammelte Politische Schriften*, 3rd expanded edn, J. Winckelmann (ed.) Tübingen: Mohr, 1–25.

—— ([1903, 1905, 1906] 1975) *Roscher and Knies: The Logical Problems of Historical Economics*, trans. G. Oakes, New York: Free Press.

—— ([1904–5] 1958) *The Protestant Ethic and the Spirit of Capitalism*, trans. T. Parsons, New York: Charles Scribner's Sons.

—— ([1904, 1905, 1917] 1949) *The Methodology of the Social Sciences*, trans. and ed. E. A. Shils and H. A. Finch, New York: Free Press.

—— ([1907] 1977) *Critique of Stammler*, trans. Guy Oakes, New York: Free Press.

—— ([1908] 1975) "Marginal Utility Theory and the Fundamental Law of Psychophysics," trans. L. Schneider, *Social Science Quarterly* 56: 21-36.

—— ([1913] 1981) "Some Categories of Interpretive Sociology," *The Sociological Quarterly*, trans. E. Graber, 22: 151–80.

—— ([1915] 1946a) "Religious Rejections of the World and their Directions," in H. H. Gerth and C. W. Mills (trs and eds) *From Max Weber: Essays in Sociology*, New York: Oxford University Press, pp. 323–59.

—— ([1915] 1946b) "The Social Psychology of the World Religions," in H. H. Gerth and C. W. Mills (trs and eds), *From Max Weber: Essays in Sociology*, New York: Oxford University Press, pp. 267–301.

—— ([1915] 1951) *The Religion of China*, trans. H. H. Gerth, New York: Free Press.

—— ([1917] 1946) "National Character and the Junkers" in H. H. Gerth and C. W. Mills (trs and eds) *From Max Weber: Essays in Sociology*, New York: Oxford University Press, pp. 386–95.

—— ([1919] 1946) "Politics as a Vocation," in H. H. Gerth and C. W. Mills (trs and eds) *From Max Weber: Essays In Sociology*, New York: Oxford University Press, pp. 77–128.

—— (1922) *Gesammelte Aufsätze zur Wissenschaftslehre*, Tübingen: Mohr.

—— ([1922] 1976) *Wirtschaft und Gesellschaft: Grundriss der verstehenden Soziologie*, 3 vols, 5th rev. edn, ed. J. Winckelmann, Tübingen: Mohr.

—— ([1922] 1978) *Economy and Society: an Outline of Interpretive Sociology*, trans. E. Fischoff *et al.*, eds. G. Roth and C. Wittich, 2 vols, Berkeley, CA: University of California Press.

White, J. B. (1990) *Justice as Translation*, Chicago, IL: University of Chicago Press.

Wieacker, F. (1968) *Rudolph von Ihering*, Stuttgart: F. Koehler.

—— (1969) "Rudolph von Ihering," *Zeitschrift der Savigny-Stiftung für Rechtsgeschichte*, 86: 1–36.

Windelband, W. (1907) "Über Norm und Normalität," *Monatsschrift für Kriminalpsychologie und Strafrechtsreform*, 2: 1–13.

INDEX

abstraction 21, 120, 122, 136–65:
see also Jellinek, on abstraction;
Marx, and Marxism,
abstractions in; Rickert, on
abstraction
abstraction, Max Weber on 12,
131, 134, 136, 142, 151, 153,
155: abstract concepts, need
for 149, 154; for causal analysis
149, 164, 177; in law 137–8,
139, 190 n. 9; purposive 170; in
the Roman law tradition 131
action, Ihering on 40, 53:
external stage of 27; interest as
source of human 121; internal
stage of 27–30
action, Max Weber on: *see also*
human conduct, Max Weber
on; beliefs about 101–2; the
category of 10, 31, 36, 171, 184
n. 7; the causes of 36, 40–1, 43,
53, 86, 101, 176, 178;
explanations 161; instrumentally
rational 36, 38, 101, 176, 178;
purposive rational 36, 38, 53,
115; rational 92; rational,
model of 36; the stability of
customary 81; the theory of 30;
traditional 136–7, 178; types of
77; uniformities of 42, 67, 80,
82–3, 90–2, 100–1, 121–2, 185
n. 7; value-rational 36–8, 66,
84, 86, 178, 185 n. 7; and
sociology 87, 175

Aegidy, L. 4
Albrow, M. 179 n. 2, 180 n. 4
American social science,
influence of continental legal
thought on 180 n. 5
*Archiv für Sozialwissenschaft und
Sozialpolitik* 143
associations, Max Weber on:
category of 104; political,
formation of 108
attributing purposes, Ihering on 175
Austin, J. 111
Austin, J.L. 18–21, 26, 40, 167–9
authority, Max Weber on 79:
forms of 102
authority, law as a product of
political 111
authority, patriarchal, Ihering on
103

Bachofen, K. 184 n. 2
Bacon, F. 166
von Bar, K. 4–5, 126–7
Beard, C. 180 n. 5
Bekker, I. 4
Bentham, J. 11
Bentley, A. 181 n. 5
Beseler, K. 4
biology (and biological), Max
Weber on: analogies 34; causes
34, 39–41, 88–91, 106, 113, 118,
163, 174–5; facts 118, 121;
morality rooted in 88; science
of evolutionary 36

protestant asceticism, Max Weber
 on 61
protestant behavior, Max Weber
 on 42
psychological coercion, Ihering
 on 48–9, 84, 106
punishment 57
purpose (and purposes) 21–2, 26,
 42, 56
purpose (and purposes), Ihering
 on: attributing 175; collective
 78; identity of 49; and Law 96;
 law of 11, 27–30, 33, 71; social
 52–3, 83, 92, 109; as a
 world-forming principle 26
purpose (and purposes), Max
 Weber on 31, 36, 38, 53, 115,
 170; attribution of 86, 88;
 objective 182 n. 3; social 52–3,
 91
purpose-relative construction of
 concepts, Max Weber on 142,
 153

Radbruch, G. 5, 7, 10, 58–62,
 64–5, 126, 130, 133, 136, 183 n.
 9, 188 n. 5, 188 n. 8: adequate
 cause, theory of, and criminal
 liability 187 n. 5; condition
 complexes, concrete, in 130;
 law and decisions in 62; law
 values in 62, 183 n. 10; legal
 causality in 5; philosophy of law
 in 10; social view of law in 62
Ranke, L. 3
rational action, Max Weber on
 92: instrumentally 36, 38, 101,
 176, 178; model of 36
 purposive 36, 38, 53, 115
rational choice theory 12, 34–6,
 38–9, 117
rationalization, Max Weber on 92,
 139, 172, 176
rationalizations of habit 43
reason: and presumptions 15–16;
 in settling disputes 15
Rehbinder, M. 180 n. 4
Rheinstein, M. 180 n. 4
Rickert, H. 124, 133, 136–7,

143–5, 183 n. 10, 189 n. 4; on
 abstraction 144; on causal
 explanation 124; on historical
 science 124
religion, Tönnies on 184 n. 5
religious ideas and interests, Max
 Weber on 176
rights, struggle for, Ihering on 55–6
Rome (and Roman): agrarian
 history 181 n.7; Roman law 21,
 25, 137–40, 159, 171, 177, 179
 n. 1
Rome (and Roman), Max Weber
 on: agrarian history, study of 4,
 181 n. 7; law 10; legal concepts
 167
Roscher, W. 6, 8
Rosenberg, A. 182 n. 4
Ross, E. 180 n. 5
Rümelin, G. 126, 145, 189 n. 5

Salmon, W. 188 n. 6
Savigny, K. 3, 55, 70, 139, 184 n. 6
Schulz, F. 131, 138, 140
science 181 n. 1: see also law (and
 legal), science; Rickert, on
 historical science
Seagle, W. 181 n. 6
Shils, E. 180 n. 4: on charisma
 186 n. 6
Sica, A. 182 n. 5
Simmel, G. 133, 136, 143, 147,
 188 n. 2: on money 143, 183 n.
 6; on objective meanings 182 n.
 6; on sociology 133, 147
skepticism, Max Weber on 161–3
Social Democrats 185 n. 1
social forces: see Durkheim, on
 social forces; Marx, and
 Marxism, on social forces;
 Spencer, on social forces;
 Tönnies, on social forces
social purposes, Tönnies on 92
social science (and social
 sciences), Max Weber on 1–2,
 7, 95, 124, 126, 137, 148, 155,
 157, 159, 166, 170–2:
 conceptualization in 141, 151,
 157, 167–70